In Search of
TUTANKHAMUN

In Search of
TUTANKHAMUN

The discovery of a king's tomb

Written and illustrated by
Giovanni Caselli

PETER BEDRICK BOOKS
New York

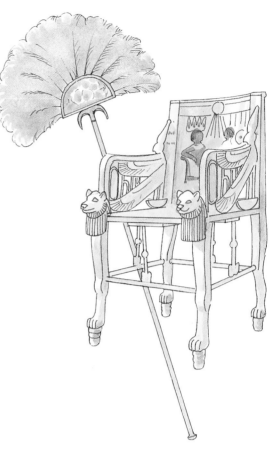

To Satzang and Zaffron

Published by
Peter Bedrick Books
156 Fifth Avenue
New York, NY 10010

Published by agreement with
Franklin Watts, London

Acknowledgments

The author and publishers would like to thank A.C.T.A.
Florence for use of the photographs on pages 36-37, and
Archeologica Viva for the image of Akhenaten on page 35.

Library of Congress Cataloging-in-Publication Data

Caselli, Giovanni, 1939-
  In search of Tutankhamun : the discovery of a king's tomb. -- 1st
American ed.
     p. cm.
  Includes Index.
  Summary: Describes the discovery of the tomb of the Egyptian king
Tutankhamun and what it revealed about everyday life in his time.
  ISBN 0-87226-543-9 (hc.)
  1. Tutankhamun, King of Egypt--Tomb--Juvenile literature.
2. Egypt--Antiquities--Juvenile literature. [1. Tutankhamun, King
of Egypt--Tomb. 2. Egypt--Antiquities. 3. Egypt--Social life and
customs--To 332 B.C.] I.Title.
DT87.5.C47 1999
932'.014'092--dc21
                                          98-44348
                                              CIP
                                               AC

Printed in Hong Kong / China

First American edition 1999

Contents

Discovering Ancient Egypt

The huge, mysterious buildings left by the ancient Egyptians attracted visitors to the Nile Valley from ancient Greek times onward. From the end of the 18th century A.D., when Napoleon invaded Egypt and the country was occupied briefly by France, scholars from Europe began to explore ancient Egyptian remains. These scholars found and identified many of the monuments that are so well known today.

In the bare desert hills they excavated tombs of kings and nobles. The tombs were painted inside with scenes of ancient Egyptian life, and they contained mummies and many precious objects that had been buried with them. The world was fascinated by news of the finds.

19th-century explorers

Teams of French and Italian scholars, dressed in exotic costume, traveled through Egypt and recorded what they found. In the center of this group is Jean-François Champollion (1790-1832). In 1822, after many years of studying the Greek and Egyptian writing on a stone found at Rosetta, Champollion figured out how to read ancient Egyptian hieroglyphs.

A paradise for archeologists

The River Nile flows from Sudan to the Mediterranean Sea. The great number of ancient remains in the Nile Valley make it a paradise for archeologists.

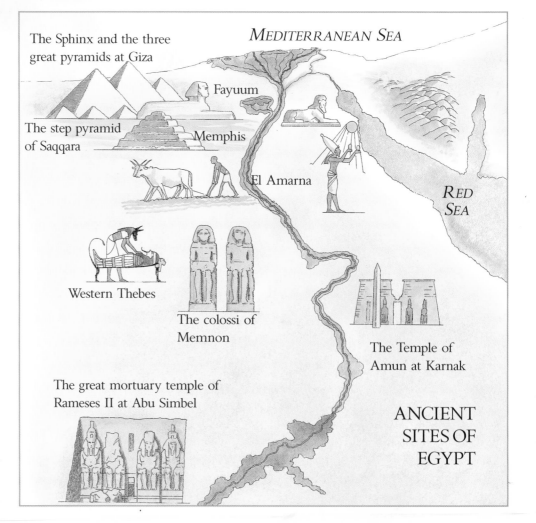

MEDITERRANEAN SEA

The Sphinx and the three great pyramids at Giza

Fayuum

The step pyramid of Saqqara

Memphis

El Amarna

RED SEA

Western Thebes

The colossi of Memnon

The Temple of Amun at Karnak

The great mortuary temple of Rameses II at Abu Simbel

ANCIENT SITES OF EGYPT

The Valley of the Kings

The pharaohs of the Egyptian New Kingdom had their tombs built in a narrow valley beyond the cliffs of the Theban Hills on the west bank of the Nile. For centuries the Egyptians have called this desolate area "Biban al-Muluk," which, translated from Arabic, means "The Valley of the Kings."

Tomb robbers

Treasured objects were buried along with the pharaohs and, over the centuries, robbers ransacked most of the tombs. Only a few tombs were left unspoiled, because they were difficult to find or to enter.

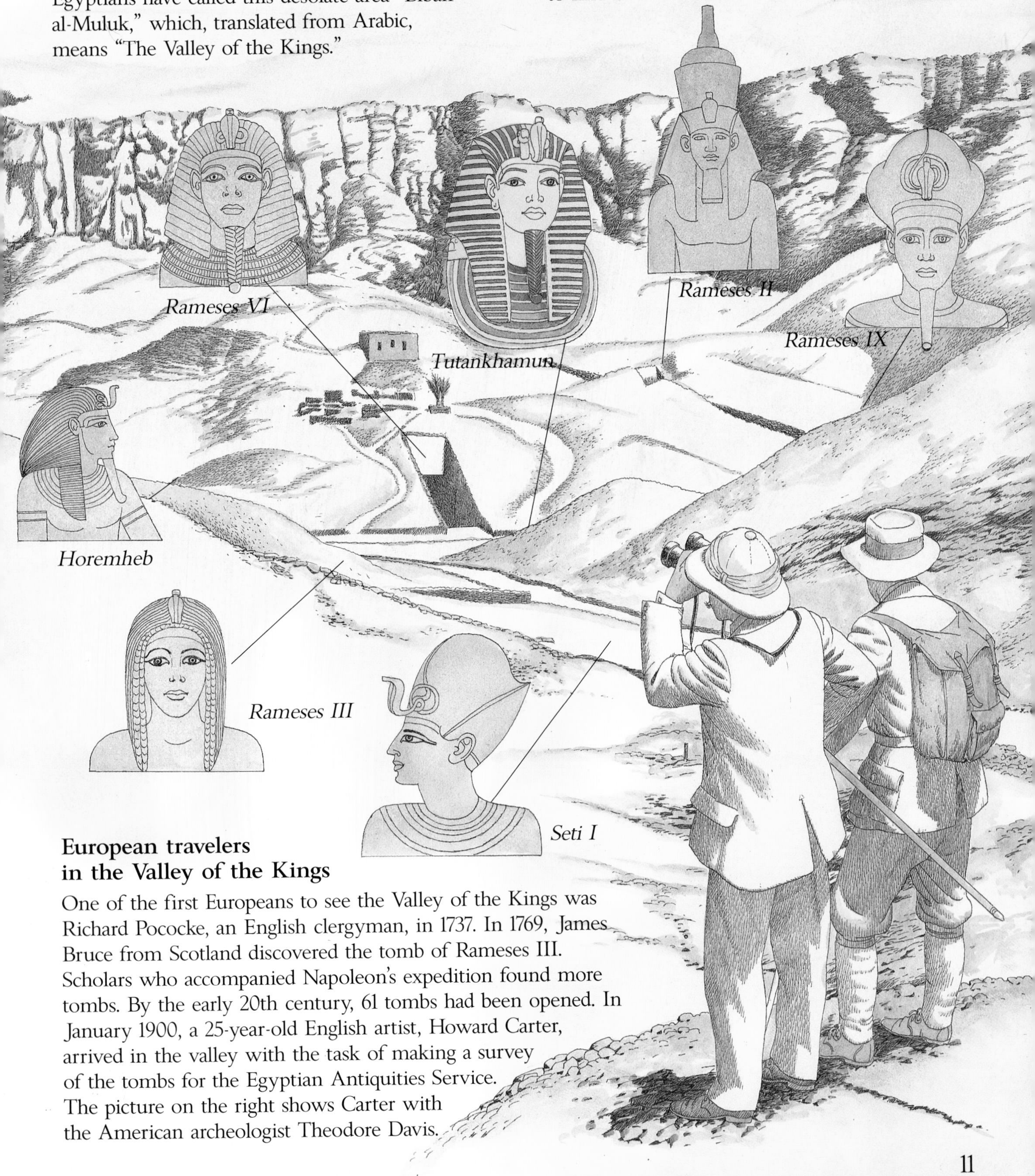

Rameses VI

Tutankhamun

Rameses II

Rameses IX

Horemheb

Rameses III

Seti I

European travelers in the Valley of the Kings

One of the first Europeans to see the Valley of the Kings was Richard Pococke, an English clergyman, in 1737. In 1769, James Bruce from Scotland discovered the tomb of Rameses III. Scholars who accompanied Napoleon's expedition found more tombs. By the early 20th century, 61 tombs had been opened. In January 1900, a 25-year-old English artist, Howard Carter, arrived in the valley with the task of making a survey of the tombs for the Egyptian Antiquities Service. The picture on the right shows Carter with the American archeologist Theodore Davis.

11

Howard Carter

Howard Carter was born in London in 1874. His father was an artist, and Howard followed in his footsteps. As a boy, Howard often went with his father to see the Egyptian collection belonging to the Amherst family, and in 1891 he started work for the Amhersts, making drawings of their artifacts. Through his work he met several important archeologists. In September 1891 Carter made his first journey to Egypt, as an artist in a team led by the archeologist Percy Newberry.

Howard Carter, aged 17, working as an archeological artist at Beni Hasan, 1891

Tut-ankh-amun—the first clue

In 1906, in the Valley of the Kings, Edward Ayrton found a cup with the name Tut-ankh-amun on it. It was a clue that this pharaoh's tomb was in the Valley. Theodore Davis searched but did not find it.

Lord Carnarvon (right) and his daughter, Lady Evelyn Herbert, with Howard Carter, 1922

Between 1902 and 1914 Theodore Davis, an American millionaire and archeologist, had permission (the "concession") from the Egyptian government to excavate in the Valley of the Kings. Sometimes Carter worked with him. They discovered several tombs, all robbed in the past and practically empty.

In 1914 the concession went to Lord Carnarvon, who since 1906 had excavated at various sites on the Nile with Carter.

Lord Carnarvon, the collector

George Edward Stanhope Molyneux Herbert, fifth Earl of Carnarvon, collected Egyptian antiquities. In 1921, when the Amherst collection was dispersed, he acquired this fragment of a stone head of Akhenaten, which Howard Carter had found at El Amarna. Akhenaten was the father of Tutankhamun.

Carter was convinced that the tomb of Tutankhamun must lie somewhere in the Valley of the Kings. But, by 1922, little had been found. Then, on November 4, workmen told him they had found a step.

Clearing rubble revealed steps leading down to a blocked doorway. Carter made a hole in the top of this and held his flashlight up to it. The space behind the doorway seemed to be full of debris. Then he discovered that the plaster blocking the doorway had impressions of seals on it. He sent a telegram to Lord Carnarvon: "At last have made wonderful discovery in Valley: a magnificent tomb with seals intact. Re-covered same for your arrival. Congratulations."
On November 23 Carnarvon and his daughter, Lady Evelyn Herbert, arrived in Egypt. What would they find in the tomb?

Lord Carnarvon and Howard Carter in the Valley of the Kings

The Way into the Tomb

The steps into the tomb were cleared again, and Carnarvon and Carter examined the doorway closely. They soon realized that the tomb had already been broken open and resealed at least twice before. Small objects found in the stairway indicated that the tomb must have been opened in about 1050 B.C., some 200-300 years after Tutankhamun's burial.

Beyond the first door, the archeologists entered a passage that descended to another doorway. Carter's hands trembled as he made a hole in the top-left corner of the door.

At the second doorway

It took a while for Carter's eyes to get used to the darkness beyond the hole he had made in the second doorway. "Can you see anything?" asked Lord Carnarvon, full of suspense.
"Yes, wonderful things!" said Carter at last.

Seals

The plaster blocking the doors was covered with impressions of large oval seals, with the name Nebkheprure on them. This was one of the names taken by Tutankhamun when he became king.

Doorways in the tomb

Once through the second doorway, Carter and Carnarvon entered the *antechamber*. Here they found two more blocked doorways, one leading to a small room called the *annex* and another to the *burial chamber*. A doorway from the burial chamber led to the *treasury*. All the doors had been broken through and re-sealed twice.

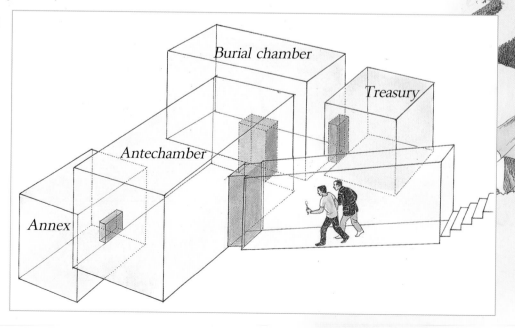

Burial chamber

Treasury

Antechamber

Annex

Through the second doorway, in the antechamber, the archeologists found objects piled high, including caskets, vases, bouquets of flowers, black shrines, beds, chairs, and parts of chariots.

There were also two life-size statues of a king, standing as if on guard by another doorway. Through this the archeologists were certain they would find the burial chamber of Tutankhamun.

Another blocked door
To gain entry to Tutankhamun's burial chamber, Carter first had to break through another doorway that had been completely sealed with plaster.

Clearing the tomb
A large team of archeologists joined Carter to photograph and record all the items found in the tomb, and preserve them so that they could be transported safely to Cairo. It took until 1932 for all this work to be completed.

The Valley of the Kings during the excavation of Tutankhamun's tomb

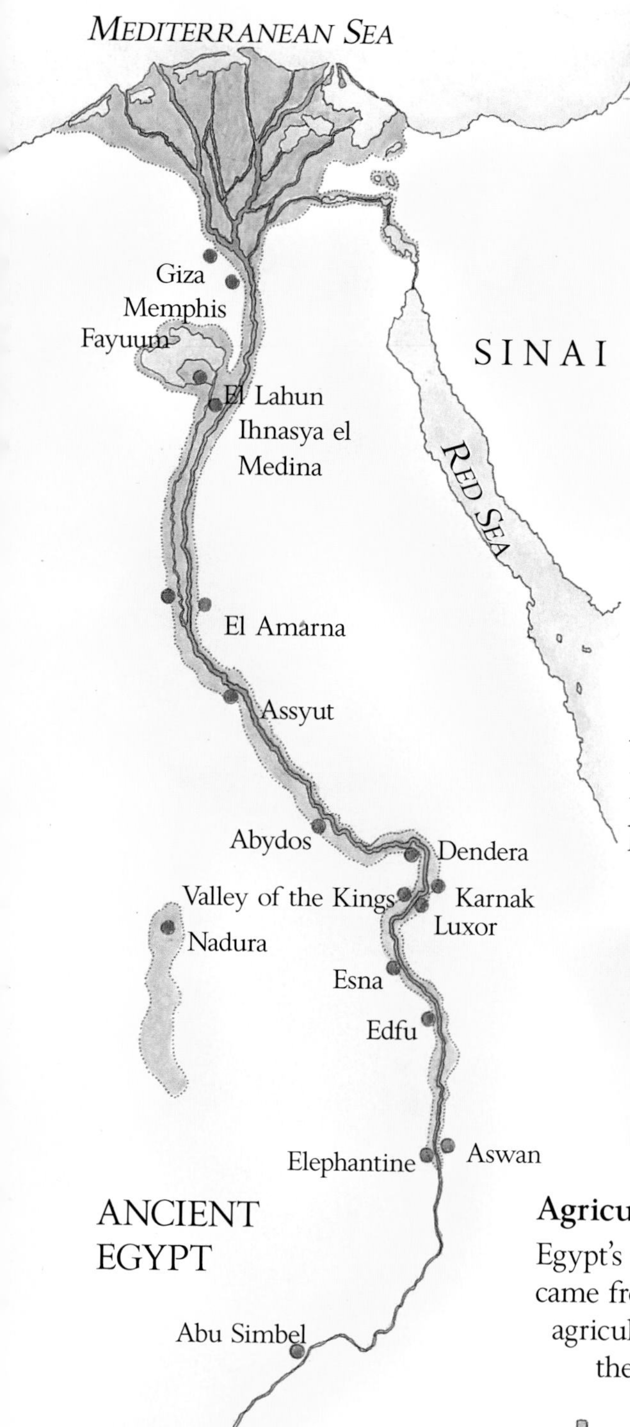

SINAI

RED SEA

Giza
Memphis
Fayuum

El Lahun
Ihnasya el
Medina

El Amarna

Assyut

Abydos   Dendera

Valley of the Kings   Karnak
                         Luxor
Nadura

Esna

Edfu

Elephantine   Aswan

ANCIENT
EGYPT

Abu Simbel

Land of the Nile

Monsoon rain falls on equatorial Africa, filling streams and rivers in the Ethiopian mountains. Some of these flow east to the Indian Ocean and some go south. But one river runs north, and after traveling 4,100 miles (6,670 km), empties into the Mediterranean Sea. The River Nile is like a long desert oasis, which explains why in ancient times this river valley became an avenue of civilization.

In 3500 B.C. there was one kingdom in the area of the Nile Delta, and another that stretched from the Delta to Aswan. In 3000 B.C. the two kingdoms united under King Menes. At this time the Egyptians developed writing, and began to build pyramids as tombs for their kings or "pharaohs."

Agriculture

Egypt's wealth came from agriculture. Each year the Nile flooded its banks, and when the water withdrew, it left behind a layer of fertile earth in which many crops could be grown. The river water was also used to irrigate the crops.

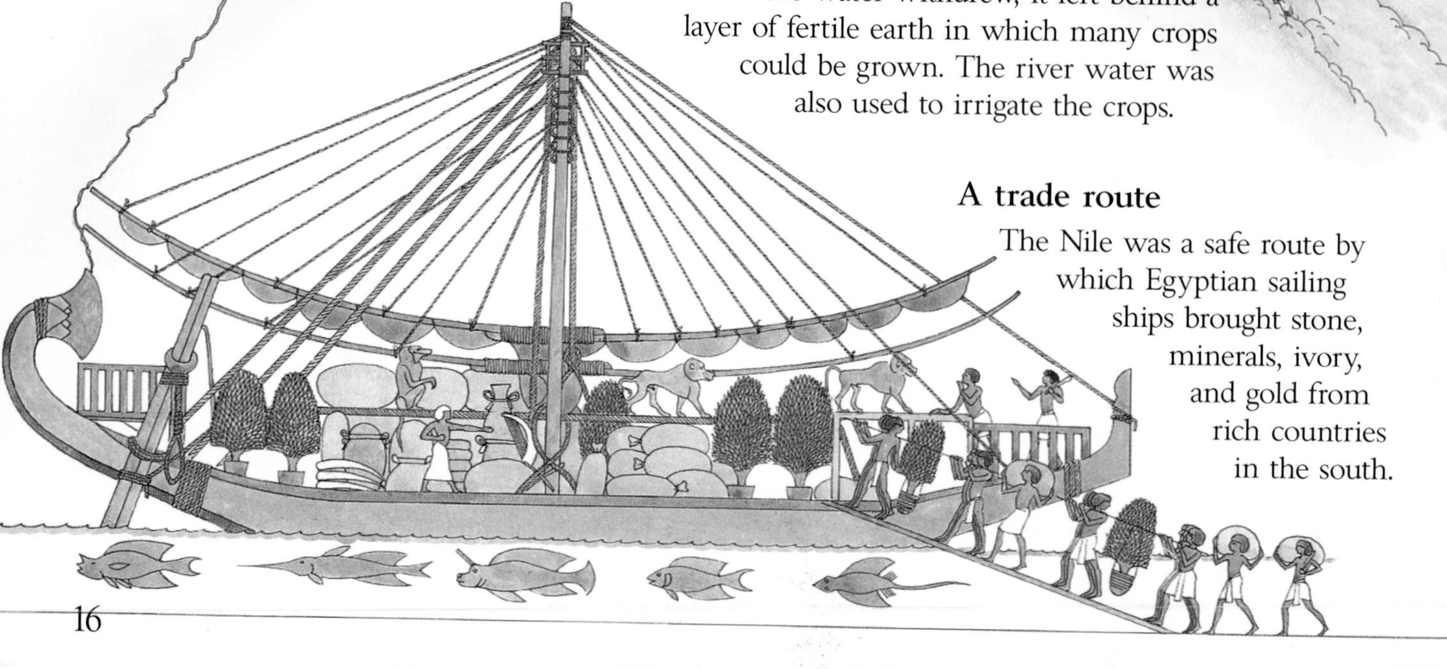

A trade route

The Nile was a safe route by which Egyptian sailing ships brought stone, minerals, ivory, and gold from rich countries in the south.

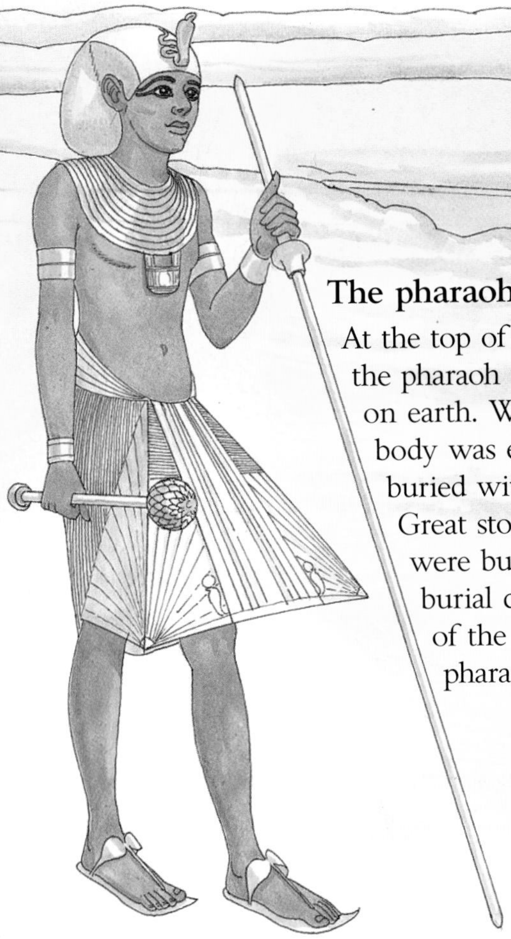

The pharaoh

At the top of the social pyramid, the pharaoh was seen as a god on earth. When he died, his body was embalmed and buried with his treasures. Great stone pyramids were built over the burial chambers of the first pharaohs.

Lifting water from the canal

Each laborer shown below lifts water from the canal using a device called a shadouf. The worker lowers the bucket into the water. Then the weight at the end of the shadouf helps lift the full bucket out again. Numerous laborers distributed the Nile water to where it was needed.

A nobleman's house

Beneath the pharaoh on the social scale, nobles ruled areas of the country. They were in charge of justice, business, and agriculture, and lived in luxurious houses, such as the one shown above, by the canals.

17

Who Was Tutankhamun?

The tomb discovered by Howard Carter and Lord Carnarvon belonged to a cemetery built during the "New Kingdom," a period of Egyptian history that began ca. 1550 B.C. Four of the kings who reigned during this period were called Amenophis.

Amenophis IV closed all existing temples and allowed people to worship only one god, the Sun, which the Egyptians called Aten. He changed his own name to Akhen-aten and built a new capital city called Akhet-aten (later renamed El Amarna). Tutankhamun, named Tutankh-aten, was his son.

The king's son
Akhenaten named his son Tutankhaten. When the boy was old enough, the pharaoh gave the prince an education appropriate for his high station in life.

Akhetaten
The new city of Akhetaten was built on the east bank of the Nile and soon grew into a splendid metropolis. It contained temples, palaces, great avenues, and gardens, and covered more than 2 square miles (5 sq km).

The King's Bridge
The king used the covered bridge over the main avenue in Akhetaten to move from his official palace to his private residence.
With his wife Nefertiti, he appeared on the balcony in the center of the bridge to speak to his subjects and distribute gifts to them.

The wife of Tutankhamun

The lid of an inlaid wooden box bears the name and picture of Tutankhamun's half-sister, who is believed to have become his wife.

Tutankhamun's mother?

Most historians believe Tutankhamun's mother was Kiya (above), a wife of Akhenaten, who died in childbirth.

Akhenaten

This statue shows the elongated face of Amenophis IV, who renamed himself Akhenaten and ruled over Egypt for 17 years, from 1353 B.C. He had several wives, of whom the principal one was the beautiful Queen Nefertiti.

On the throne

Akhenaten and Queen Nefertiti are shown here on their throne, receiving the blessing of the Sun's (Aten's) rays. Beside them are their six daughters, including Ankhesenpaaten, who some historians think became the wife of Tutankhamun.

Only the pharaoh's daughters, and not his sons, appeared in public and were represented in art. This is one reason why there is controversy about who Tutankhamun's mother was.

19

Tutankhamun's Reign

Following the death of Akhenaten there was a period of confusion during which Egypt was ruled by a mysterious king under the name of Ankhkheprure Smenkhkare-djerkhepru. Many people believe that this was in fact Queen Nefertiti, who took over the throne in an attempt to continue her husband's "revolution." Then, in 1333 B.C., a nine-year-old child named Tutankhaten was crowned king of Egypt. The city of Akhetaten was razed to the ground and Thebes became the main religious center again.

A view of the great temple complex of Amun

The coronation of Tutankhamun

The coronation of the child pharaoh took place near Thebes, in the Great Temple of Amun at Karnak. The ceremony included traditional rituals from before the time of Akhenaten.
The prince entered a shrine where the god Amun placed the blue war-crown on his head. Then the high priests placed all the crowns of Egypt, one after the other, on his head and gave him the symbols of power, the crook and the staff, to hold. Later, the king's name was changed to Tutankhamun—a sign that the old religions were being restored.

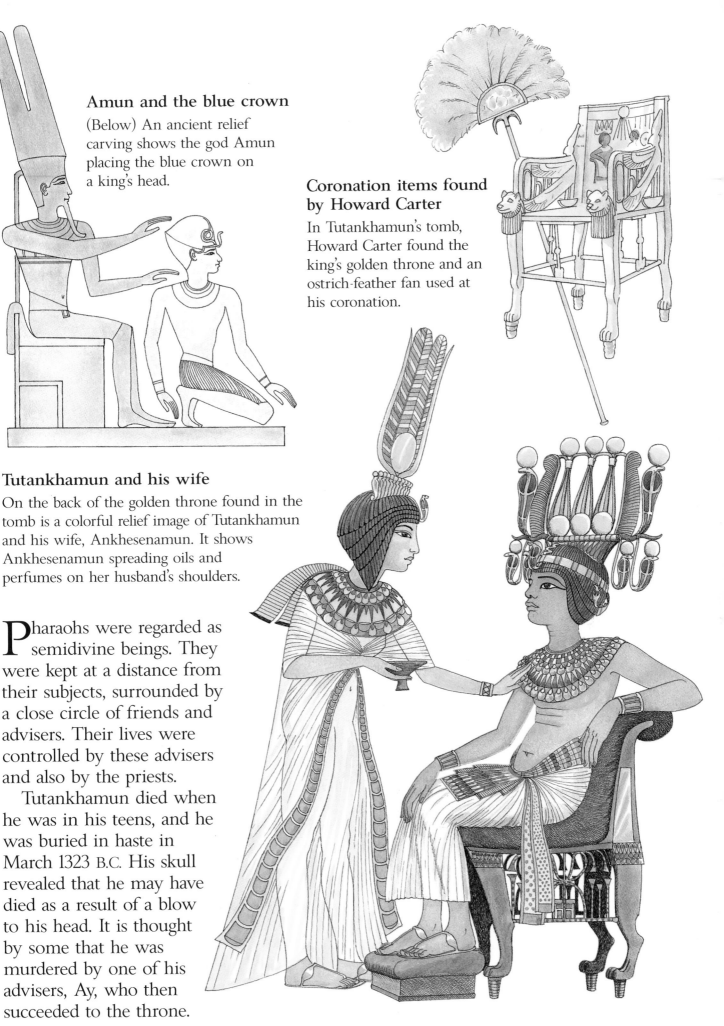

Amun and the blue crown

(Below) An ancient relief carving shows the god Amun placing the blue crown on a king's head.

Coronation items found by Howard Carter

In Tutankhamun's tomb, Howard Carter found the king's golden throne and an ostrich-feather fan used at his coronation.

Tutankhamun and his wife

On the back of the golden throne found in the tomb is a colorful relief image of Tutankhamun and his wife, Ankhesenamun. It shows Ankhesenamun spreading oils and perfumes on her husband's shoulders.

Pharaohs were regarded as semidivine beings. They were kept at a distance from their subjects, surrounded by a close circle of friends and advisers. Their lives were controlled by these advisers and also by the priests.

Tutankhamun died when he was in his teens, and he was buried in haste in March 1323 B.C. His skull revealed that he may have died as a result of a blow to his head. It is thought by some that he was murdered by one of his advisers, Ay, who then succeeded to the throne.

Tutankhamun's Tomb

Building work on the tomb intended for Tutankhamun had barely begun when the young king died, so he was buried in another, private tomb. Since it was much smaller than his own tomb would have been, the grave goods buried with him were all jammed in to fit.

Tutankhamun's tomb is cut into the bedrock of the Valley of the Kings. Sixteen steps lead down to a sloping corridor, which Howard Carter found full of rubble. The entrance doorway and all the other doorways in the tomb were filled with limestone blocks, which were then plastered over and stamped with many oval seals.

The corridor is just over 26 feet (8 m) long, 6.5 feet (2 m) wide, and 6.5 feet (2 m) high. It leads to the antechamber, which lies 23 feet (7 m) below the valley floor. The most prominent objects found here were three gilded couches in the shape of animals; two life-size painted wooden figures of the king; and a tangle of chariot parts. There were also boxes, stools, and chairs.

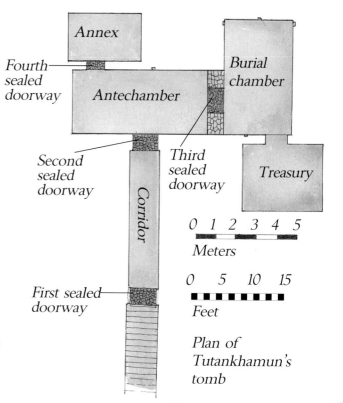

Annex

Fourth sealed doorway

Antechamber

Burial chamber

Second sealed doorway

Third sealed doorway

Treasury

Corridor

0 1 2 3 4 5
Meters

0 5 10 15
Feet

First sealed doorway

Plan of Tutankhamun's tomb

Annex
The annex lies at a lower level than the antechamber.

The jackal and nine captives
Several types of seal were found in the tomb, some attached to lengths of cord used, for example, to close boxes. This seal shows a jackal and nine captives.

Antechamber
The antechamber was piled high with grave goods, which completely covered the doorway to the annex.

The position of the wall paintings in the burial chamber

More than 600 objects were found in the antechamber, and in the annex there were another 2,000 piled up, including stone vessels, baskets, boxes, stools, chairs, and bedsteads.

Inside the burial chamber itself, the golden shrine of Tutankhamun took up nearly all the space. Around it were 11 oars and some wine jars and lamps. When Carter opened the shrine, he found that it contained four more shrines, one inside the other; the last one held the coffin with Tutankhamun's mummy.

The treasury was full of religious and funerary objects. The most important was a gilt shrine containing the embalmed internal organs of the king.

Paintings in the burial chamber

The four walls of the burial chamber had been decorated with paintings representing Tutankhamun's funeral and his meetings with various gods in the afterlife.

Scarabs

In the rubble of the entrance stairway, Carter found a green-glazed scarab (a beetle-shaped amulet).

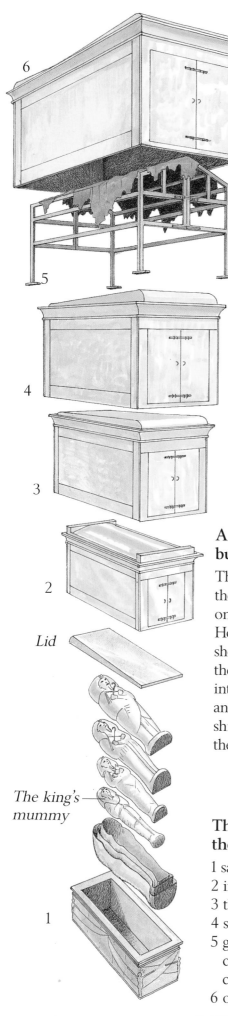

The King's Mummy

When they opened the doorway into the burial chamber, Carter and his team faced a great wall of gold—one side of a shrine measuring 16 x 11 x 11 feet (5 x 3 x 3 m). This shrine was made of gilded wood, inlaid with blue faience (pottery).

Inside its double doors was a dark brown cloth laid over a wooden frame. Under this was a second golden shrine, inside that a third shrine, and inside that the inner shrine. All the shrines were lavishly decorated with religious and funerary images and symbols. The inner shrine was a miniature representation of an ancient palace, the "Palace of the North."

Inside the smallest shrine was a sarcophagus (stone coffin), 9 x 11 x 5 feet (2.5 x 3 x 1.5 m). It had been carved out of a single block of quartzite, and its red granite lid was painted yellow to match the rest.

A plan of the burial chamber

The illustration on the right is based on a drawing by Howard Carter. It shows how tightly the shrines fitted into one another and how the outer shrine nearly filled the burial chamber.

The casing of the mummy

1 sarcophagus
2 inner shrine
3 third shrine
4 second shrine
5 gabled frame, covered with a cloth
6 outer shrine

The gold mask

Tutankhamun's mummy was found wearing as many as 100 items including amulets, jewels, a dagger, sandals, and toe- and finger-stalls made of gold. The solid gold mask (right) over the mummy's face was the most strikingly beautiful object found in the tomb. When the treasures of Tutankhamun were displayed to the public, this mask in particular caused a sensation.

Using specially designed pulleys, Carter lifted the sarcophagus lid. James Henry Breasted, who was watching, wrote: "At first we saw only a long, narrow, black void. Then across the middle of this blackness we gradually discerned fragments of granite which had fallen out of the fracture in the lid. They were lying scattered upon a dark shroud through which we seemed to see emerging an indistinct form. . ."

They had reached the first of a set of glittering coffins, shaped in the form of an Egyptian king.

The faces on the coffins

Below is the outer coffin, inside which nested two more coffins. On the left is the face on the outer coffin. Above it is the face on the second coffin, and above that the face on the third coffin. Inside the third coffin was Tutankhamun's mummy.

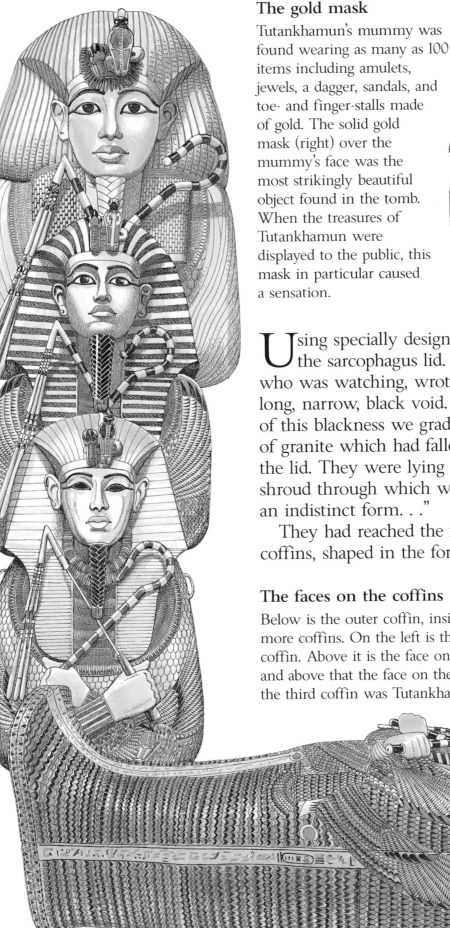

The Treasury

Howard Carter wrote a description of the tomb's treasury soon after he first opened the room in 1923. But it was not until October 1926 that he was able to start clearing this room, recording and preserving all the 500 major objects that it contained.

The main item in the treasury was a large gilded shrine mounted on a sled. This was the "canopic shrine." Inside was a beautiful stone chest containing the embalmed internal organs of Tutankhamun. Carter described the canopic shrine as "the most beautiful monument that I have ever seen."

In front of the shrine, facing the doorway, Carter saw a figure of the jackal god Anubis wrapped in cloth. Between this figure and the shrine was a model of a cow head on a stand. Anubis and the cow (Hathor) represented the Underworld.

Sections through the canopic shrine

A vertical section (above) and a horizontal section (below) through the canopic shrine show how the stone chest inside it contained four small human-shaped coffins. Inside these, wrapped in bandages and preserved in scented oils, were the internal organs of Tutankhamun.

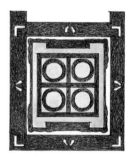

The canopic shrine

The canopic shrine (left) consisted of a gilded canopy (top) and a gilded wooden chest (second from top) inside which was a stone chest draped with linen. Around the top of the canopy were ornamental snake heads.

Cobra's head with sun disk

The canopic chest

The chest inside the canopic shrine rested on a gilded wooden sled (right). This chest was made of calcite, with details picked out in blue.

26

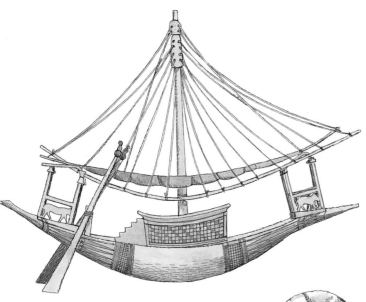

Model boats

This model sailing boat rested on the model granary. It was one of 35 model boats in Tutankhamun's tomb.

Children of Tutankhamun

A wooden box in the treasury contained two small human-shaped coffins. Inside each was an inner coffin containing a tiny mummy. One of them was wearing a gilded papier-mâché mask. Investigation showed that these were mummies of two premature babies, possibly the children of Tutankhamun.

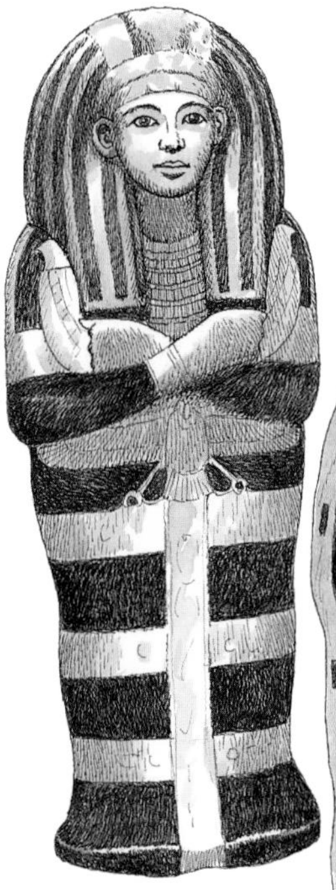

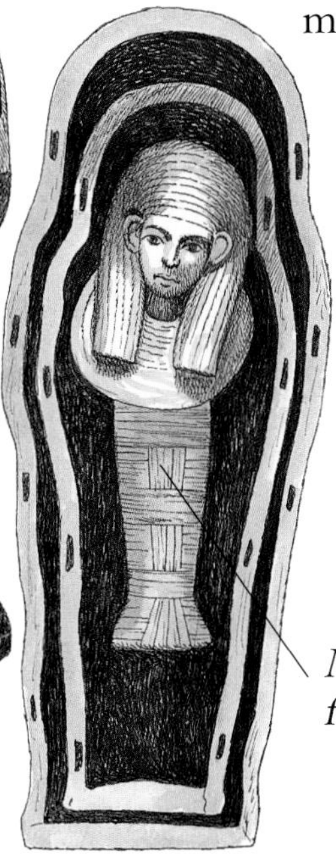

One of the calcite heads found in the canopic chest

Anubis

Anubis was the Egyptian god of embalming. He was represented with the head of a jackal or wild dog.

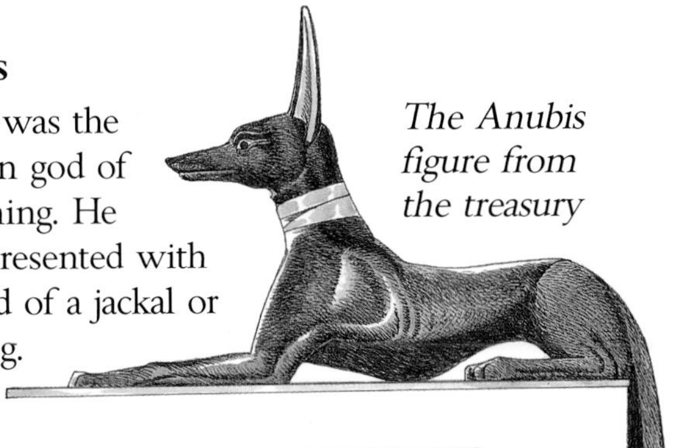

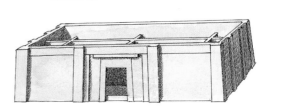

The Anubis figure from the treasury

A model granary

This model granary, with an entrance yard and 16 compartments for cereals, was made from white-painted wood. The compartments were full of seeds.

This black and gold cow's head represents the goddess Hathor

Mummified fetus

A tiny coffin

The larger of the two baby coffins is shown above with its lid removed. The mummy was a five-month-old female fetus.

The coffins inside the chest

The elaborate gold coffins (right) that contained Tutankhamun's preserved internal organs were contained in four cylindrical spaces inside the canopic chest. Each cylindrical space was covered with a lid modeled from calcite in the shape of the king's head.

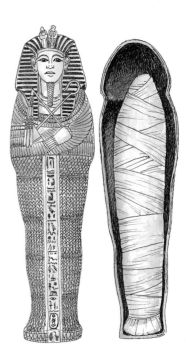

Furniture and Figures

The archeologists could scarcely believe that they had found such a wealth of precious objects in one relatively small tomb. Robbers had entered the tomb twice and must have taken away some jewelry and other items that could be easily carried through the narrow holes they had made to get in. But they had not been able to remove the splendid pieces of furniture, nor the figures of the pharaoh, gods, and sacred animals, many of which were crammed inside the treasury.

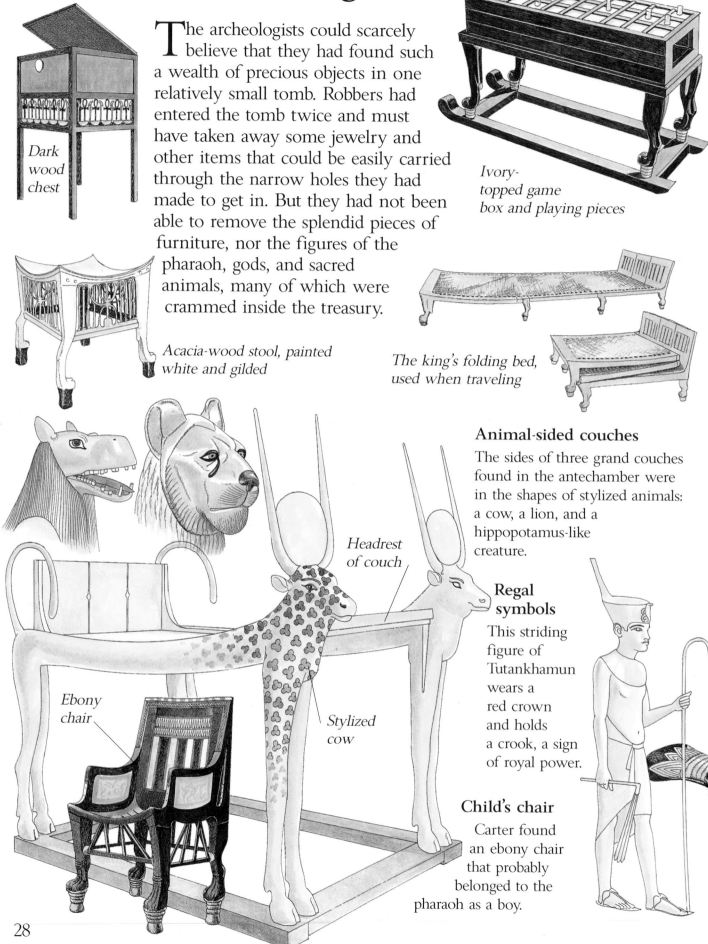

Dark wood chest

Ivory-topped game box and playing pieces

Acacia-wood stool, painted white and gilded

The king's folding bed, used when traveling

Headrest of couch

Ebony chair

Stylized cow

Animal-sided couches

The sides of three grand couches found in the antechamber were in the shapes of stylized animals: a cow, a lion, and a hippopotamus-like creature.

Regal symbols

This striding figure of Tutankhamun wears a red crown and holds a crook, a sign of royal power.

Child's chair

Carter found an ebony chair that probably belonged to the pharaoh as a boy.

28

*Box for carrying
rolls of papyrus*

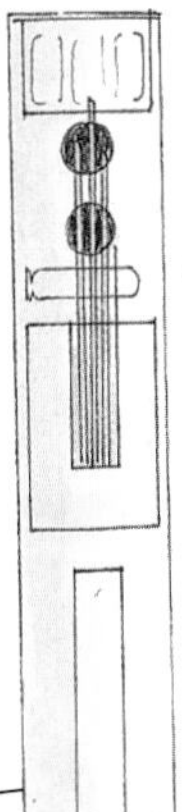

Ink palette ——

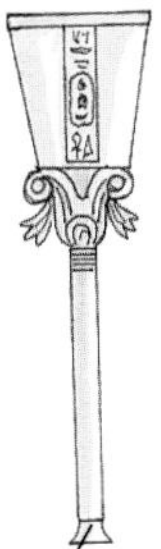

WRITING
IMPLEMENTS

*Papyrus
burnisher
(polisher)*

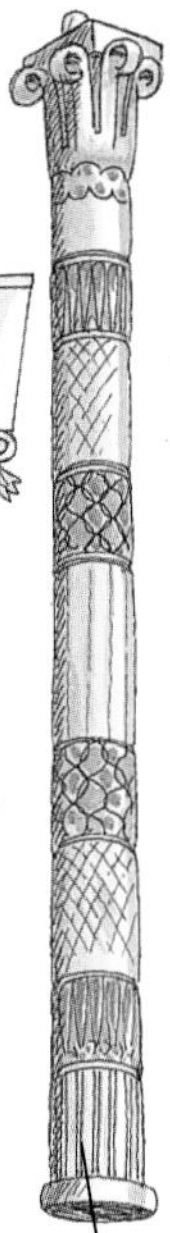

Decorated pen case

Sixty figures, showing Tutankhamun, gods, and animals, were found in the tomb. They were all made in the city of Akhetaten (renamed El Amarna), by artists working in a style developed during the reign of the pharaoh Akhenaten. In fact, some of the figures had been intended to go into Akhenaten's tomb, which was never completed.

In addition to these 60 figures, there also were more than 400 other wooden figures called "shabtis" in the tomb. These were intended to do menial agricultural work for the pharaoh in the next world.

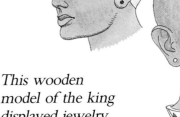

Shabti figures

413 shabtis were found in the tomb. 365 of them were workmen (one for each day of the year). The others were overseers.

*This wooden
model of the king
displayed jewelry
and clothing*

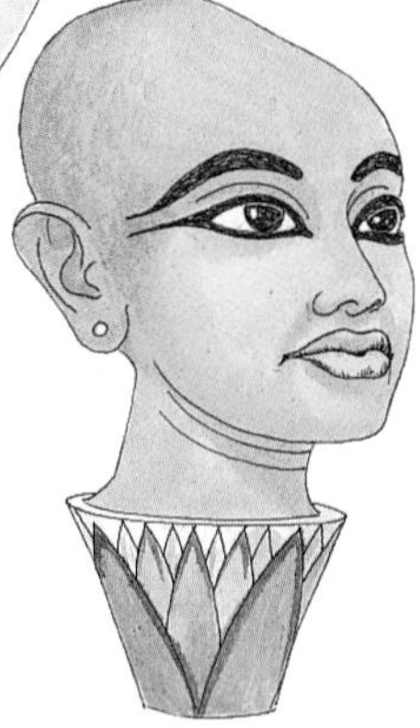

*Tutankhamun
as a child—a painted wooden head
emerging from a lotus flower*

*Three shabtis of
Tutankhamun*

Mighty hunter

This gilded statue of Tutankhamun shows him as the god Horus, standing on a papyrus boat and perhaps in the act of throwing his spear at a hippopotamus.

Incredible figure

This is one of the two life-size figures of Tutankhamun, made from gilded and blackened wood, which guarded the entrance to the burial chamber.

Tools, Weapons, and Chariots

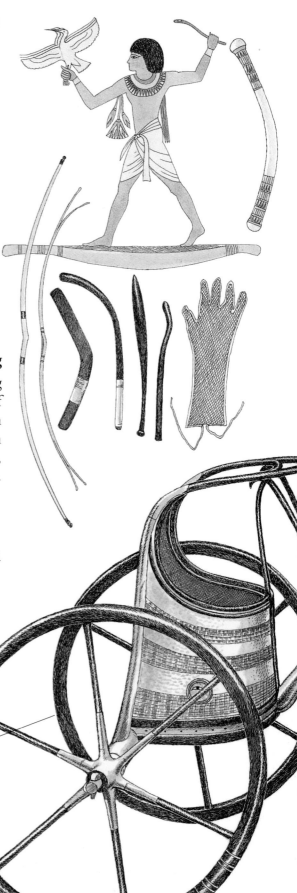

Chariots were among the most noble possessions of the New Kingdom pharaohs. Very often these pharaohs are represented standing proudly in their chariot—out hunting fowl or game, or in the middle of a battlefield shooting arrows at the enemy. War chariots were first used in Egypt about the year 1550 B.C.

Until Tutankhamun's tomb was opened, archeologists had found only two Egyptian chariots. Then, as they entered the antechamber of Tutankhamun's tomb, Howard Carter and Lord Carnarvon found a great pile of chariot parts in the left-hand corner. This one tomb alone contained the dismantled parts of six complete chariots of the most sophisticated kind.

Equipment for hunting

A tomb painting shows a nobleman hunting wildfowl in the marshes. He is using a kind of club. Many of these were found in Tutankhamun's tomb, together with boomerangs, throwing sticks, bows, arrows, and two quivers.

Two bronze swords— the small one belonged to Tutankhamun as a child

Agricultural items

These items in the tomb had a ritual purpose and were intended to be used in the next world:
1 storage jar; 2 rush basket;
3 sickle for harvesting wheat;
4 Syrian amphora;
5 hoe

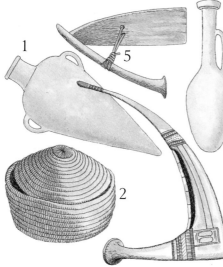

Rawhide tires

The chariots differed, depending on what they were used for. The body of one of them, made from bent wood and leather, was covered inside and out with gesso (a kind of plaster), overlaid with gold, and inlaid with brightly colored glass and stones. The typical Egyptian yoke at the end of the shaft was also overlaid with gold. This and another of the chariots were Tutankhamun's "state vehicles," used for parades and ceremonies.

Two other chariots, lighter and sturdier, were probably used for hunting.

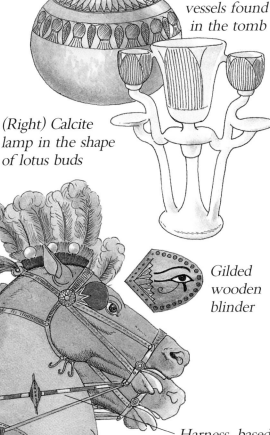

Pomegranate-shaped gold vase, one of the finest vessels found in the tomb

(Right) Calcite lamp in the shape of lotus buds

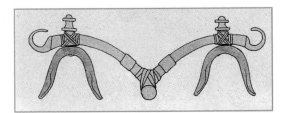

The two-horse yoke

The yoke was made of artificially bent hardwood covered with gold. It was pegged and tied into position.

Gilded wooden blinder

Harness, based on a reconstruction drawing made by Howard Carter

Fire-drill

This fire-drill found in the tomb would have been used for lighting candles and torches. Turning the bow made the stick rotate quickly in one of the holes in the block, setting alight the dried powder inside.

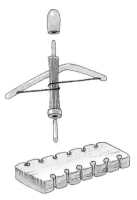

31

Underworld Journey

The old religion of Egypt had been restored after the death of Akhenaten, and Tutankhamun received a traditional "Osirian" burial. Egyptians believed the dead king would make a night-time journey, by boat, through the "Underworld," to be reborn at dawn in the realm of the gods. The gods and spirits were invoked, and many rituals were performed to ensure that he made the journey safely.

Ancient Egyptian religious books, *The Book of the Dead* and *What There Is in the Underworld*, describe the sun's journey during the 12 hours of the night. The dead king, like the dead sun, journeys through the Underworld with the main gods, and the walls of Tutankhamun's burial chamber were painted with scenes from the journey.

The protective winged goddess Isis, as engraved on the inner coffin

The king's funeral

In the painting on the east wall of the burial chamber, Tutankhamun's mummy is shown in a shrine hung with garlands. The shrine is pulled on a sled by five teams of men with mourning bands around their heads.

The Solar Boat

This drawing of the Solar Boat or Bark of the King is based on an engraving inside the second golden burial shrine. Tutankhamun is on the far left. On the far right is the god Re-Harakhti. Amun is third from the right. Behind him is Hathor. Third from the left is Osiris, Lord of the Underworld.

Welcomed in the Underworld

(Above) The south wall painting shows Tutankhamun (center) being welcomed in the Underworld by Hathor, goddess of the west. Behind him is Anubis.

Union with Osiris

(Above right) The north wall painting shows Tutankhamun as Osiris and his successor Ay (in a priest's leopard skin) at the "opening of the mouth" ritual (right); Tutankhamun being greeted by the goddess Nut in the realm of the gods (center); and Tutankhamun (in striped headdress), followed by his spirit or "ka," as he embraces Osiris, with whom he becomes one.

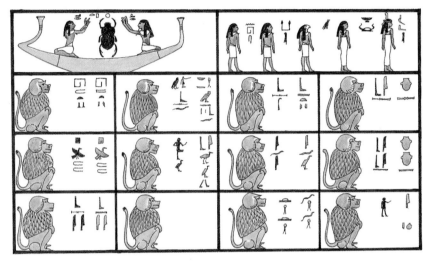

Twelve baboons

This painting on the west wall of the burial chamber represents part of the sacred book *What There Is in the Underworld*. At the top, five gods walk in front of the Solar Boat. Each baboon is associated with an hour of the night. The king must travel with the sun through the 12 hours of the night, to be reborn at dawn.

At the front of the Solar Boat is the falcon-headed sun god Re-Harakhti

"The Curse of the Mummy"

After the burial chamber had been opened in February 1923, Howard Carter and Lord Carnarvon took a rest from their excavations. Soon, Carnarvon fell ill. A mosquito bite on his cheek had become infected. Then he developed pneumonia, from which he died on April 5.

His sudden death gave rise to a morbid legend about "the curse of the mummy." Journalists reported that a writer called Marie Corelli had predicted that anyone intruding into a sealed tomb would receive "dire punishment." There were other mysterious stories: for example, that Carnarvon's dog had howled inconsolably through the night of his death and then died itself; that on the same night an unexplained power failure had plunged Cairo into darkness; and that on the day the tomb had been opened, Carter's canary had been eaten by "the pharaoh's cobra."

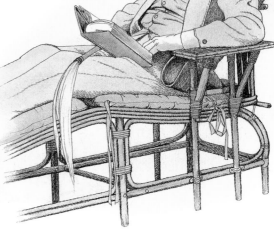

Lord Carnarvon had always been weak, after he had been injured in an automobile accident in 1901

Egyptomania in Hollywood

A 1932 Hollywood movie called *The Mummy* starred Boris Karloff and Zita Johann (above). It tells the story of an Egyptian mummy (played by Karloff) who returns to life in the 20th century. The filmmakers modeled the appearance of the mummy on that of the mummy of Rameses III.

For some 20 years, the death of anyone connected with the discovery of the tomb or with Lord Carnarvon was said to be caused by "the mummy's curse." On the other hand, it was pointed out that many of those people who had been most closely involved with the excavation suffered no harm. Howard Carter himself died of a heart attack in 1939—just before his 65th birthday.

In his later years Carter was often in Egypt, supervising work at the tomb. It is said that while there he discovered the location of the tomb of Alexander the Great and stated that "this secret will die with me." This is probably also a legend.

Carter was buried at Putney Vale in London. His gravestone reads:

HOWARD CARTER
Archaeologist and Egyptologist
Born May 9, 1874—died March 2, 1939

The discovery of Tutankhamun's tomb and the legend of the mummy's curse caused "Egyptomania," the fashion for all things Egyptian, to spread through 1920s Europe and America. The same kinds of fads had occurred at other times since Napoleon's day, whenever an important new find was made.

More recently, various exhibitions around the world, showing the treasures from Tutankhamun's tomb, have kept the interest alive, and in 1970s New York there was even a fashion called "Tutmania."

An article in The Connoisseur *magazine, February 1979, proves the enduring interest in ancient Egypt*

Following the recent opening of the Temple of Dendur and 'Treasures of Tutankhamun' at New York's Metropolitan Museum of Art, an exhibition sanctioning the current phenomena of 'Egyptomania' will be at the Metropolitan Museum from 16 January to 11 March 1979. Included are some fifty prints, drawings and ephemera of the eighteenth, nineteenth and twentieth centuries. The subject matter ranges from cemetery gates to cigarette advertisements.

'Living, healthy, and youthful forever and ever . . .'.

John Loring

Egyptomania: The Nile Style

A steely stare
The impassive face of Akhenaten, Tutankhamun's father, inspires respect. Looking at it, it is easy to understand how people could believe that such a man could curse those who dared to open his tomb.

Treasures of Tutankhamun

The treasures from Tutankhamun's tomb are now mostly on display at the Cairo Museum. The most stunning and important is the mask (left) found on the pharaoh's mummy. It is made from burnished gold, with blue glass stripes in the headdress and the false beard. The vulture's head on the brow, a symbol of the king's rule over Upper Egypt, is made from solid gold, with a glass beak. The cobra, a symbol of the king's rule over Lower Egypt, is gold decorated with blue faience, cornelian, lapis lazuli, and quartz. The eyebrows and eye makeup are lapis lazuli, the eyes quartz and obsidian.

Mummification preserved the body so that it was ready to receive the soul, and also made the dead pharaoh resemble the god Osiris. This mask represents Tutankhamun as Osiris. It is probably a lifelike picture of the young king's face.

Stunning headgear

The gold diadem (below) decorated with precious stones and glass was found on the mummy's head.

Fit for a pharaoh

At religious ceremonies, Tutankhamun sat on this "ecclesiastical throne."

Impressed

The canopic shrine (left) was "so lovely," said Howard Carter, "that it made one gasp in wonder and admiration."

Guardians

The shrine is surrounded by the protective figures of four goddesses: Isis, Nephthys, Neith, and Selkis.

Royal footwear

On the royal sandals there are pictures of captives who would be symbolically crushed under the king's feet as he walked.

Canopic vessels

The embalmed internal organs (liver, lungs, stomach, and intestines) of Tutankhamun were kept in four small coffins like the one on the right. Made of beaten gold, these coffins were elaborately decorated inside and out.

Elaborate couch

The cow head from one of the couches found in the antechamber (see page 28) represents the goddesses Hathor and Nut—it carries the solar disk between its horns.

Chronology

B.C.

ca. 6500 Farming begins in the Nile Valley. Villages combine and grow to form the kingdoms of Upper and Lower Egypt.

ca. 3100 Menes, King of Upper Egypt, conquers Lower Egypt and builds a new capital at Memphis. He becomes first king of the 1st Dynasty. Dynasties I and II are called the **Archaic Period.**

ca. 2680-2180 The **Old Kingdom** or **Pyramid Age** (Dynasties III-VI). Pharaohs of the 3rd Dynasty include Djoser, who builds the step pyramid at Saqqara. Pharaohs of the 4th Dynasty build the three straight-sided pyramids at Giza. 5th Dynasty pharaohs build the pyramid of Abusir and temples devoted to the sun god Re.

ca. 2180-2040 **1st Intermediate Period** (Dynasties VII-X) A troubled time of civil wars and foreign invasions.

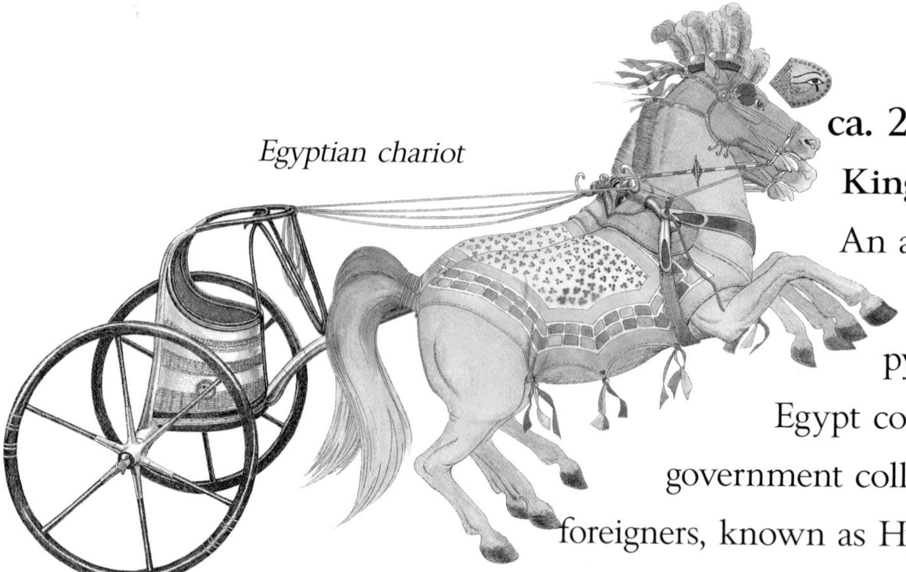

Egyptian chariot

ca. 2040-1650 The **Middle Kingdom** (Dynasties XI-XIII) An age of great achievement. Kings are buried in brick pyramids near the Fayuum. Egypt conquers Nubia. Eventually government collapses as foreigners, known as Hyksos, invade the Delta.

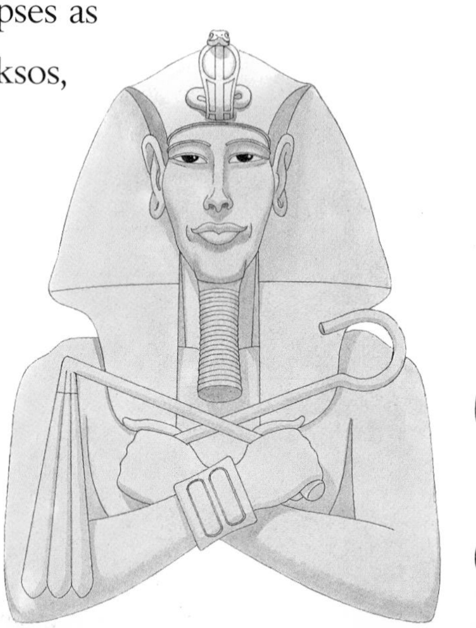

ca. 1750-1650 **2nd Intermediate Period** (Dynasties XIV-XVII) The Hyksos rule the Delta. Then 17th Dynasty pharaohs, based in Thebes, lead a revolt against them.

ca. 1550-1070 The **New Kingdom** (Dynasties XVIII-XX) Having driven out the Hyksos, Egypt goes on to build the greatest empire of the day. Akhenaten (right) and Tutankhamun reign toward the end of the 18th Dynasty.

Building works by kings make the temple of Amun at Karnak the biggest in Egypt. Temples at Luxor and the tombs in the Valley of the Kings are also built. Akhenaten builds Akhetaten (now El Amarna).

The 19th Dynasty includes Rameses I and II and Seti I and II. The 20th Dynasty includes pharaohs from Rameses III (left) to Rameses XI, who build many temples.

ca. 1070-663 3rd Intermediate Period (Dynasties XXI–XXV) The kings are weak, and the tombs in the Valley of the Kings are robbed. The descendants of Libyan mercenaries rule as Dynasties XXII-XXIII and the country splits into five small kingdoms. The kings of Nubia then conquer Egypt and rule as Dynasty XXV.

663-332 The **Late Period** (Dynasties XXVI-XXX) Egypt is conquered by Persians, then by Greek armies led by Alexander the Great.

332-323 Egypt is a province within Alexander's empire. After his death, his friend Ptolemy rules.

323-30 Egypt is ruled by the Ptolemies.

30 B.C.-A.D. 395 The Romans rule Egypt as a province of their empire.

A.D.

395-640 Egypt is a province of the Byzantine or Eastern Roman Empire.

French and Italian scholars

Howard Carter (left), Lady Evelyn Herbert, and Lord Carnarvon

640-1517 The Arabs invade Egypt, which becomes a province of their empire and then (in 969) an independent Muslim state.

1517-1798 Egypt is ruled by Turkey.

1798-1805 Egypt is ruled by France.

1805-1882 Turkey again rules Egypt.

1882-1922 Egypt is part of the British Empire.

1922-1952 Egypt is an independent kingdom.

1952- Egypt is an independent republic.

Glossary

amulet An object worn or kept as a charm against evil.

calcite Translucent soft stone used for lamps and delicate vessels.

canopic A word describing a jar (a "canopus") with a lid, designed to contain the internal organs that were removed from a person's body when it was embalmed. The lid was made in the shape of an animal or human head.

cornelian A reddish semiprecious stone.

dynasty A succession of rulers from the same family. There are 30 dynasties in ancient Egyptian history.

embalming Preserving a dead body, generally by treating it with oils, spices, and perfumes.

Tutankhamun's ka stands behind him as he embraces Osiris

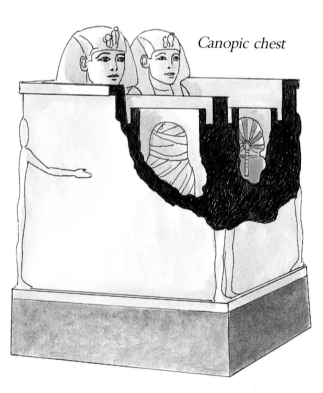

Canopic chest

faience A colored glazed pottery.

funerary Having to do with a funeral.

gesso A plaster surface, used as a base for decoration.

gilded Covered or overlaid with gold.

ka One of three spirits, which the ancient Egyptians believed was released when a person died. It lived on in the tomb, like a "double" of the person.

lapis lazuli A deep-blue stone.

lotus An Egyptian and Indian water lily.

mummy A body that has been preserved after death. In ancient Egypt, it was only pharaohs and very important people who were mummified at first. From ca. 2000 B.C. more people were mummified.

New Kingdom A period of ancient Egyptian history starting ca. 1550 B.C. About 30 pharaohs from the 18th, 19th, and 20th Dynasties ruled Egypt during this period. They included Tutankhamun.

obsidian A dark volcanic type of rock resembling green bottle glass.

opening of the mouth ritual A ritual that was performed at the entrance of a tomb before the mummy was carried inside. The mummy in its coffin was held upright, and a priest touched its lips with special tools. Ancient Egyptians believed that this act would make the mummy able to see and feel again.

papyrus A tall plant that grows in water. The ancient Egyptians used its stems to make a material for writing on. The word "paper" comes from papyrus.

Shabtis from Tutankhamun's tomb

pharaoh The name used for a king in ancient Egyptian times.

pyramid A huge monument of stone, with a square base and triangular sides sloping upward to a point. The ancient Egyptians built pyramids over the burial chambers of their pharaohs.

sarcophagus A stone coffin, often with carvings on it.

scribe A "writer," meaning a person whose job was to copy documents. Ancient Egyptians believed that in the afterlife the pharaoh became a scribe to the sun god.

shabti A small statue or figure of the dead person that the Egyptians put in the tomb with his or her mummy. Many shabti figures were put in the tombs of pharaohs buried during the New Kingdom. The figures represented the dead king, and worked on his behalf in the afterlife.

Sphinx An ancient imaginary monster with a human head and the body of a lion, lying down. The later Greek version also has wings. A huge stone sphinx was built at Giza in ca. 2540 B.C.

Underworld The world of the dead, as it was imagined by ancient religions.

The "opening of the mouth" ceremony

Egyptian Gods

Amun From the Middle Kingdom period onward, Amun was the supreme god in the Egyptian religion. The Temple of Amun was built at Karnak.

Anubis The god of embalming, Anubis is represented with a human body and the head of a black jackal.

Aten This god represented one part (the sun's disk) of the sun god Re-Harakhti. During his reign, the pharaoh Akhenaten made Aten the only god that Egyptians were allowed to worship. Afterward, in the time of Tutankhamun, the old religion was restored, with Amun as the supreme one of very many gods.

Amun

Hathor This goddess of love, dancing, and joy was represented as a cow or with some features of a cow's head.

Horus This god of the sky was shown as a man with a hawk's head. He was believed to be the son of Isis and Osiris. The ancient Egyptians believed that Horus "lived" in their pharaoh, giving the ruler godly power.

Isis Believed to be the wife and sister of Osiris and the mother of Horus, Isis was greatly revered.

Second from the right, Nut welcomes Tutankhamun to the realm of the gods. On the left Tutankhamun embraces Osiris

Nut This goddess of the sky was the mother of Osiris, Isis, Seth, and Ra.

Osiris The "king of the Underworld," Osiris was represented as a mummy, with green skin and wearing a white crown. Egyptians believed that he had once been king of Egypt; his brother Seth had murdered him and scattered the pieces of his body. His sister Isis bandaged the pieces together, making him the first mummy, and so he became king of the Underworld. He is believed to be the son of Nut and Geb, the god of the earth and the husband of Isis.

Re-Harakhti This is a personification of the sun god Re in the shape of Horus, the falcon, carrying the solar disk on his head.

Re-Harakhti

Index

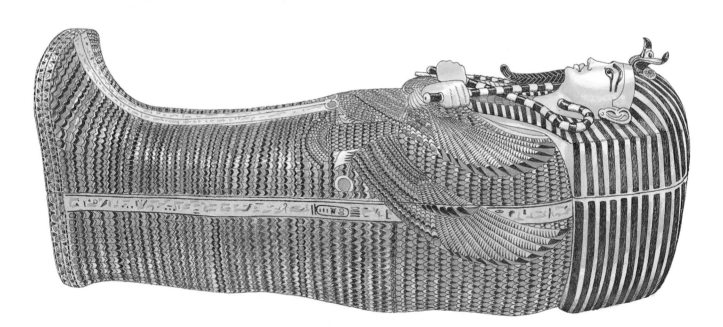

18.95

– – B Tutankhamun C
Caselli, Giovanni.
In search of Tutankhamun.

ENCYCLOPEDIA OF
FAMILY HEALTH

THIRD EDITION

ENCYCLOPEDIA OF
FAMILY HEALTH

THIRD EDITION

CONSULTANTS

David B. Jacoby, M.D.
Johns Hopkins School of Medicine

Robert M. Youngson, M.D.
Royal Society of Medicine

VOLUME 11

OSTEOPATHY — PHYSICAL THERAPY

MARSHALL CAVENDISH
New York • London • Singapore

MEDICAL CONSULTANTS

Second Edition
David B. Jacoby, M.D.
Johns Hopkins School of Medicine
Associate Professor of Pulmonary and Critical
Care Medicine

Third Edition
Robert M. Youngson, M.D.
Fellow of the Royal Society of Medicine
Officer of the Order of St John of Jerusalem
Diploma in Tropical Medicine and Hygiene
Fellow of the Royal College of Ophthalmologists

CONTRIBUTORS TO THIRD EDITION

David Arnot   Tom Jackson
Deborah Evans   Nathan Lepora
Leon Gray   Fiona Plowman
Joanna Griffin   Alison Tarrant
Tim Harris   Aruna Vasudevan
John Jackson

Picture Credits
(b – bottom; t – top; r – right; l – left; c – center)

Cover: Dynamic Graphics: John Foxx & Images 4 Communication b/l, b/r;
PhotoDisc: Don Farrall b/c, Keith Brofsky t/r, Russell Illig c.

Alan Hutchinson Library: 1476t; All-Sport: 1447c/r, 1447b/l, 1448; Beecham Group: 1550;
Biophoto Associates: 1537t/r; Bruce Coleman Ltd: 1500 all, Jessica Ehiers 1465t; Bubbles:
1520, 1521; Camera Press: 1515; Camilla Jessel 1559c; Cardiologic UK Ltd: 1472t; Charles
Day: 1484; C James Webb: 1557t/l, 1451l, 1457t/l, 1498c/r, 1499c/l, 1500b, 1512b/l, 1512b/c,
1512b/r; Colorific: Mary Fisher 1499b/l, Penny Tweedie 1545; Colorsport: 1446; Corbis:
Ariel Skelley 1490, Becky Luigart-Stayner 1502, Chris Hamilton 1494, Dann Tardif/LWA
1518b, James A Sugar 1513t/r, Javier Pierini 1497c/l, Jogi Inc 1467, John Garrett 1472b, Jose
Luis Pelaez Inc 1553t, Lester V Bergman 1533, 1565t/r, Michael Keller 1548, Rick Gomez
1526, Roy Morsch 1491, Stephen Welstead/LWA 1517t, 1519, Tom Stewart 1450, 1516;
Dynamic Graphics: John Foxx & Images 4 Communication 1461, 1466, 1571; The
Fotomas Index: 1452; Getty Images: 1512t, 1534, 1565t/l, 1574, 1577, Brad Martin 1459,
Carol Kohen 1544b, Chris Cole 1544t, Eric Bouvet 1463, Larry Dale Gordon 1497t/r,
Laurence Monneret 1558, Stephen Marks 1557t/r; Hulton/Archive: 1528t; Images: 1449
all, 1540; Image State: 1564; Imagingbody.com: 1528b, Raquet/Eurelios 1478; Jerry
Harpur: 1483, 1498t, 1569t/l, 1569c/l; King's College Hospital Medical School: Medical
Unit 1503; London Scientific Photos: 1500t, 1500c/t; Medicine Ltd: Sandoz Products Ltd
1507 all; National Portrait Gallery: 1549t/r; Nordisk-UK: 1487t/r; Nottingham Rehab:
1493; Paul Brierley: 1529 all; Paul Windsor: 1561, 1563; PHIL: Armed Forces Institute of
Pathology, C Goldsmith, J Katz & S Zaki 1508, Charles N Farmer 1513t/l, Dr Shirely E
Maddison 1509, Dr W Winn 1510; Phil Babb: 1480, 1524 all; PhotoDisc: Don Tremain 1457,
1477, Doug Menuez 1460, Keith Brofsky 1511, 1514, 1551c/r, 1553b, Russell Illig 1474, Steve
Mason 1465b; Photos.com: 1497t/l, 1497c/m; Rex Features: 1506t, Action Press 1562t,
Elizabeth Welch 1560, Everett Collection 1539, Lehtikuva Oy 1475, Phanie Agency 1477t,
1569t/r; Robert Harding: 1522, 1537t/r; Robert Hunt Library: 1499t; Roger Payling: 1532,
1555; Ron Sutherland: 1479, 1552, 1581; Science Photo Library: 1496 all, 1517t, 1535, Blair
Seita 1453b, Catherine Pauedras/Eurelios 1506b, CC Studio 1580, Custom Medical Stock
Photo 1455t, Geoff Tompkinson 1554, Hank Morgan 1488, 1547, James King Holmes 1575,
Jerrican Laguet 1573, John Greim 1454, 1518t, 1566, Joyce Photographics 1471, Larry
Mulvehill 1578, Martin Dohrn 1481, Michael Gilbert 1469, Dr P Marrazzi 1546, Sinclair
Stammers 1468, Sue Ford 1470, Will & Deni McIntyre 1455b, 1456, 1481, Will McIntyre
1495; Vision International: Anthea Sieveking 1568; Zefa: 1453t, 1476b, 1505, 1527, 1536,
1538, 1570, 1576, 1579; Zoe Dominic: 1559t/l.

Marshall Cavendish
99 White Plains Road
Tarrytown, NY 10591-9001

www.marshallcavendish.com

© 2005, 1998, 1991 Marshall Cavendish Corporation

Library of Congress Cataloging-in-Publication Data

Encyclopedia of family health / David B. Jacoby, Robert M. Youngson.--
3rd ed.
    p. cm.
Includes bibliographical references and index.
  ISBN 0-7614-7486-2 (set)
  ISBN 0-7614-7497-8 (vol 11)
1. Medicine, Popular--Encyclopedias. 2. Health--Encylopedias. 1. Jacoby, David
B. II. Youngson, R. M. III. Marshall Cavendish Corporation. IV. Title
RC81.A2E5 2004
610'.3--dc22   2003065554
Printed in China
08 07 06 05 04 5 4 3 2 1

Marshall Cavendish

Editor: Joyce Tavolacci
Editorial Director: Paul Bernabeo
Production Manager: Alan Tsai

The Brown Reference Group

Project Editor: Anne Hildyard
Editors: Jane Lanigan, Sally McFall
Designers: Jeni Child, Reg Cox, Karen Frazer
Picture Researcher: Clare Newman
Indexer: Kay Ollerenshaw
Illustrations: Samantha J. Elmhurst
Managing Editor: Tim Cooke
Art Director: Dave Goodman

CONTENTS

KEY TO COLOR CODING OF ARTICLES

HUMAN BODY

DISEASES AND OTHER DISORDERS

TREATMENTS AND CURES

PREVENTION AND DIAGNOSIS OF DISEASE

HUMAN BEHAVIOR

Osteopathy

The art of manipulation and massage that led to osteopathy has been practiced since ancient times, but in the last century the idea has become more accepted that osteopathy can achieve success when conventional medicine cannot help.

Osteopathy is a system of medicine that diagnoses and treats disorders of the bones, muscles, ligaments, and joints. It is also a therapy that recognizes all parts of the body and takes into account such factors as people's health, lifestyle, environment, diet, and stressors.

The osteopath is a highly trained practitioner who uses his or her hands to treat the body when illness arises. He or she works to restore body control mechanisms, to relieve pain and discomfort, and to improve joint mobility (see Joints).

Although massage and manipulation have existed since ancient times, the art and science of osteopathy actually originated in the United States in the late 19th century. Its founder, Andrew Taylor Still, had qualified as a doctor, but like many of his contemporaries, he was skeptical of many of the methods then used. He had developed a consuming interest in the structure of the body during his childhood and he chose osteopathy (bone disease) as the name for his system of healing to underline the principle that structure governs function. Although this was doubted by the medical profession of his day, modern research has proved him right. The self-regulating activities that keep numerous body functions within proper limits (homeostasis) are closely related to the structural components by different reflexes of the nervous system (see

▲ *The most common strains and sprains that are treated by osteopaths are sports injuries, particularly those that arise in contact sports.*

Homeostasis). By normalizing the relationships of joints (especially of the spine), muscles, ligaments, and connective tissue, an osteopath can treat the whole body.

Scope of osteopathy

Most people who consult an osteopath do so because they have pain and restricted movement somewhere (often in the lower back, the neck, or the shoulders). These injuries arise for a variety of reasons that range from accidents to rheumatism. However, an osteopath can often resolve these problems faster and more completely than rest in bed or drugs.

Some scientists believe that massage can speed healing by softening the scar tissue, and improving the metabolism and blood flow, but this is not proved (see Massage). Osteopaths may also use ultrasound or heat therapies (see Heat Treatment).

Medicine divides diseases into two principal categories: organic and functional. Organic illnesses are those that destroy or permanently alter some body tissue or system; examples are cancer, tuberculosis, cirrhosis of the liver, and coronary artery disease. Functional illnesses occur when the body is not working properly, because of infections, changes in blood pressure, or recurring symptoms of migraines or asthma, for example. Many so-called psychosomatic illnesses are given this label because no obvious medical reason can be found for the disorder (see Psychosomatic Problems). Anxiety, stress, and emotional or personality problems often accompany these disorders, with the resulting symptoms of muscular tension, disturbed circulation, and altered nerve and hormonal supply. By treating these associated symptoms manually, osteopathy has a strong, constructive role to play in the healing process.

Osteopathic treatment is actually suitable for males and females of all ages. It is especially suitable for growing children, since if potential disorders are detected and treated at this early stage, future disabilities can be prevented (see Growth). Strains, sprains, falls, and other minor injuries generally are painful for only a short time (see Sprains); but the long-term effects that are caused by muscular and ligamentous shortening, fibrosis, and minor derangements in the joints are very common. Eventually, lack of exercise, obesity, aging, or a subsequent injury can reveal these

▲ *Babies who suffer from asthma or ear infections, or have had a difficult birth, can benefit from cranial osteopathy—the manipulation of the subtle motion of the cerebrospinal fluid.*

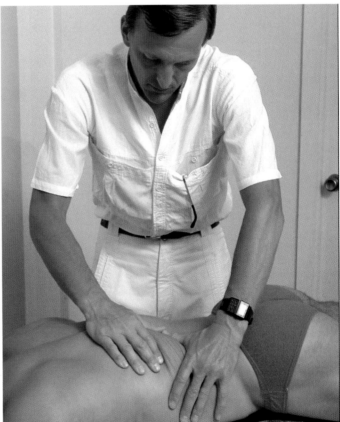

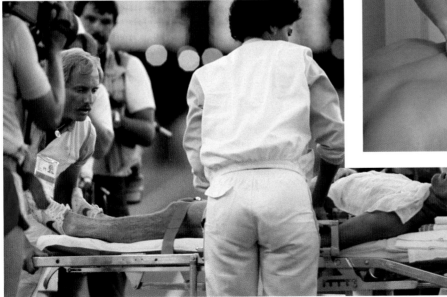

◄▲ *Olympic athletes (left) seem equally prone to muscular injuries that can benefit from the healing manipulation of an osteopath (above). Leg injuries usually heal very quickly. More troublesome are back strains; these may require a lengthy course of treatment before they heal.*

What causes the popping sound that occurs when the osteopath adjusts my spine?

Each vertebra in the spine has four bony projections that form joints with adjacent vertebrae. Each of these joints is enclosed by a fibrous capsule with synovial fluid inside as a lubricant. When the spine is manipulated, the joint surfaces are forced apart, disturbing the pressure equilibrium inside the joint capsule. The resulting pop is similar in principle to cracking the knuckles. The sound is louder because it goes along the bones of the spine.

My 14-year-old brother has developed a curvature of the spine. Can osteopathy help?

The answer depends on the reason for the curvature. If it is caused by an accident or poor posture, a complete cure can be expected. However, a few children develop a more severe hereditary curvature (scoliosis). Regular osteopathic treatment during the growing phase can usually reduce the degree of curvature, but surgical splinting of the spine may be needed.

The osteopath that I have consulted for lower-back pain has advised me to have all my shoes fitted with a higher heel on one foot. Why is this?

It may be that you have a primary short leg—the bones are shorter in one leg than the other. This is fairly common, owing to either an earlier fracture or the bones' growing at different rates. A primary short leg unbalances the pelvis, forcing the spine to bend to one side and form curves in compensation. The unequal pressures and muscular tensions of this posture can cause strains and backaches. Although most human spines are flexible enough to adapt to a small difference in leg lengths, a heel insert or a specially modified shoe may be necessary to level off the pelvis, and so correct the imbalance and spinal pressure.

weaknesses (see Aging; Obesity). If they are left untreated, an increased susceptibility to injury or the onset of arthritis can occur.

Osteopathy is not a substitute for medicine or surgery in diseases when conventional medicine is clearly more effective. However, it can help treat most muscle and bone disorders, functional illnesses, and chronic diseases that can seriously affect the structure of the body.

Training

Osteopaths study a number of medical disciplines including anatomy, physiology, pathology, biochemistry, and neurology, as well as osteopathic diagnosis and treatment. The distinctive feature of the training is the development of great sensitivity of the hands, an essential requirement for proper diagnosis, and the corresponding artistry and subtlety in the application of treatment to the body. Diagnosis of a problem can involve initial X rays, blood and urine tests, and also referral to specialists, in addition to manual techniques (see X Rays).

Theory and practice

All the various bodily systems function normally by very sophisticated processes of communication and control. The role of the muscles and bones is actually much greater than simply providing support and a framework for the body. The muscles, for example, besides enabling physical work and self-expression, also affect bone structure and posture, circulation, metabolism, and hormonal balance (see Bones; Muscles).

Osteopathy is specifically concerned with the way disturbances and injuries of a mechanical nature can negatively influence other bodily processes and contribute to poor health. A central part of this theory has been called the osteopathic lesion. In medical terms, a "lesion" is a disturbance of the structure or function of the body, such as a wound, tumor, or chemical abnormality. In osteopathic practice, a "lesion" is a more complex and subtle disturbance that may appear as a source of pain or discomfort, yet be unnoticed by the patient or in a routine

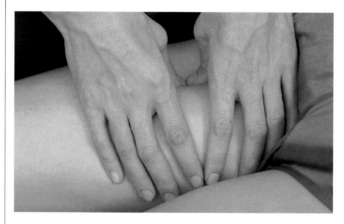

◄▼ *Massage often forms part of the manipulative therapy performed by an osteopath. It can revitalize tired, aching muscles as well as treat more serious problems. Leg muscles are prone to aches, as well as pain resulting from injuries such as pulled, torn, or knotted muscles.*

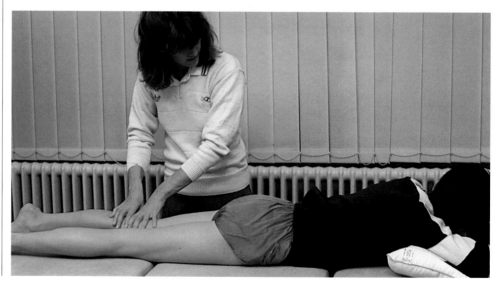

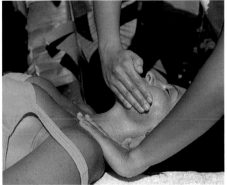

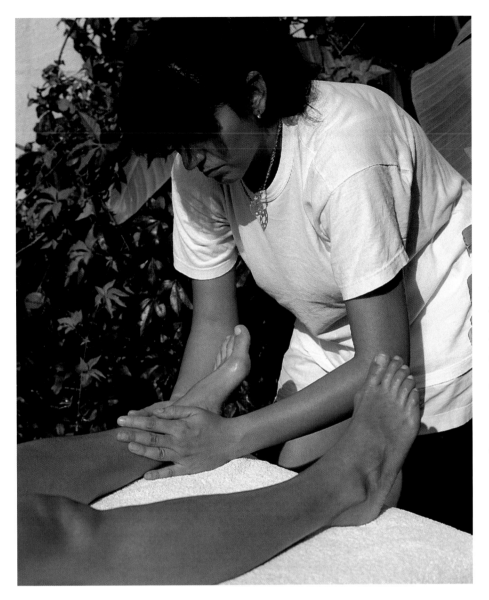

◀ ▲ *Osteopathy is also effective for treating areas far from the spinal cord, such as the ankles (left) and jaw (above).*

Treatment

A typical session with an osteopath generally lasts for between 20 and 30 minutes. Once the cause of the pain or illness has been determined, the osteopath will then decide if manipulation is safe and desirable, and if so, what type of treatment to apply.

Spinal manipulation is often accompanied by soft tissue work—for example, massage, stretching, and putting the joints through their full ranges of movement. Some osteopaths practice a specialized form of manipulation that is applied to the head and upper neck. This is known as cranial osteopathy, and it is a very gentle treatment that is particularly useful for treating young children and for treating functional disorders such as migraines, sinusitis, and visual disturbances (see Migraine; Sinusitis).

The number of osteopathic sessions needed for a particular condition will vary widely among individuals, but most osteopaths prefer not only to resolve the main problem but also to improve the patient's general mobility and health, in order to prevent future problems.

medical examination. The osteopathic lesion, discovered by careful touch examination and specific tests, may be an area of contracted muscle or a shortened ligament anywhere in the body (see Ligaments). It frequently occurs as a change in normal joint movement in the spinal column (see Spinal Cord).

The vertebrae themselves are passive structures that are pushed or pulled around by the forces of gravity, trauma, and muscular or ligamentous action. The distinctive contribution of osteopathy is to seek out and then correct these disturbances by manual methods, supplemented when necessary by other therapies, especially change in the diet and the environment. Local pain or discomfort from muscle spasm or irritation of the nerve roots is thus gradually relieved, and altered circulation is achieved, along with beneficial effects for the overall health of the person.

From the osteopathic point of view, a spinal lesion is generally the largest single contributing factor in this vicious circle of functional and organic disorder. The correcting influences of manipulation are therefore applied to restore the natural defenses and at the same time to encourage the tendency of the body to restore body controls, thereby restoring the patient's good health and his or her general well-being.

Dangers

There are some diseases and conditions for which manipulation is undesirable or even dangerous. The practitioner's skill and experience should determine whether or not they try to treat spinal disk herniation, osteoarthritis, or severe sciatica (see Osteoarthritis; Sciatica). However, tuberculosis, malignancy, acute arthritis, various bone diseases, fractures, and severe cases of herniated disks that cause neurological symptoms should not be manipulated under any circumstances. A qualified osteopath can detect conditions such as these and then make appropriate referrals. This is the major advantage that an osteopath has over a chiropractor.

> **See also:** Arthritis; Back and backache; Chiropractic; Fibrositis; Manipulation; Physical therapy; Posture; Rheumatism; Slipped disk; Sports injury; Ultrasound

Osteoporosis

This condition of unusually light and fragile bones causes 238,000 hip fractures in the United States each year. Women are four times more likely than men to suffer from the disease. However, osteoporosis is preventable.

My grandmother has a humpback. It seems to have occurred gradually since her 70th birthday. She calls it her dowager's hump and says that it's not worth worrying about because it doesn't hurt. Is she right? What caused it?

A dowager's hump is the result of osteoporosis, in which the bones become smaller, lighter, and less robust than normal. Over the years, some of the bones in your grandmother's spine have become squashed and others have collapsed into a wedge shape, so that the spine has bent into a hump. Your grandmother is right not to worry about it; it is not life-threatening, it often causes no pain, and severe cases are rare.

Can I avoid osteoporosis if I drink plenty of milk?

Some of the constituents of milk are essential for bone growth, but milk cannot prevent osteoporosis, which is a condition of old age and its accompanying changes in the balance of the body's hormones or chemical messengers. By all means drink plenty of milk, but don't expect it to work wonders.

Is it true that women on hormone replacement therapy (HRT) do not develop osteoporosis?

Hormone replacement therapy (HRT) may be given to women who suffer from severe problems associated with menopause. One of these problems is the failure of the ovaries to produce the hormone estrogen, and it is thought that a lack of estrogen is a cause of osteoporosis. HRT usually consists of estrogen and progesterone. Evidence suggests that HRT does seem to prevent or reverse osteoporosis to some extent, but HRT is now known to pose some serious health risks, which must be weighed against its few and relatively slight benefits.

▲ *Elderly people are prone to osteoporosis. The weakened bones can cause minor deformities, falls, and fractures.*

The bones in the body are not dead, as some people imagine. They are living material that is constantly changing. When such changes involve a loss of bone, the condition is called osteoporosis.

Causes

The most common cause of osteoporosis is aging. From middle age onward everyone's bones become lighter. This change is generally more marked in women after they have been through the menopause. However, it is only when an excessive amount of bone is lost that the symptoms of osteoporosis arise (see Aging).

There are other, more complicated causes of osteoporosis, most of which are rare. In such cases the loss of bone is usually a result of drastic changes in the body that have been brought about by another illness. In these instances, the osteoporosis is described as secondary, since it is an effect of the initial (primary) illness and will disappear if the primary illness is cured. Many cases of secondary osteoporosis are diseases of the hormonal system (see Endocrine System).

There is one relatively common secondary cause that is generally described as immobilization—a term meaning simply that the patient must stay in bed for some reason. Therefore, osteoporosis is often seen in the bones of a single limb, which cannot be moved because of pain, paralysis, or a broken (fractured) bone (see Fractures).

Symptoms

Osteoporosis may cause no symptoms at all, or it may give rise to bone pain and backache. In advanced cases there may be deformities such as loss of height or a bent spine. The bones tend to break easily from even minor accidents or trivial strains.

The most commonly caused fracture is the collapse of one of the spinal vertebrae (small bones). This may not hurt, or it may cause severe pain over that bone, which tends to improve without treatment over two or three months. In the long run, several of these fractures may occur and cause the spine to shorten and bend.

The other common fracture site is the hip, which is particularly vulnerable in older people, whose poor balance and general stiffness make them likely to fall. If an elderly patient has osteoporosis, a relatively minor trauma will often be enough to break the hipbone (see Hip).

Diagnosis

The diagnosis of osteoporosis is confirmed with X rays and bone densitometry nuclear scans, which can measure bone density and estimate the risk of future osteoporotic fractures. Women generally have these tests done when they reach menopause.

Blood tests may be used in order to rule out another disease that has similar symptoms or to see whether there is a disease, such as an overactive thyroid, that may be causing secondary osteoporosis.

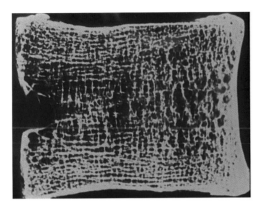

▲ *This X ray of a normal vertebra shows bone with both a normal calcium content and a regular structure.*

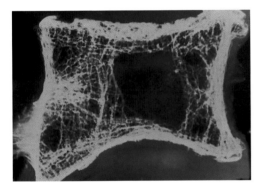

▲ *Osteoporosis in this vertebra shows up clearly. The affected areas look blacker than normal bone would.*

HOW OSTEOPOROSIS AFFECTS THE SPINE

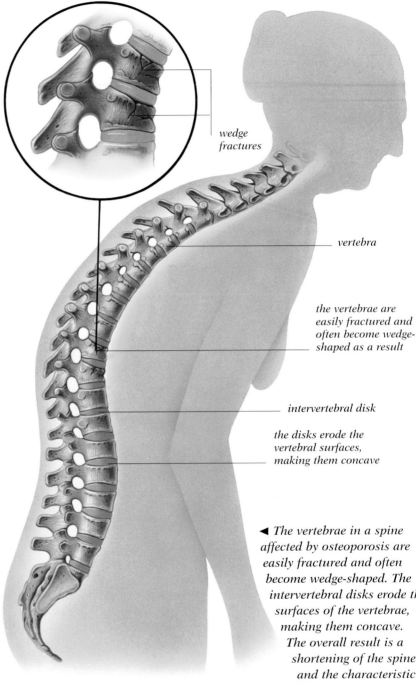

wedge fractures

vertebra

the vertebrae are easily fractured and often become wedge-shaped as a result

intervertebral disk

the disks erode the vertebral surfaces, making them concave

◄ *The vertebrae in a spine affected by osteoporosis are easily fractured and often become wedge-shaped. The intervertebral disks erode the surfaces of the vertebrae, making them concave. The overall result is a shortening of the spine and the characteristic humped look.*

Dangers

Left untreated, osteoporosis can seriously restrict mobility and cause disability. Repeated fractures may confine a sufferer to a wheelchair. Hip and other types of fractures that cause immobilization are associated with a high death rate in elderly patients.

The associated back troubles may also affect the nerves leading from the spine to the limbs, causing considerable pain and weakness. In the most advanced cases, the back can become bent almost double, and breathing may become very difficult.

Treatment

The patient should make efforts to become as mobile as possible. Regular exercise promotes strong bones and also prevents their deterioration. Following a fracture, the patient is encouraged to start moving at the earliest possible opportunity. To give the bones the best possible conditions for growth, a calcium-rich diet is advised (see Diet). For women, hormone replacement treatment (HRT) may help retard further bone loss (see Estrogen), but this must be considered against the increased risk of heart disease, breast cancer, and stroke. Alendronate is a drug that can build bone and prevent fractures, although its optimal use has not yet been discovered.

Outlook

Although aging, lack of exercise, and a calcium-poor diet can all aggravate osteoporosis, the disease can be prevented with calcium supplements, regular exercise, and, if the disease is really severe, HRT. There are drugs that can prevent or slow the rate of osteoporosis, so no one should needlessly have to suffer this debilitating disease without any alleviation.

See also: **Back and backache; Bones; Calcium; Exercise; Hormone replacement therapy; Hormones; Menopause; Thyroid**

Otitis

My husband has had otitis but needs to travel by airplane. Is this going to be dangerous?

No. However, the air pressure in the cabin of the aircraft does vary during takeoff and landing, so flying may be very uncomfortable if your husband is unable to equalize the air pressure on either side of his eardrum. He should try swallowing, chewing gum, or holding his nose while gently blowing through it.

One of my younger sister's friends had to stop going to the local pool because she was told swimming causes otitis. Is this true?

Swimming is fine when you have healthy ears. The trouble starts when a swimmer ignores the inflammation that is the first sign of otitis; the condition would then be aggravated by swimming. Occasionally, otitis is an adverse reaction to swimming. People who know that they have this tendency should protect their ears with earplugs or a swimming cap.

What should I do if my young son puts something in his ear that cannot be removed easily?

Any foreign material in the ear should be removed by a doctor or nurse as soon as possible. Trying to remove it yourself can damage the eardrum. Similarly, too much earwax should be treated medically. It can be softened with mineral oil before being syringed by a trained nurse or a doctor.

Do people suffering from otitis ever need hospital treatment?

The ear lies very close to the brain, so if infection is not controlled there may be a risk of meningitis, and this must be treated in a hospital. However, this should not happen if otitis is treated early.

Thanks to antibiotics, otitis—an infection of the ears—is not a serious disorder. However, it is still important for sufferers to seek early treatment to help prevent the recurrence of ear problems.

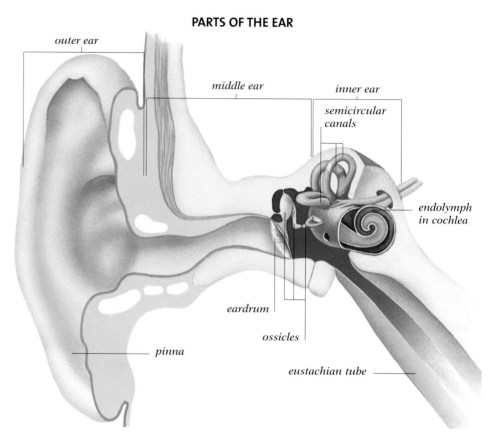

PARTS OF THE EAR

outer ear

middle ear

inner ear

semicircular canals

endolymph in cochlea

eardrum

ossicles

pinna

eustachian tube

Each ear consists of three parts, and these combine to make it the organ of both hearing and balance. The outer ear—the visible part—receives sound waves, which are transmitted via the eardrum to the middle ear. Here the waves are reduced and made stronger by three bones, called the ossicles. The waves then pass through another membrane and into the inner ear. In this inner compartment, the sound vibrations are converted into electrical impulses, and these travel along a pair of nerves to the brain, which interprets them as sound.

There are membranes between the three parts of the ear. These membranes help to prevent infection, particularly of the highly sensitive inner ear. However, the process of transmitting information in the form of sound can still be interrupted by infection. There are three types of infection—otitis externa, otitis media, and otitis interna. These relate directly to the outer ear, middle ear, and inner ear respectively.

Otitis externa

Otitis externa is inflammation of the skin of the outer ear caused by bacteria or fungi. The condition usually arises if the ear is not dried properly after getting wet—for example, after swimming—or if the skin is very sensitive and has a tendency to develop eczema.

The canal leading to the middle ear may also become affected if the wax in it is disturbed (see Earwax). Irritation may occur if this part of the ear is explored with a sharp instrument, such as a matchstick or a cotton swab.

In such instances the ear may become red and itchy, and sometimes there is a watery discharge. Drops and ointments are good for clearing up mild cases of inflammation. However, if the infection is very severe and painful, antibiotics are usually given orally. This is particularly the case when it may not be just the outer ear that is affected.

It is always important for people to remember that any unskilled treatment or exploration of the ears is extremely unwise.

Otitis media

Otitis media, a middle-ear infection, is usually the result of a bacterial infection or a viral infection of the nose and throat. The infection reaches the ear along the eustachian tube, the passage that leads from the back of the nose to the middle ear. Such complications are very common in children and may follow an illness such as measles, tonsillitis, or a common cold.

Acute otitis media can cause an extremely painful earache and fever together with muffled hearing. This is due to a buildup of fluid in the middle ear, which normally contains only air.

When a doctor suspects a bacterial infection, he or she will prescribe antibiotics. Occasionally, the eardrum perforates to discharge the pus, or the eardrum may have to be drained surgically to get rid of the pus. However, once the infection has cleared up, the eardrum heals and there should be no further trouble.

If a person suspects a middle-ear infection, he or she should consult a doctor immediately. Antibiotics can prevent mastoiditis—the spread of infection to the mastoid cells or the skull cavity—which in the past was a serious complication of otitis media.

Otitis media is a common condition in babies and young children, who may not even complain of an earache but may feel ill and possibly have a fever. For this reason doctors always examine the ears of young children who have a fever. *Hemophilus*, a bacterium often found in the respiratory tract, is a common cause of otitis media. Since it also causes meningitis, children are immunized against *Hemophilus* (see Meningitis).

▲ *Even if only a slight ear infection is suspected, it is best to avoid swimming. Those people who are prone to ear infections should wear earplugs or a swimming cap.*

Chronic otitis media

Occasionally otitis media recurs when infection enters the middle ear through a hole in the eardrum that has been discharging pus. In such cases the earache persists, and a slight discharge of pus may continue. Impaired or painful hearing may follow as the eardrum and ossicles become scarred, so prompt treatment is important to prevent such a recurrence.

With careful cleansing the infection can be controlled. However, when the bone becomes affected, surgery may be needed. Serious defects in the eardrum may be repaired by grafting.

Otitis interna

Infection of the inner ear, otitis interna, is now very rare because antibiotics are normally given before this stage is reached. However, it may occur if a middle-ear infection has been allowed to spread, causing deafness and giddiness. Treatment should be given immediately in such cases, before any permanent damage to hearing occurs.

See also: Antibiotics; Deafness; Dizziness; Eczema; Hearing; Infection and infectious diseases; Mastoiditis; Pus

▲ *A simple ear examination will reveal any reduction in hearing due to fluid in the middle ear. This can be treated easily and there should be no permanent damage.*

Outpatients

Questions and Answers

My mother has just spent some time in the hospital following a heart attack. Will she have to continue visiting the outpatient clinic when she gets better?

That depends on her health coverage. Many people in the United States have private health coverage, and each case will be followed up by the specialist concerned in his or her office, rather than having the patient go to an outpatient clinic.

I am scheduled to have a minor surgical procedure in an outpatient clinic. Is surgery safe in this setting?

Yes. Many surgical procedures can be safely performed at an ambulatory surgery center, particularly minor procedures. Throughout your surgery your physical status will be constantly monitored. The same level of care will continue during your recovery period.

Can I take a friend with me to my hospital appointment?

Certainly. The specialist may allow you to bring your friend in when you have your appointment, but you should always ask first.

If I am late for my outpatient appointment, will the doctor still see me?

That depends on how late you are. Most doctors see several patients in a morning or afternoon session, so if you arrive before the end of your session you may still be seen. However, if you are very late, the doctor is unlikely to be able to see you, since most doctors have a very tight schedule.You should always call the hospital if you think you are going to be late, and the staff will advise you.

When people think of going to a hospital, most imagine wards with long corridors of bedrooms. However, much of the day-to-day work of a modern district general hospital is carried out in an outpatient clinic.

▲ *Both occupational and physical therapists help patients in outpatient clinics. Here a physical therapist shows a patient exercises to improve the mobility of her wrist.*

When a doctor feels that a patient should have the benefit of the advice and treatment of a hospital specialist, he or she will usually refer the patient to the part of the hospital outpatient clinic where that particular specialist practices. The patient who is being referred will need to take a referral from the doctor to the specialist; this referral will detail the condition that needs to be investigated and treated.

The specialist has all the resources of the hospital to enable him or her to investigate the patient's case and to treat the patient once a clear diagnosis has been made. Many cases can be handled in this way without the patient's needing to stay in the hospital. However, people who are referred to one of the surgeons practicing at a hospital will probably need to be admitted for surgery at some point.

Use of outpatient clinics

There has been a great expansion in the use of outpatient facilities in hospitals in recent years, and every effort is made to avoid admitting people unless it is absolutely necessary. This practice is better for patients, who generally prefer not to be away from home. It is also better for hospitals, because keeping people in means that services have to be provided on a 24-hour, seven-day-a-week basis, which can be very expensive.

Some people need complicated tests even though they are not ill enough to require the level of nursing care that the staff of a surgical or medical unit provides. In view of this, many hospitals have created special wards that are halfway between a ward and an outpatient clinic. These wards may vary from an investigation unit that takes patients in for tests first thing in the morning, then closes at 5:00 P.M. or 6:00 P.M. every night, to five-day wards that are open 24 hours a day during the week but that then cut the cost to the hospital by closing on weekends.

The tests that investigation wards carry out include all forms of endoscopy. The benefit of endoscopies in general is that they require only sedation—under which the patient feels sleepy and can breathe on his or her own (see Sedatives)—not a full-scale general anesthetic, under which the patient is unconscious and requires artificial ventilation to breathe (see Anesthetics). As a result, the patient will usually be able to go home the same evening after coming into the hospital for an endoscopy.

In other cases a whole series of blood tests can be carried out in an investigation ward—for example, investigating the control of the level of blood sugar in a diabetic by measuring his or her blood sugar level every few hours during an entire day.

Outpatient investigations and tests

Almost all of the tests that may be performed on patients in a hospital ward can also be carried out in an outpatient clinic. Because so many people are sent for blood tests from ordinary general hospitals, there is nearly always an area set aside—often near the outpatient clinic—where specially trained technicians take all the blood specimens. From here the specimens are sent to the hospital's pathology laboratory for analysis.

Tests can also be carried out on urine samples that are supplied by patients. Alternatively, a patient may be asked to bring in a specimen—of sputum, for example, if he or she has a cough, or of feces if the patient is suffering from an intestinal disorder.

Just as the laboratory will perform tests on outpatients, so too does the X-ray department. If a patient is sent to see a specialist, he

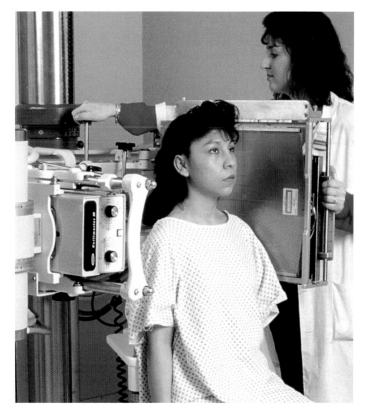

▲ *An outpatient is being prepared for a neck X ray. An X ray in this region may be used to diagnose fracture, whiplash, or curvature of the spine.*

or she may be asked to go to the X-ray department as a result of the visit. Many of the more simple X rays can be carried out there and then, and the patient may be able to go straight back to the specialist with the X rays.

Some X rays can be performed only by appointment, and the patient may have to wait to have these done. Barium swallows (see Barium Liquids), enemas, and IVPs (kidney X rays) are examples of X rays that patients might have to wait for.

Aside from X rays and blood tests, there are many other tests that are performed on an outpatient basis. Many of the patients passing through an outpatient clinic are likely to have an electrical recording of the heartbeat (an ECG; see Electrocardiogram). Heart patients may also have ultrasound studies done on the heart, just as pregnant mothers attending the prenatal clinic may have a routine ultrasound scan of their babies.

Like ultrasound scans, radioactive isotope scanning techniques have added a great deal to the investigation of various medical problems. Radioactive isotopes are used for diagnosis, and many large hospitals have a large nuclear medicine department where these tests are performed; here again, many of the patients involved are outpatients.

Outpatient treatment

One of the largest hospital departments is likely to be the pharmacy, from which all the drugs are dispensed for both the outpatients and the inpatients. The pharmacy of a large hospital is likely to contain the widest possible range of drugs and, because it buys them in bulk, it should obtain them from the drug companies

▲ *In larger hospitals, the pharmacy will be able to offer a wider range of drugs than are available at ordinary drugstores.*

Questions and Answers

If I feel unwell, can I go to the nearest hospital outpatient clinic?

No. You should telephone your doctor. Hospital outpatient clinics are for people receiving short-term or continuous treatment from particular specialists.

If you have an urgent problem, you can go to the emergency room (ER) of the nearest hospital. However, you should do this only for a genuine accident or emergency. These departments are always very busy. You must also remember that the doctors and nurses decide on the order in which patients are seen on the basis of severity of medical condition, not on a first-come-first-serve basis, so you might have to wait a long time.

All in all, the best thing to do is to see your own doctor unless you have a really urgent problem such as a badly bleeding wound.

I have been to the outpatient clinic at my local hospital three times now, and I have seen a different doctor each time. Why does this happen?

There are many possible reasons. The staff will usually comprise a specialist doctor and his or her junior colleagues. In many cases it is usual for the specialist to see a new case and then hand the patient over to another doctor. In addition, junior doctors tend to change positions fairly frequently and move to a new job every six months. However, you can soon expect to see the same doctor fairly regularly.

If my doctor doesn't think I need to be admitted to the hospital, but I am too ill to attend an outpatient clinic, how can he or she get a specialist's opinion?

In some cases a specialist may be willing to visit you at home. However, it might be impossible for him or her to come within a reasonable time, or he or she may feel, after discussing the problem with your doctor, that you should be admitted to the hospital.

at a cheaper rate than an ordinary drugstore would be offered. The pharmacy may deal only with drugs in the form of medicines, pills, and ointments. A hospital's specialists may also ask for all sorts of other medical items such as surgical boots, surgical corsets, and elastic stockings, all of which are obtainable from the department that supplies surgical appliances.

Outpatients may also need other hospital services. One department that has a large number of outpatients attending it is the physical therapy department. People who require remedial treatment for all kinds of conditions go there. A patient in need of physical therapy could have recently left a hospital bed after a stroke, for example, or he or she might have attended the outpatient clinic directly with a complaint such as a frozen shoulder.

In the same way that a patient may be referred to have therapy as an outpatient, he or she can also have speech therapy or osteopathy, have a hearing aid fitted, and receive counseling from the hospital's social work department.

▲ *When people visit the outpatient clinic they will have to wait their turn. Some hospitals provide toys to entertain young children.*

An increasing number of surgical procedures are also being performed in outpatient clinics. It has always been the case that minor operations, such as the removal of sebaceous cysts or the freezing of warts, were done under local anesthetic and carried out on an outpatient basis. Many hospitals have an operating room in their outpatient clinics especially for this purpose. There has also been an increase in the use of mini D & Cs (see Dilatation and Curettage) in which a woman's uterus is scraped clear of material—following a miscarriage, for example. Surgeons now frequently perform in their own offices procedures that involve, for instance, injections to treat hemorrhoids or varicose veins.

Radiation therapy—usually for cancer—can be carried out on outpatients. The only difficulty with this is that the treatment itself can make people feel ill, so that outpatient radiotherapy has to be reserved for those patients who are not badly affected by their underlying disease. Since this treatment is often given daily, patients need to live within easy reach of the hospital they are visiting if this is to be a practical option.

Day hospitals

Another of the growth areas in outpatient care has been an innovation: day hospitals. A large general hospital might have not only a geriatric day hospital for the elderly, but also a psychiatric

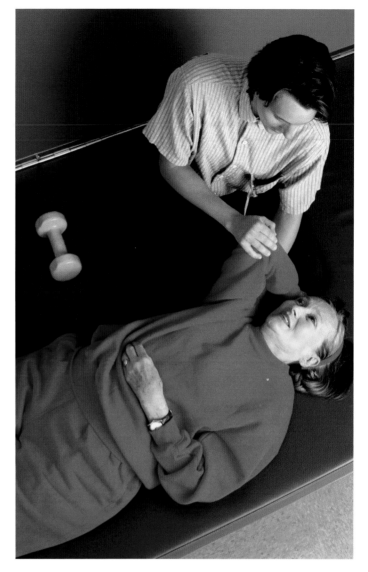

▲ *Most large hospitals have a physical therapy department, which outpatients who are convalescing at home can attend. Physical therapy can be a vital postoperative service.*

day hospital for people recovering from psychiatric illnesses. These day care institutions provide a place for people in both geriatric and psychiatric groups who have difficulty coping entirely by themselves in the community but who are able to cope if they are given the support provided by a visit once, twice, or even five times a week to the day hospital. This type of hospital may also be an appropriate place for active treatment in the form of physical therapy or other types of remedial care.

The modern outpatient clinic is now much more than a place where patients go to be given pills by a doctor or to be advised whether or not to have an operation. Such a wide range of medical tests and treatments can be performed in an outpatient clinic that today, hospital admission is reserved for those who really need it.

See also: Endoscopy; Geriatric medicine; Laboratory tests; Pathology; Physical therapy; Radiotherapy; Scans; Ultrasound; X rays

Hints for attending an outpatient clinic
Beforehand, ask if you need to fast.
Let the receptionist know when you arrive, or if you need to leave the waiting area at any time before your appointment.
If the appointment is for a child, or you need to bring a child along with you, take his or her favorite toy or book.
Allow time after your first visit; the doctor may need to send you for tests in other departments.
Bring all your medicines in their original pharmacy bottles.
Be prepared to give a urine specimen when you arrive; some hospitals ask you to bring one from home.
Expect a complete physical examination on your first visit.
Do not wear too many tight-fitting clothes that are difficult to take off.
Write down beforehand any questions that you want to ask the doctor.
Don't be afraid to ask about anything that you may want to know.
Take a relative or friend along if you think you may become worried or confused.

Ovaries

Questions and Answers

My doctor tells me that there is a chance that I may have to have one of my ovaries removed. Will I be less fertile?

No. What usually happens when one ovary is removed is that the other one grows slightly larger and takes over the work of both ovaries. The single ovary may even release two eggs each month.

When do a girl's ovaries first begin to work?

The ovaries may begin to release their first hormones as early as a girl's seventh year. The effects of the hormones can be seen in a subtle change in her body shape, making it appear more womanly. The changes are followed by the start of breast development. The sooner these changes begin, the earlier a girl will have her first menstrual period.

Is it true that the Pill interferes with the way the ovaries work?

Yes. The Pill contains artificial sex hormones, similar to those made by the ovaries, and it prevents eggs from maturing. Its hormones alter the body's natural monthly rhythm of hormone production, and this prevents the release of eggs. In effect the body is tricked into thinking that it is pregnant, so the ovaries get the message that they need not release any eggs for the time being.

What happens to the ovaries and their eggs after menopause?

At menopause the ovaries stop making hormones and as a result also stop releasing mature eggs. The mature eggs that remain in the ovaries fail to develop any further. As time passes, the ovaries gradually shrink and become full of fibrous tissue. This tissue largely obliterates the remaining eggs.

The ovaries do more than produce and release eggs that are ready for fertilization. Their other vital role is to produce hormones that maintain a pregnancy and give a woman's body its feminine shape.

The ovaries are the parts of the female reproductive system that are designed to produce and release mature ova (egg cells). When an ovum meets and is fertilized by a male sperm, this event marks the start of a new human life. From the first menstrual period right up to menopause, usually one egg is released each month; this release can take place from either ovary. However, sometimes two or even more eggs may be released by an ovary in one month. The ovaries are also essential parts of a woman's hormonal system.

SITE, STRUCTURE, AND FUNCTION OF THE OVARIES

▶ *The ovaries are covered by a layer of cells. The cells that are destined to become eggs pass into the substance of the ovaries, where they are surrounded by a follicle membrane (egg sac). Each month a single follicle matures and bursts on the surface of one of the two ovaries, and an ovum is released. The corpus luteum then develops at the site of the egg's follicle. If the egg is fertilized, the corpus luteum grows and secretes the hormones that maintain pregnancy.*

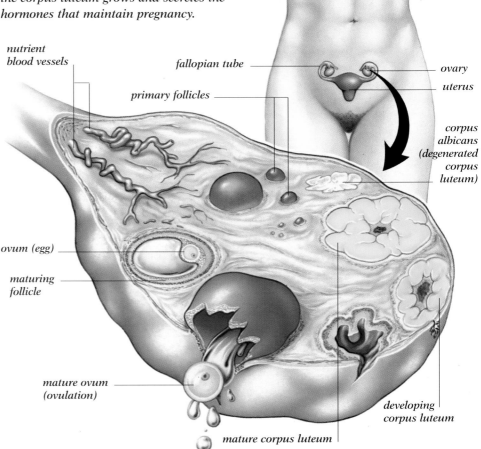

nutrient blood vessels

fallopian tube

primary follicles

ovum (egg)

maturing follicle

mature ovum (ovulation)

mature corpus luteum

ovary

uterus

corpus albicans (degenerated corpus luteum)

developing corpus luteum

Location and structure

The ovaries are two gray-pink almond-shaped structures each measuring about 1⅕ inches (3 cm) long and about ⅖ inch (1 cm) thick. They are found in the pelvis, the body cavity bounded by the hip or pelvic bones, and lie one on each side of the uterus. Each ovary is held in place by strong elastic ligaments. Just above each ovary is the feathery opening of the fallopian tube, which leads to the uterus. Although they are very close together, there is no direct connection between the ovary and the tube opening.

In a mature woman, the ovaries have a rather lumpy appearance. The reason for this can be seen by looking at an ovary's internal structure under a microscope. Covering the ovary is a layer of cells called the germinal epithelium. It is from these cells that the eggs or ova form; thousands of immature eggs, each in a round casing or follicle (the egg sac), can be seen clustered near the ovary edge.

More noticeable are the follicles that contain eggs in various stages of maturation. As these follicles enlarge, and after their eggs have been released, they produce the characteristic bumps on the ovary surface. The center of the ovary is filled with elastic fibrous tissue that supports the follicle-containing outer layer.

Ovulation

Under a microscope, the maturing follicles of the ovary can be seen as tiny balls enclosing a small mound of cells. In the center of the mound is the egg cell. A mature follicle forms a conspicuous swelling on the ovary about ¾ inch (2 cm) across. Exactly how the follicle ruptures to release the mature egg cell is not known. The ovum is then wafted by the feathery ends (fimbria) of the fallopian tubes into the tube openings.

In their role as egg producers, the ovaries also act as endocrine glands (see Endocrine System). The ovaries function under the control of the pituitary gland at the base of the brain. The pituitary makes a hormone called follicle-stimulating hormone (FSH), which travels in the bloodstream to the ovaries. FSH stimulates the follicles and causes the ova to mature; it also causes the secretion of the hormone estrogen. Under the influence of estrogen, the lining of the uterus thickens in preparation for receiving a fertilized egg. Estrogen also stimulates the buildup of body proteins and leads to fluid retention.

After a follicle has ripened and burst, another pituitary hormone, luteinizing hormone (LH), goes into action and brings about the development of the corpus luteum in the empty follicle. The corpus luteum helps to establish a pregnancy and also makes and releases its own hormone, progesterone. If the egg is not fertilized within 14 days, the corpus luteum shrinks, progesterone production is shut off, and the lining of the uterus is shed as the monthly menstrual period (see Menstruation). FSH production then begins again and the whole cycle is repeated. If, however, the egg has been fertilized, the corpus luteum continues working until the placenta is established. There is no menstrual bleeding in this case.

Ovary development

Ovary development is largely complete by the time a female fetus is in the third month of life in the uterus, and few major changes will take place until puberty. By the time a baby girl is born, her two ovaries contain a total of between 40,000 and 300,000 primary follicles, each containing an immature egg. At most only 500 of these eggs will be released, and probably no more than six will go on to develop into new human beings.

▲ *Few of the eggs released by a woman's ovaries will be fertilized; fewer will go on to develop into a new human life.*

When the ovaries first start making estrogen, they are not yet capable of releasing mature eggs, but this early estrogen stimulates the physical changes of puberty, such as the growth of the breasts, the widening of the hips, and the growth of pubic hair. This happens at least a year before a girl has her first period, and it is a signal that the estrogens have stimulated the production of mature eggs.

What can go wrong

Aside from the normal failure of the ovaries at menopause, the most common problem is the formation of ovarian cysts. These growths, which are usually benign, can grow very large, making a woman's abdomen swell as if she were pregnant. Many small ovarian cysts disappear of their own accord, and cysts usually do not cause pain unless they become twisted within the ovary.

Ovarian cancer is another quite common, and very dangerous, condition. Treatment with a drug called Taxol has been effective in some cases, and an early diagnosis improves the outlook.

A doctor can examine the ovaries by feeling, or palpating, them from the outside, but for a more thorough internal examination a laparoscopy is used. After a general anesthetic, carbon dioxide gas is injected into the woman's pelvic cavity. The gas shifts the position of the intestines so that they no longer obscure the ovaries. The laparoscope is then inserted through an incision near the navel. This allows the surgeon to look directly at the ovaries and to take a tissue sample— a biopsy—if it is required.

See also: **Conception; Estrogen; Hormones; Menopause; Pituitary gland; Puberty; Uterus**

Overdoses

Questions and Answers

If I take two aspirins for a headache and they have no effect, how long should I wait before taking more?

Most medication is meant to be taken three or four times a day, with usually four hours as the shortest safe interval between doses. If your headache is really persistent, you could take two aspirins every three hours. However, if you are still suffering from a headache in two days' time, you must go to a doctor, rather than take any more aspirin.

Is it safe to take medicine that you can buy over the counter as often as you want?

No. The fact that some medicines are available without a doctor's prescription does not mean that there is no risk of overdose. It is vital to follow the manufacturer's instructions carefully even when taking the mildest medication.

I have been taking iron tablets for a year. Could their effect build up to an overdose?

No. The body excretes what it cannot absorb; any excess iron passes out of the body in urine and feces. However, an overdose can occur if a substance such as iron is given in sufficiently large amounts to do immediate harm.

If I accidentally gave my one-year-old too much baby aspirin, what would the symptoms be?

The symptoms of overdose may be delayed for 24 hours and include rapid and deep breathing, lethargy, vomiting, fever, tinnitus, and possibly convulsions and coma. These effects are unlikely unless several times the normal dose is taken; one extra tablet is unlikely to do any harm. Use caution when giving aspirin to children, as it may cause Reye's syndrome.

Many people think of an overdose of drugs purely in terms of attempted suicide. Accidents with prescribed medications, however, are just as common as the deliberate misuse of such drugs.

Overdoses, whether deliberate or accidental, have become a major concern among doctors. Everyone should be aware of the possibility of overdoses, because a tragedy can almost always be avoided if people follow a few simple rules about when and how to take medication. An accidental overdose rarely happens because a doctor or a pharmacist makes a mistake in prescribing, making up, or labeling a medication. The majority of overdoses arise out of a user's carelessness with either prescribed or, in some instances, illegal drugs.

People should take care with all medications, not just the ones that are obviously potent. Even commonplace medications, such as acetaminophen, can kill if taken in large quantities. The same is true of many household chemicals.

Children and overdose

Children are the most likely victims of an accidental overdose. They are much more seriously affected than adults, partly because of their small body size and partly because medications intended for adults are exactly that—they can harm a child even if a tiny amount is given. Most medications for children are specially prepared with children in mind, and are usually given in doses of one teaspoonful (5 ml). Children should not be given medications other than those that are specifically meant for them.

Medication taken by a pregnant woman can affect the fetus. Therefore, no medication should be taken during pregnancy unless a doctor has been consulted beforehand (see Pregnancy).

▲ *An accidental drugs overdose can result from an abuser's mixing heroin with other drugs, or unknowingly injecting a purer form of the narcotic than usual. Deliberate overdoses are also common among drug abusers.*

Medications can also be passed on from a mother to her baby during breast-feeding. The simple and necessary precaution is for her to first consult a doctor before taking any drugs.

Most overdoses among children occur because they get hold of and swallow their parents' medications out of curiosity. Therefore, it is common sense for parents and others always to store medications where children cannot get at them. People should remember that children can usually climb or crawl quite far, and that they are always acquiring new skills (see Accident Prevention).

To children, tablets look just like candy, so to prevent such potentially fatal comparisons, parents should not let their children see them taking medications. Another reason for taking medications out of sight of children is that young children learn by imitating grown-ups; if they see a parent taking tablets, they may copy him or her.

Adults and overdose

The greatest risk for adults is forgetting whether or not they have taken a particular pill, or medication, and then taking another just to be sure. If this happens two or three times a day, or just once with a potent drug, an overdose may occur.

Taking another dose just to be sure is most likely when a patient has to take several different medications each day. To avoid mistakes, he or she should put the whole of the day's pills in a small container. The patient should also check—by reading the label carefully—that the pills to be taken really are what he or she thinks they are. Also, the patient should always check the instructions, however familiar they may be. Doctors and nurses do this every time they give a patient medication.

▲ *People should read the label each time they take a medication. In this way they can check what the pills are, their dosage, and any other instructions for their use.*

People should never take medication from a container that does not have a label, or from one where the label has become unreadable, even if they are sure they can recognize the contents. There are literally thousands of medications available today, and as there are not enough combinations of color, size, and shape for them all to look different, mistakes can be made in identification.

Even doctors and nurses can sometimes be in doubt about the identity of a pill or capsule and will have to refer to a complicated chart. Everyone should be equally careful identifying his or her own medicines. The checking process takes only a minute.

Doubting the medicine

Sometimes a particular medication does not have the expected or desired effect, and the patient starts to feel doubtful. This situation is potentially dangerous, because the patient may be tempted to increase the dose slightly, or to take the drug at shorter intervals. Although it is clear that this is not what the doctor recommended, the practice commonly occurs, sometimes with tragic results.

Another temptation, which is especially strong for those who are already unwell and think they cannot spare the time to get to a doctor, is to take medication that has been prescribed for someone else on the assumption that it might help. This too can prove fatal.

Similarly, it is unwise for people to take additional medicines, even those bought at a drugstore, while they are already on a course of specific medication. The old and new medications could interact

Questions and Answers

I am terrified that my four-year-old son will accidentally take one of my contraceptive pills. What would happen if he did?

If your son were to take one of your pills, it would probably not do him much harm. However, there is the danger that he would eat the whole lot, and this might cause vomiting. If you think that your child has swallowed any drugs, you should take him to a hospital immediately. More to the point, why leave pills where your son can get hold of them? If you take more care to secure them, then you'll have no need to worry.

What should I do if I find someone who has overdosed on drugs? Should I make him or her vomit?

If you do suspect that someone has taken an overdose, either accidentally or on purpose, the first thing to do is call the Poison Control Center or 911. Immediate hospital treatment is vital in all cases of suspected overdose.

Whether or not you should make the patient vomit depends on how long it has been since the overdose was taken, and whether or not the patient is unconscious. If he or she is unconscious, check for breathing or a pulse. If there is neither, and you are trained, you should carry out CPR after calling 911. If the patient is unconscious, never try to induce vomiting. In such cases, the overdose will have already entered the body's system. Also, when someone is senseless there is a real danger that vomit will enter his or her lungs and cause death.

If you are confronted by someone who has swallowed a bottle of sleeping pills within the last 30 minutes, you can save his or her life by inducing vomiting. Try to talk the person into making him or herself vomit. Wait for the ambulance. When it arrives, give the paramedics the bottle of whatever drug has been taken, even if it is empty. This is vital for diagnostic purposes when the patient reaches hospital. The vomited material should also be retained and given to the paramedics.

Safety with drugs

Keep all medications in a lockable, dark cupboard, out of the reach of children. Use childproof containers. Do not let children handle medications, or see you taking them.

Do not keep medications longer than a year, or after their expiration date. After that time, destroy what is left. To avoid environmental contamination, it is best to seek the advice of—or return medications to—a pharmacist for safe disposal.

Never treat any problem yourself for longer than a week without consulting your doctor.

Do not take any medication during pregnancy, or while breast-feeding, without first seeking the advice of your doctor.

If you are taking any medication prescribed by a doctor, you should mention this if you then go on to consult another doctor.

If a doctor has prescribed a course of medication, always complete the course. If in doubt, ask a doctor or a pharmacist.

Always read the directions on the label, and take exactly the recommended dose.

If you are advised not to drink, drive, or operate machinery while taking a medication, be sure to follow this advice. To ignore it could be dangerous.

If a medication you have used according to the instructions fails to have the expected or desired effect, consult your doctor.

Tell your doctor of any side effect experienced from a medication.

Only give young children medications that are described on the package as being suitable for them. Always give a child the dose that is specified for his or her age group.

with each other and cause side effects. Alternatively, the two drugs could potentiate each other—that is, exaggerate each other's effects. Patients should, therefore, always consult their doctor before taking any medication if they are already taking another drug that has been prescribed for a particular condition or complaint.

Symptoms of overdose

Symptoms of an overdose vary according to the medication involved and the amount taken. However, indications of a mild overdose—which should still be reported to a doctor—include dizziness, faintness, blurring of the vision, drowsiness, difficulty in concentration, and a mild degree of mental confusion. There may also be some disorientation since victims of an overdose may not know where they are or how they came to be there. Patients suffering from a more serious overdose may collapse, be difficult to awaken from a deep sleep, or may finally slip into a coma.

Outlook

If a patient is found and transported to a hospital in time, the outlook is generally good. The hospital plays the major role in any treatment. There are three things that a doctor can do: resuscitate the patient in the intensive care unit; do gastric lavage, also known as a stomach washout; and give chemical antidotes. Highly effective antidotes are available for narcotic and acetaminophen overdoses. If treatment is given early enough, the patient usually recovers with no ill effects. The important point about overdoses is that prevention makes more sense than cure.

See also: Amphetamines; Coma; Drug abuse; Heroin; Medicines; Narcotics; Suicide

Oxygen

How can you tell if a person is short of oxygen?

If a person is blue around the lips, the level of oxygen in the blood is lower than it should be.

My husband is in the hospital and must have oxygen. Will he always need this extra supply?

No, he is unlikely to need extra oxygen when he leaves the hospital. The usual reason people are given oxygen in the hospital is that they have an acute heart problem or an infection in the chest when they already suffer from a long-term chest ailment. The extra oxygen helps them with the immediate difficulty, and it is controlled very carefully.

What is an oxygen debt?

If you walk or run a long distance, your muscles use most of the oxygen in the bloodstream, but your heart and lungs work hard to keep the level as high as possible and the system remains in balance. However, if you use a lot of energy over a short time, as you do, say, if you run fast for 200 yd. (200 m), your muscles use up more oxygen than the heart can provide. They do this by drawing on an oxygen store in a compound called myoglobin. Once the stored oxygen is used up, it needs to be replaced; this is the oxygen debt.

I often feel tired and lethargic. Is this because I am short of oxygen?

No, probably not. Everybody feels tired sometimes, but oxygen shortage is rarely the cause. Some heart or lung conditions can make a person breathless with any sort of exercise. Anemia, however, can cause a person to become tired and listless, and it does involve a low oxygen level. Consult your doctor if you are worried.

People cannot live for more than a few minutes if their oxygen supply is cut off. Oxygen is the single most important substance on which human life depends; therefore, breathing and the transportation of oxygen throughout the body are crucial functions for human existence.

Oxygen is an odorless, tasteless, and colorless gas. Its main source on Earth is from living green plants. Oxygen also makes up about one-fifth of the air that people breathe, and the function of the lungs, the heart, and the blood vessels is primarily to carry oxygen from the air to the body's cells, where it is needed to produce the energy that the tissues need to stay alive.

What oxygen does

Oxygen is essential for the production of energy in the body. An automobile burns gasoline with oxygen, and a log fire uses both wood and the oxygen in a room to produce heat; the body's cells use oxygen in exactly the same way: they burn up their fuel—usually in the form of sugar—with oxygen to produce energy. This chemical reaction produces the same waste products in automobiles, log fires, and the body's cells—carbon dioxide and water. Although some of the body's cells are able to function for a short while without oxygen, the brain cannot manage without it.

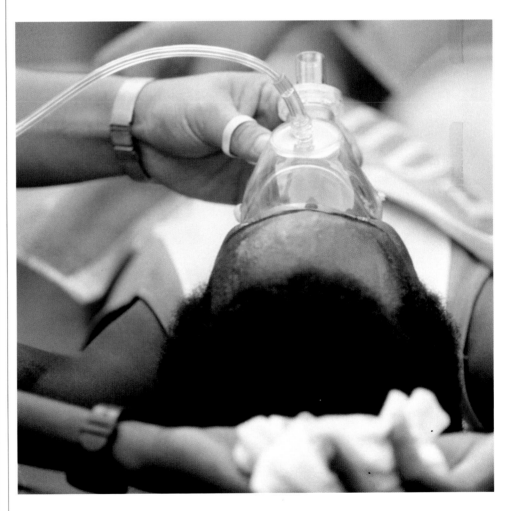

▲ *Oxygen-enriched air is being given to this athlete through a face mask after he was injured while running a marathon.*

THE PATH OXYGEN TAKES THROUGH THE BODY

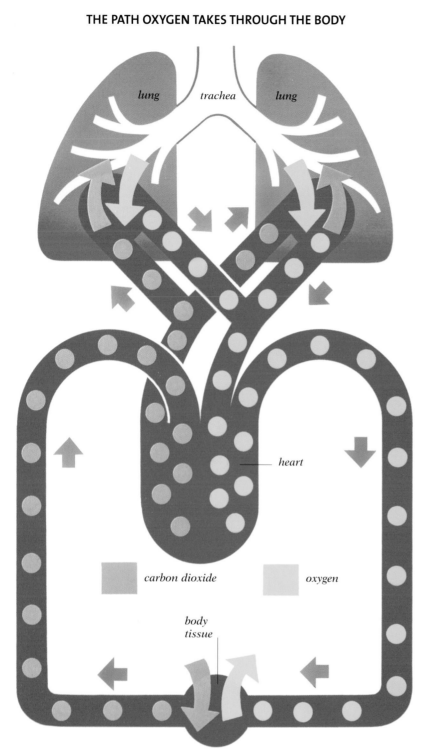

◄ Oxygen from the lungs is transported around the body in the blood. The cells exchange oxygen for carbon dioxide, which is returned to the lungs and then exhaled.

embolus or blood clot, or pneumonia) and those with heart complaints that keep the lungs short of blood (for example, congestive heart failure). A lack of oxygen shows up as blueness around the lips and tongue, a condition that is called cyanosis.

Hemoglobin is the red pigment in blood that takes up oxygen in the lungs and carries it to the tissues where it is released. Saturated hemoglobin is hemoglobin that is full of oxygen; it is red. Hemoglobin with insufficient oxygen looks purple. Therefore, an excess of low-oxygen hemoglobin leads to the blue look of cyanosis.

Associated conditions

Almost any type of lung condition can lead to the patient's developing a low level of oxygen in the bloodstream. Chronic bronchitis is perhaps the most common of these complaints (see Bronchitis), and it is often combined with emphysema. Emphysema is a disease in which the lung tissue is destroyed to such a great extent that fewer air sacs than normal are available for the exchange of oxygen between the blood and the tissues (see Emphysema).

A lack of oxygen is also associated with acute attacks of asthma. The condition is prevalent during severe spasms among asthmatics, which may also lead to chronic bronchitis.

Pneumonia may also lead to cyanosis, and it may be necessary to give oxygen to people who have suffered from a heart attack, because the flow of blood—and therefore the delivery of oxygen to the body's tissues—will have been drastically reduced by the attack (see Heart Attack).

Giving extra oxygen

An oxygen mask is the most common way for oxygen to be administered to a patient. The type of mask that is used in hospitals allows doctors to regulate the percentage of oxygen in the air that the patient breathes. The aim is to raise the amount of oxygen in the bloodstream until it reaches normal levels. The level of oxygen in the blood can be monitored by taking samples of arterial blood.

Some people find wearing an oxygen mask over the face very uncomfortable, so they may be given oxygen through nasal cannulas instead. These are simply tubes which run under the nostrils, and through which the extra oxygen can be inhaled by the patient as needed. A tube can also be inserted directly into the windpipe—a medical process known as transtracheal oxygen.

Babies and small children can be put inside an oxygen tent. If the baby has been born prematurely, the oxygen can be fed directly into the incubator. Great care is needed in giving oxygen to premature babies, because too much can lead to a disease that causes blindness (see Premature Babies).

Oxygen from the air is inhaled, then absorbed by the lungs and carried in the blood to all the body tissues. When the amount of oxygen needed for a particular physical task is greater than that available at the time, the difference is known as an oxygen debt. A person makes up the shortfall in oxygen supply by panting and breathing in deeply, so as to take in as much oxygen as possible—for example, immediately after a period of strenuous physical exertion.

Oxygen deficiency

There are two main groups of people likely to suffer from a shortage of oxygen in the blood: those with a lung disease (such as pulmonary

The oxygen cycle

Green plants are the main source of oxygen for all animals, including humans. In plants a chemical reaction called photosynthesis is initiated by sunlight. Carbon dioxide and water absorbed by the plant form starch in the leaves and release oxygen. Oxygen is breathed in by animals, and carbon dioxide is exhaled and used by plants, forming a continuous cycle of interdependence. Animals, including humans, eat plants, and the starch is broken down into sugars that release energy when they react with oxygen.

oxygen

carbon dioxide

▼ *Sea air is thought by some to be especially invigorating because it has a higher proportion of ozone, a form of oxygen.*

Oxygen chambers

Low levels of oxygen in the body's tissues may be treated by putting the patient into a small chamber with oxygen which is more concentrated than usual, and which is also supplied at a higher than normal pressure. This is called hyperbaric (high-pressure) oxygen. The treatment has a small but valuable place in modern medicine. It is used to treat carbon monoxide poisoning, or when people are distressed from inhaling acrid smoke, or in cases of gas gangrene (see Gangrene).

High concentration

If a person on a ventilator (artificial respirator) breathes a high concentration of oxygen—more than 60 percent—for a prolonged period of time, he or she can develop a lung injury (see Artificial Respiration).

Another potential problem with oxygen therapy is its effect on patients with a chronic obstructive pulmonary disorder (COPD) such as emphysema, or chronic bronchitis (see Pulmonary Disorders). For some reason, when a patient with chronic obstructive pulmonary disease is given oxygen, his or her breathing can slow or stop.

Because of such problems, the level of oxygen that is administered to a patient in a hospital is always carefully controlled and monitored.

See also: Arteries and artery disease; Asthma; Blood; Breathing; Chronic obstructive pulmonary disease; Exercise; Heart; Lung and lung diseases; Oxygen therapy; Pneumonia; Sugars

Oxygen therapy

Questions and Answers

My sister recently had a premature baby, and he had to be kept in an incubator for nearly a month. The doctors seemed worried about giving him oxygen. Is it true that oxygen can be dangerous to a newborn baby?

Doctors are now fully aware of the dangers to low-birth-weight babies of excessively high concentrations of oxygen. These can induce a serious and potentially blinding retinal problem called retrolental fibroplasia, and a serious lung disorder called bronchopulmonary dysplasia. Therefore, great care is exercised in using oxygen therapy for premature babies.

My doctor has advised me not to pay any attention to the hype about oxygen therapy on the Internet. Is the medical profession against oxygen therapy?

No. Oxygen therapy is very important, even lifesaving, in cases in which, as a result of disease, a patient's organs and tissues are not getting enough oxygen. Orthodox physicians' objection to oxygen and ozone as commodities for sale to healthy people has to do with claims that these substances can enhance health. There is no evidence that supplementary oxygen can do so in normal people, and ozone (trioxygen) is a dangerous poison.

Is hyperbaric oxygen different from ordinary oxygen?

The term "hyperbaric" means "of higher than normal pressure." The extra pressure is supposed to allow the oxygen to penetrate deeper into the circulatory system and body fluids, but hyperbaric oxygen is just regular oxygen and differs in no way from the oxygen you breathe in continuously in the atmospheric air.

Oxygen is by far the most vital element for human life and health. Failure to get an adequate supply of oxygen to the tissues causes a range of diseases in which the intake of oxygen to the blood, or the supply of blood to the tissues, is reduced. Oxygen therapy is often an essential part of medical treatment.

The atmosphere is about 20 percent oxygen, so the oxygen people breathe is considerably diluted, mainly by the inert gas nitrogen. Atmospheric oxygen is mainly in a molecular form; each molecule contains two atoms. A small proportion is in the form of ozone, the molecule of which contains three atoms of oxygen (see Molecular Biology). Ozone is a powerful and poisonous chemical agent.

Atmospheric oxygen, when inhaled, is capable of fully saturating the blood returning from the lungs so that all the tissues of the body get an adequate supply. Oxygen is necessary for the "burning" (oxidation) of food materials to provide the energy every cell needs to function efficiently. The brain, especially, requires a large, continuous supply. Deprivation of oxygen for more than a few minutes will usually produce serious brain damage and is often fatal.

There is no medical reason to give supplementary oxygen to people with normal heart and lung function unless they have ascended to altitudes at which the pressure of the atmosphere

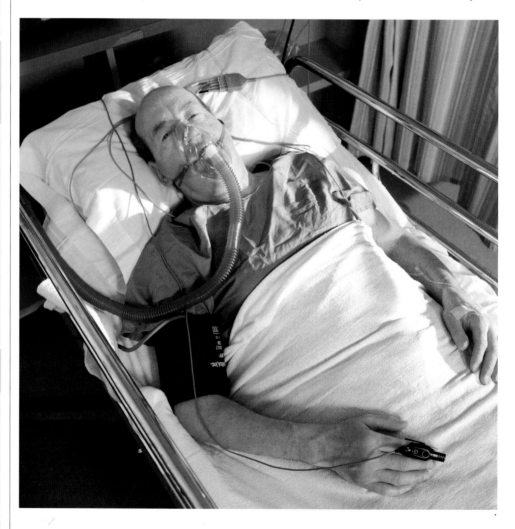

▲ *A man receives oxygen therapy in the hospital through an oxygen mask. The level of oxygen given to a patient is carefully monitored, as too much can cause complications.*

◄ A U.S. Navy diver aboard a submarine examines a decompression chamber, where hyperbaric oxygen is used to treat divers suffering from decompression illness.

with wheels. These are intended for nonmobile use in hospitals or homes. Smaller compressed-gas cylinders can be provided for use outdoors.

A greater quantity of oxygen can be stored in a smaller container if the gas is liquefied. Oxygen becomes a pale blue liquid at −297°F (−183°C). Liquid oxygen is made by cooling oxygen gas to change it to a liquid form. This is often used by people who are more active because larger amounts of liquid oxygen can be stored in smaller, more convenient containers. However, there are greater storage problems with liquid oxygen than with the compressed gas.

The third method of supplying oxygen is a device called an oxygen concentrator, which removes a proportion of the nitrogen from atmospheric air, thereby raising the concentration of oxygen. This is a cheap way to obtain supplemental oxygen and can be used in the home, but the devices consume electricity, produce heat, and are bulky and sometimes noisy, .

Oxygen tents, once commonly used, have now been largely abandoned, partly because of the danger of fire—oxygen strongly supports combustion and will cause a glowing cigarette to burst into flame—and partly because of the development of efficient masks. Plastic nasal oxygen probes are less efficient than well-designed and properly used masks.

is well below that at sea level. But certain lung diseases, especially chronic obstructive pulmonary disease (COPD), interfere with the passage of oxygen from the air into the blood, and additional oxygen may be necessary (see Chronic Obstructive Pulmonary Disease). Many patients with COPD require intermittent or even continuous supplementary oxygen in order to raise the amounts in the blood to a safe level. In many cases supplementary oxygen is given to patients in their own homes. There are some other conditions in which oxygen at high pressure (hyperbaric oxygen) can be medically helpful.

Methods of delivery

People who watch medical dramas and soap operas on television may conclude that every patient who is brought into the emergency room requires nasal prongs to supply additional oxygen. This is far from the case. Only a small proportion of injured or seriously ill people actually need extra oxygen.

Oxygen can be dispensed in one of three ways. Most commonly it is supplied as a gas under pressure in strong steel or aluminium cylinders from which it is released by way of a pressure-reducing valve. Such cylinders are often fitted with a pressure gauge that provides an indication of how much oxygen is left in the cylinder and with a flow-rate meter calibrated in liters per minute. The largest cylinders are very heavy and are often mounted in strong frames

Hyperbaric oxygen

This form of oxygen therapy makes use of oxygen at a pressure two to three times more than the normal atmospheric pressure. It may be applied by placing the patient in a pressure chamber filled with air or oxygen. The amount of oxygen that passes into the body is increased roughly in proportion to the increase in pressure over atmosphere. It is possible to increase the oxygen in the body by about sixfold by this means. At high pressures, oxygen dissolves in the blood plasma, and hyperbaric treatment makes it possible to maintain life even in the absence of hemoglobin, the normal oxygen carrier of the blood. Hyperbaric oxygen is used much less often than standard oxygen therapy by mask but has been shown to be effective in a range of conditions in which oxygen by mask has had little useful effect. These conditions include infections by germs that reproduce at low oxygen levels (anaerobic organisms), particularly gas gangrene and tetanus (see Gangrene); decompression sickness; carbon monoxide poisoning; radiation sickness; and bone marrow infection (osteomyelitis).

See also: Bends; Blood; Brain damage and disease; Breathing; Circulatory system; Lung and lung diseases; Oxygen; Ozone layer; Plasma; Premature babies

Ozone layer

Can ozone act as a pollutant?

Ozone is a highly reactive chemical. In the atmosphere it protects us from the sun's radiation, but if it forms at ground level it can damage lung tissue. Exposure to ozone can also trigger asthma and other respiratory problems. Ozone pollution on the ground happens when sunlight reacts with hydrocarbons and nitrogen oxides in automobile fumes. It tends to form in summer and is the main ingredient in smog.

Why are dark-skinned people less likely to get skin cancer?

Skin color comes from a brown pigment called melanin, a protein which occurs in the epidermis (the outer layer of skin). Melanin is produced in epidermal cells called melanocytes. In dark-skinned people melanocytes are more active. This is because such people originated in warm climates, and their skin has developed a natural protection against the sun's harmful rays. Lighter skin becomes tanned when exposed to sunlight, but tanning does not give full protection. Dark skin is thus less at risk from skin cancer than pale skin.

Will ozone depletion affect plants?

Plant studies show that although higher-UV radiation harms plants, some species may not be affected by it and may even thrive. Plants of the same species may also react differently. When soybeans were exposed to extra UV radiation (an ozone loss of 16 percent), one variety's growth declined by 25 percent, while another's was unaffected. A smaller reduction in the ozone layer might also affect agriculture because farmers could be forced to replace crops that are good but sensitive to UV radiation with less sensitive, and possibly less productive, crops.

Human use of environmental chemicals has badly damaged the ozone layer, which is the Earth's only protection from the sun's harmful rays. Scientists fear that increases in skin cancer and disastrous climate changes will result.

Ozone (O_3) is a rare, poisonous type of oxygen, produced by the action of electrical discharges—such as lightning—on oxygen molecules. The gas is found naturally in the Earth's stratosphere and forms a shield around the Earth called the ozone layer. This layer acts as a barrier between life-forms such as humans and harmful ultraviolet (UV) radiation from the sun. There is concern that people's use of environmental chemicals, particularly chlorofluorocarbons (CFCs) found in aerosols, is damaging the ozone layer, potentially leading to global warming.

The ozone layer lies between about 9 and 30 miles above the Earth's surface, and absorbs damaging UV radiation from the sun. Ozone is created when powerful UV rays split molecules of oxygen (O_2) into two atoms. A single oxygen atom (O) then combines with a molecule of oxygen (O_2) to form ozone (O_3).

However, ozone breaks down if it meets a single oxygen atom (O). Here, the ozone molecule and oxygen atom combine to form two molecules of oxygen ($2O_2$). This breakdown of ozone happens slowly in the stratosphere and there is always a net surplus of the gas, but the total amount of ozone is very small. Even at its most concentrated, there are only eight molecules of ozone to 1 million molecules of other gases.

The ozone layer varies naturally from region to region and from season to season. Most of the ozone is created above the tropics, but then weather systems push it toward the north and south poles. As a result, the highest levels of ozone occur at the poles and the lowest in the tropics. The amount of ozone peaks in the spring (September in the southern hemisphere) and reaches a low point in the fall.

Levels of ozone also vary naturally from year to year, with higher amounts recorded when there is increased sunspot activity, or dark spots on the sun.

The stratosphere lies above the troposphere, which is the lowest layer of atmosphere and the part in which humans live. The troposphere contains most of the water vapor in the air, so this is where most clouds form. Between the troposphere and the stratosphere lies a boundary called

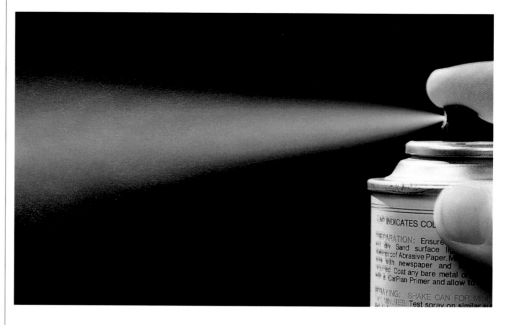

▲ *The CFCs that power aerosols are probably destroying the ozone layer—our only protection from the sun's ultraviolet rays. A worldwide treaty now limits CFC production.*

the tropopause. This boundary lies about 10 miles above sea level at the equator but is just 5 miles above the poles. The ozone layer occurs just above the tropopause and varies in height in the same way, lying lowest at the poles and highest at the equator.

Ozone hole

In the mid-1980s, scientific researchers made a discovery—a hole had appeared in the ozone layer above Antarctica. This hole was recorded from late August to late November, as the southern hemisphere moved from winter to spring. Since then, the hole has continued to appear every southern spring.

The evidence for the hole came from scientists in Antarctica who were using ground-based instruments to measure ozone, and from NASA researchers. NASA started monitoring ozone in November 1978, when it launched the Total Ozone Mapping Spectrometer (TOMS) instrument on board the Nimbus 7 spacecraft. In 2004, balloons, aircraft, satellites, and the space shuttle missions are used to measure ozone levels worldwide.

These measurements show clearly that the ozone layer has thinned all around the Earth. After allowing for natural variations, scientists found that ozone had declined by about 3 percent per decade between 1978 and 1991. The decline increases with latitude; above the United States, Europe, and Australia, the decline for the period was 4 percent. Although the scientists found no drop in ozone over the tropics during this time, more recent measurements have shown that ozone is now decreasing there as well. The ozone over the Arctic also shows unusually high losses in spring.

However, the most dramatic changes are still to be found over Antarctica. Every southern spring, about 95 percent of the ozone in the lower stratosphere is destroyed. Higher up, above 15 miles, about half the ozone disappears. Ozone destruction at the poles increases when there is a stronger polar vortex (air spiraling above the poles), with lower temperatures and more stratospheric clouds.

After some weeks, the depleted ozone layer above the Antarctic has been found to break up and be carried away by winds. As a result, the ozone can temporarily thin at higher latitudes, too. This effect has been observed as far north as Australia. After a few months, however, the ozone is regenerated.

The discovery of the ozone hole rang alarm bells with scientists about the amount of UVB—the band of ultraviolet radiation with wavelengths between 280 and 320 nanometers (nm)—getting through to the Earth's surface. If there was less ozone, less UVB would be absorbed in the stratosphere, and it was feared that increased UVB radiation would cause biological damage to humans, triggering more skin cancers and eye cataracts, and suppressing the body's immune system. Extra UVB radiation might also harm trees and plants or microscopic marine life. Some scientists think that the ozone hole may also have a serious affect on the Earth's climate. This has spurred researchers to find out more about the ozone layer, and many governments are taking steps to stop its destruction.

Increased radiation?

UV radiation from the sun can be separated into three bands: UVA, UVB, and UVC. The ozone layer filters out UVC, which is the most active and therefore the most dangerous. For significant amounts of UVC to get through to the Earth's surface, the ozone loss would have to be enormous. The ozone layer also absorbs some UVB, the next most harmful band of radiation, so any thinning of ozone would

▲ *The hole in the ozone layer—shown in white—over Antarctica. UV radiation is shown in purple. Different altitudes are shown by a Boeing 727 (7 miles), Concorde (9 miles), and an ER-2 research plane (11 miles).*

allow more UVB through. UVA, which is not absorbed by ozone, used to be considered harmless; however, now it seems that UVA may also be involved in causing skin cancer.

Levels of UVB radiation vary naturally from region to region. UVB is strongest near the equator and weakest at the poles. On average, the level of UVB is a thousand times greater at the equator than at the poles. UVB radiation also increases with altitude and is affected by cloud cover.

Scientists report that there was no significant increase in UVB in American cities between 1974 and 1985. However, it is thought that this was probably because the UVB was absorbed by pollution on the ground (see Pollution). By contrast, UV radiation in the Antarctic has at times increased by a factor of two to three.

Effects on health

Predicting the effects on health of decreased ozone is not an exact science, because there are so many factors involved, including the actions people may take to protect themselves against the sun.

Questions and Answers

Does extra UV radiation harm marine life?

Radiation from the sun can penetrate tens of yards into clear seawater. Some scientists are worried that increased UV radiation will harm microscopic plants (phytoplankton) and animals (zooplankton), which live near the surface of oceans. The food chain in the sea starts with plankton, so if they are harmed, all living organisms in the oceans (and some on land) would find food scarcer. Recent studies on phytoplankton in the seas around Antarctica suggest that they photosynthesize less when directly below the hole in the ozone layer. However, the domino effect that ozone depletion might have on other marine life is not known.

Is sunburn dangerous?

People receive as much as 70 percent of their lifetime's exposure to sunlight in the first 18 years of life. Epidemiological studies indicate that one to three episodes of acute sunburn in early childhood predispose the individual to skin cancer. So it is important to protect skin from overexposure to UV radiation.

How can I avoid sunburn and help reduce the risk of skin cancer?

The American Academy of Dermatology and the Skin Cancer Foundation recommend a number of steps. Both adults and children should try to avoid the sun when it is at its strongest—between 10 A.M. and 3 P.M. Use sunscreen with a factor of at least SPF15 on all exposed areas of the body. Reapply every two hours, even on cloudy days, after swimming or sweating. Wear clothes that cover sensitive areas of the body. Hats should have wide brims to shade both the face and the neck. Avoid exposure to UV radiation from sunlamps. Sunscreen should be applied frequently on children aged six months or older; babies under six months should be kept out of the sun entirely.

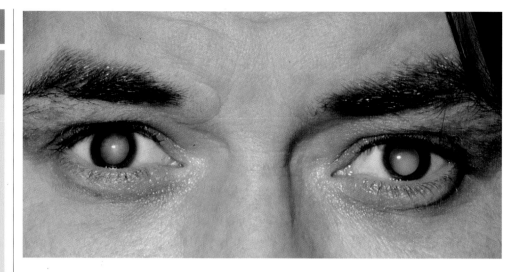

▲ *The milkiness typical of cataracts can be seen in this patient's eyes. Aging is the most common cause of the disease, but radiation is now an increasing cause in all age groups.*

Scientists estimate that a 1 percent loss of ozone produces an increase of between 1 and 2 percent in UVB. This in turn leads to a 2–4 percent increase in the number of cases of two types of skin cancer: basal cell carcinoma and squamous cell carcinoma.

Every year, about 800,000 cases of these carcinomas are diagnosed in the United States. UVB radiation is blamed for more than 90 percent of such cancers. When UVB radiation is absorbed by skin cells, it can break bonds in the cells' DNA. Most of this damage is repaired by proteins made inside the cells. However, if the damage is not repaired, the faulty DNA can trigger cancer.

Studies have shown that, like UVB levels, basal cell carcinoma and squamous (scaly) cell carcinoma correlate with latitude. Light-skinned people who live closer to the equator are more likely to get these cancers than people with darker skin who live nearer the poles (see Melanin).

Both basal cell and squamous skin cancers appear as red nodules or blotches and occur where the skin is most exposed to the sun—the face, neck, hands, and arms. Because both cancers are more common in people who work outside, long-term exposure to sunlight seems to be one cause. Both forms of skin cancer are simple to treat if detected early enough.

A more dangerous cancer, melanoma, can develop rapidly from a harmless-looking mole to a life-threatening disease. In the United States in 2001, 29,000 men and 22,400 women were diagnosed as having malignant melanoma. The estimated deaths from this disease were 5,000 men and 2,800 women. Usually this cancer appears on men's trunks and women's legs.

Studies suggest that people who develop melanoma have in the past received high doses of UV radiation that caused acute burning (usually sunburn). Other studies suggest that the risk of melanoma increases if people were overexposed to UV radiation as children. Some scientists suspect that exposure to UVA, which is not absorbed by ozone, is a factor in melanomas.

A causal link

Evidence linking melanoma to UV radiation has come from studies of a rare disorder that is caused by a defect in a gene for repairing damaged DNA. In this disease, called xeroderma pigmentosum, the faulty gene is unable to make the enzyme needed to repair DNA damaged by UV radiation. Research shows that people who have the faulty gene are 1,000 times more likely to develop melanoma than people who are carrying healthy copies of the gene.

The incidence of melanoma in the United States has been increasing since the 1940s. However, this increase is probably not linked to ozone loss, because levels of UVB radiation in the country have not increased significantly. Also, melanomas are slow to develop, taking up to 20 years to appear. As a result, even if an individual is exposed to extra UVB radiation—as he or she would be in Antarctica—any effect may take years to show up. The rise in melanoma cases is most likely caused by both the huge increase in recent years in the number of people taking vacations in the sun and the production of CFCs (discussed below).

Further evidence suggests that UV radiation suppresses the body's immunity so that the skin's immune system cannot attack forming cancer cells. There is a fierce debate among

► *A scientist launches a weather balloon in Antarctica. The data it sends back from the stratosphere will be used to evaluate the state of the ozone layer.*

scientists about whether this suppressed immunity also increases the risk of catching an infectious disease.

Increased UVB radiation is also thought to cause an increase in cataracts. There is medical evidence that in some mountainous countries where UVB levels are naturally high, such as Tibet and Bolivia, there is a high incidence of cataracts.

Ozone eaters

Scientists first raised concerns about the damage to the ozone layer in the early 1970s. The United States, Britain, and France wanted to build a commercial fleet of supersonic aircraft, and this plan provoked a discussion about whether the aircraft's exhaust gases (nitric oxide) would speed up ozone destruction. The debate prompted intensive scientific research, which centered on the stratosphere.

By the mid-1970s, U.S. researchers had proved that stable synthetic chemicals and gases released into the Earth's atmosphere might be eating away at the ozone layer. Examples of such chemicals are chlorofluorocarbons, or CFCs, a group of gases that contain chlorine, fluorine, and carbon. Halons—or bromofluorocarbons (found in fire extinguishers)—which contain bromine, fluorine, and carbon, also cause ozone loss.

CFCs are used to propel aerosols from spray cans and in the cooling coils of refrigerators and air conditioners. They are also produced in the manufacture of industrial solvents and Styrofoam. CFCs were developed in the United States in 1928, but it was only after 1950 that they were used in large quantities. Industrialized countries use 80 percent of CFCs, but developing countries are now using more of these chemicals.

CFCs are very stable compounds. Once they escape from an aerosol can or an old refrigerator, they enter the atmosphere and slowly diffuse upward. After many years they reach the stratosphere. This part of the atmosphere is bombarded constantly with powerful UV radiation, some of which severs the weak carbon-chlorine bonds in CFC molecules. It is the released chlorine atom that breaks down ozone. Just one chlorine atom can catalyze the breakdown of 100,000 ozone molecules. That is why CFCs are so instrumental in the destruction of the ozone layer.

Repairing the hole

The discovery of the ozone hole inspired an international effort to phase out the use of the chemicals that cause the damage. In 1987, most of the nations that were using CFCs adopted the Montreal Protocol, a treaty committing them to reduce the emission of CFCs by 50 percent by the year 2000.

In 1990, an amendment to the treaty called for all manufacture of CFCs, carbon tetrachloride (found in solvents), and halons to stop by 2000. In 1992, the timetable for phasing out ozone-eating chemicals (which differs for developing countries) was brought forward by four years. By January 1993, 95 percent of countries that were using ozone-depleting chemicals had signed the Montreal Protocol. However, the benefits of these agreements will not be seen for several years, because CFCs are so long-lived.

Bringing on substitutes

Scientists have developed substitutes for CFCs. Some of these are halocarbons, such as HCFC-22, which can replace CFC-12 in refrigeration and air-conditioning systems. In the electronics industry, water-based cleaners are increasingly replacing CFCs. Another innovation is nonpressurized or pump spray bottles, which replace spray cans that use CFCs as propellants.

International efforts to prevent the ozone layer from further destruction have had some effect. In May 1996, researchers from the National Oceanic and Atmospheric Administration reported that they had seen a reduction in ozone-depleting chemicals in the Earth's atmosphere. This decline in atmospheric chlorine derived from CFCs and other halocarbons should have been repeated in the stratosphere by 2000, as the gases in the lower atmosphere slowly diffuse up into the middle stratosphere.

When the concentrations of ozone-depleting chemicals that are in the stratosphere fall, the impact on the springtime Arctic ozone thinning should be seen immediately. However, it will be much longer before the hole over Antarctica can repair itself. In recent years, because so much chlorine and bromine have built up, the ozone is completely destroyed each spring. The hole in the Antarctic ozone layer will probably not close before 2050.

See also: Cancer; Cataracts; Melanoma; Skin and skin diseases; Sunburn

Pacemaker

The development of pacemakers for the heart has been one of the most dramatic advances in medical technology. It has saved many patients from either death or disablement.

Questions and Answers

My mother is going to have a pacemaker. Will there be a large bump on the surface of her skin?

Because modern pacing boxes are about the size of a matchbox, a bump is unavoidable. Pacing boxes are usually fitted on the front of the chest, about 2 in. (5 cm) below the middle of the collarbone. If your mother is of average weight, most of the bump will be lost in the breast tissue.

If my pacemaker fails, will my heart stop beating?

Only a minority of patients with a pacemaker are so dependent on it that the heart would stop completely if the pacemaker ceased working. Most patients would have the symptoms of a very slow pulse rate: dizziness, blackouts, or lethargy on exertion. The pacemaker is designed to prevent sudden failure, but there is still a small risk of failure if there is a sudden shift of pacing wire; this can occur soon after the pacing system has been put in, if at all. Attend a pacemaker clinic regularly to have the electrical function of your unit checked. The batteries will run down, but the clinic will have warning and will replace the pacing box.

If I needed to have a pacemaker fitted in an emergency, how quickly could it be put in?

Many doctors could put a temporary pacing wire into the heart without using X rays to guide them. It would take two or three minutes to get some pacing activity. In an emergency, it is possible to get a heart working again by passing a wire directly into it through the chest wall by means of a long needle or by delivering pulses of electricity via electrodes attached to the skin. However, there is usually time to get the patient to X-ray facilities.

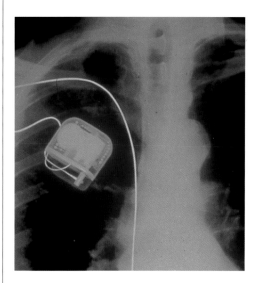

▲ *This chest X ray shows the two main components of a pacemaker in place: the pacing box and the wire to the heart.*

People rely on the regular beating of their heart to stay alive. A regular heartbeat depends upon the heart's own natural pacemaker, the sinoatrial node. The sinoatrial node initiates impulses that spread through the heart by a system of specialized electrical conducting tissues. The entire electrical timing system is called the conducting system of the heart (see Heart).

Who needs a pacemaker

Unfortunately, the heart's natural pacing system can sometimes fail to work properly. This can occur as a result of ischemic heart disease (muscle damage from a deficiency of the blood supply). A heart attack may also lead to difficulties in the conducting system, and this requires urgent surgery to insert a pacemaker. Often, a pacemaker is a temporary measure, since the heart is able to recover its function of controlling its own timing. If and when this occurs, the temporary pacemaker will be removed.

The majority of patients who require a permanent pacemaker are those whose conducting system has broken down completely. Special muscle cells conduct the electrical impulses that control contraction. These are destroyed by ischemia. The condition is more common in elderly people. Most patients who need pacemakers are over the age of 65 (see Aging).

When the heart stops conducting electrical impulses properly, the heart rate slows down; this condition is called "heart block," or arrhythmia. The condition may be variable, with different manifestations or degrees of severity. It can lead to sudden attacks of fainting and unconsciousness. The heart may even stop completely; without emergency treatment death may result. Patients may also suffer from a continuously slow pulse rate. This may be ideal for keeping patients well while they are resting, but a slow pulse leads to disabling lethargy and makes exertion impossible.

How a pacemaker works

The basic principle in the various types of pacemaker is exactly the same. Two parts make up the pacing system. First, there is some electronic means of producing regular electrical impulses that are of the correct strength and duration to cause the ventricles (the main pumping chambers of the heart), to beat. Second, the impulse is conducted to the

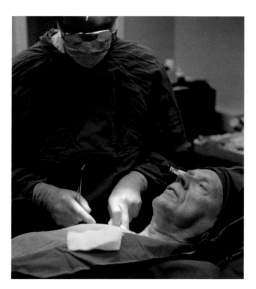

▶ *A pacemaker is inserted with the help of X rays to guide the wire to the heart.*

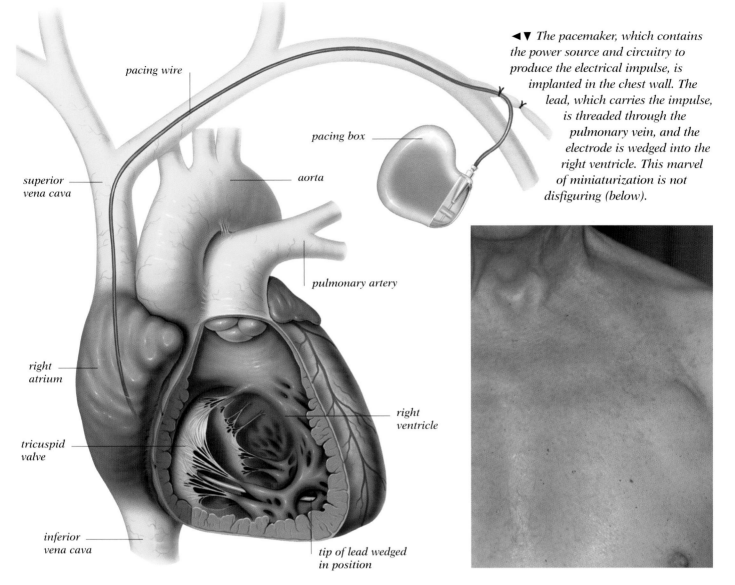

pacing wire

pacing box

superior
vena cava

aorta

pulmonary artery

right
atrium

right
ventricle

tricuspid
valve

inferior
vena cava

tip of lead wedged
in position

◄▼ The pacemaker, which contains the power source and circuitry to produce the electrical impulse, is implanted in the chest wall. The lead, which carries the impulse, is threaded through the pulmonary vein, and the electrode is wedged into the right ventricle. This marvel of miniaturization is not disfiguring (below).

heart by a wire, called a pacing lead, whose tip is implanted in the ventricles. If the impulses are strong enough, and there is good electrical connection between the wire and the muscle of the ventricle, a heartbeat will result from each impulse.

To coordinate the timing of the heartbeat, the pacing box receives electrical signals from the heart muscle. This enables it to know when there has been a heartbeat, so that it does not send another impulse until the heart is ready. This is called "demand pacing" and is almost always the system used, because it allows the heart specialist to program the pacemaker.

The pacing box is then set at a given rate, for example, 60 beats per minute. This means that the box will produce an impulse every second unless it senses that the heart has produced a beat on its own. If the heart does produce a beat, then the pacing box will wait for another second before it produces its next impulse (see Pulse).

Putting in a pacemaker

Two types of systems are used. The first is temporary: a pacing wire is passed through the skin, via a special needle, into a large vein, usually around the shoulder. It is then passed into the right atrium, through the tricuspid valve, and into the tip of the right ventricle, where it makes contact with the heart muscle. The position of the

wire is followed on an X ray so that it can be guided to the right position. If it is fixed to the skin, it is unlikely to become dislodged. The other end of the wire is attached to a pacing box that remains outside the patient's body.

For a permanent system, the same principle is used. Once the wire is connected to the pacing box, and the electrical connection between the wire and heart is ensured, the pacing box is sewn into a special pocket under the skin of the chest. Although the pacing box is only the size of a matchbox, it has enough battery power to produce impulses for years (more than 10 years in some cases). For long life, the pacemaker may use a radioactive atomic battery. Some pacemakers have an electrode in the right atrium that fires before the electrode in the right ventricle.

Pacing has saved many patients' lives. The effect of pacing has also helped prevent disabling symptoms such as recurrent blackouts—problems that occur mainly in the elderly. Age is no bar to having a pacemaker. An alternative to a pacemaker is an automatic implanted defibrillator, which delivers a jolt of electricity to restart the heart if the ventricles are fibrillating (quivering).

See also: **Blackouts; Heart attack; Heart disease**

1473

Pain

The parts of the brain that receive and analyze painful stimuli have close connections with the parts that have overall control of blood circulation, the heartbeat, and the condition of the peripheral blood vessels. Even a small degree of pain causes some change in a person's pulse rate, blood pressure, or both. If pain is severe, the circulation can be swamped by these influences: the blood vessels dilate and the blood pressure drops so low that unconsciousness results. This process is the same for any severe unpleasant stimulus, though people vary as to what degree of pain causes fainting.

Does acupuncture work only psychologically to relieve pain?

Psychological factors are very important in any method of pain relief, because of the considerable psychological component in our appreciation of pain. However, it is likely that there is a genuine physiological mechanism at work in some methods of acupuncture.

Is it true that some people feel pain more easily than others?

Yes. The threshold above which a person interprets a stimulus as being painful varies hugely for both psychological and physical reasons. Hence, different people require different amounts of painkillers or local anesthetics for pain caused by identical stimuli.

Can chronic pain cause a person to become emotionally disturbed?

Severe depression can result from prolonged suffering. Often the personality seems to be changed as the pain takes over the person's whole life. However, such severe pain is not very common.

Pain is the body's protective warning system, signaling injury and disease. It tells people to avoid harm and to seek medical attention for painful illnesses or injuries.

Pain can come in many forms. Individual sufferers may describe it as sharp, dull, aching, gripping, or throbbing. Minor degrees of pain are normal functions of the body and also part of its repertoire of sensory contact with the outside world. Through the experience of pain, people learn to avoid unpleasant elements in the world; the prospect of pain warns a person against repeating an action that has caused him or her pain in the past.

In disease, more severe and distressing pain arises generally from the persistent presence of some harmful stimulus in a particular part of the body. Occasionally, pain may be caused by a malfunction, due to some kind of damage, of the nerve fibers that carry and analyze painful stimuli within the nervous system.

A large section of the nervous system participates in the sensations of pain, from the peripheral nerves to the most sophisticated thinking areas of the cerebral cortex in the brain. There are many different types of pain. Each depends on various stimuli that cause it, and the way in which those stimuli are analyzed by the nervous networks in the spinal cord and brain. Cultural and social factors also play an enormous role in determining the mind's response to the perception of pain.

The purpose of pain

The ability to feel pain is vital to the well-being of humans. This can be seen from situations in which the whole or parts of a person's body lose their ability to discern pain. In leprosy, for example, the nerves to the hands and feet become so damaged that pain is no longer felt in these areas; as a result, sufferers damage their hands and feet continually and sometimes unknowingly without feeling any pain (see Numbness).

▲ *Pain acts as a warning to a person that part of the body has been injured. He or she should then seek medical attention if further damage is to be avoided.*

PATHWAYS OF PAIN

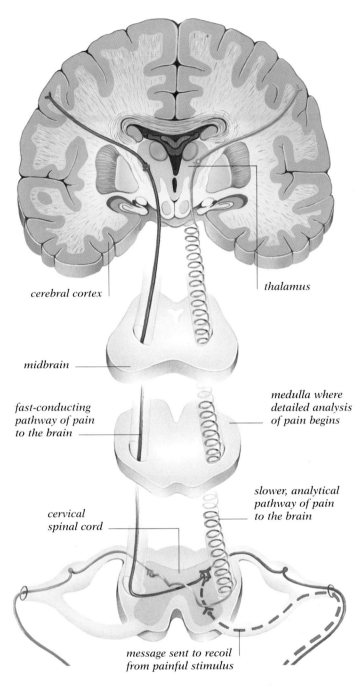

cerebral cortex

thalamus

midbrain

fast-conducting
pathway of pain
to the brain

medulla where
detailed analysis
of pain begins

cervical
spinal cord

slower, analytical
pathway of pain
to the brain

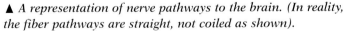

message sent to recoil
from painful stimulus

▲ *A representation of nerve pathways to the brain. (In reality, the fiber pathways are straight, not coiled as shown).*

A few people are from birth in the dangerous state of being unable to feel any pain; they must be protected from injuring themselves. Such injuries would cause severe physical damage to anyone who did not heed the warning messages conveyed by the pain system. People do not touch boiling saucepans, for example, because the very few times they have done so, the pain has reminded them of the tissue damage that can occur.

Pain from the internal organs warns a person in the same way of the presence of a disease. For example, indigestion may warn a person to eat less rich, spicy food during his or her next meal. The paradox is that while the most distressing aspect of a disease may

▲ *A stiff, painful shoulder is one of the first signs of repetitive strain injury (RSI).*

be pain, it is pain—its character and its position—that enables a doctor to detect the cause of the complaint and prescribe treatment. When a person has abdominal pain, it is dangerous for him or her to cover it up with painkillers, since this may mask the development of painful symptoms that could herald the presence of a serious disorder. However, once a doctor is sure of a diagnosis, any painful symptoms can be treated as necessary.

How pain occurs

Painful stimuli inside or outside a person's body excite otherwise unspecialized nerve endings in the skin and elsewhere. The nerve endings are attached to nerves of two different types: one is fast-conducting and conveys its information to the spinal cord rapidly (see Reflexes); the other also takes its information to the spinal cord, but more slowly. This helps the brain to distinguish between two types of pain—pricking pain that is felt immediately, and can therefore be reacted to, or pain that is dull and aching.

Peripheral nerve endings make many contacts with the network of fibers in the spinal cord. The fibers are responsible for the initial analysis of all sensations, but pain in particular. A second nerve fiber then takes this more organized information upward to the brain. Again this happens by two different pathways—one leads to the thalamus (the main sensory relay station deep in the brain) fairly directly; the other takes a more branching course, making many connections with centers in the brain stem before it also arrives at the thalamus. This enables the cortex—the part of the brain where pain is actually perceived—to obtain fast reports of the painful situation, and also more slowly arriving but more heavily analyzed information coming by the slow pathway.

The thalamus, which analyzes information for presentation to the cerebral cortex, has rich connections with the areas of the brain that are concerned with the maintenance of emotional tone and the areas concerned with arousal. As a result, before the perceiving brain receives information, especially of painful stimuli, it is already aware of a person's emotional state and is affected by his or her levels of arousal.

The final arbiter as to whether pain is perceived is the cerebral cortex. It seems that large areas of this part of the brain participate

Questions and Answers

Can a man really feel the physical pain of his partner's childbirth?

Probably not. However, if a man is very close to his wife or partner, his brain may synthesize some of the distress (if any) of childbirth, although this is unusual. Of course, not actually feeling the pain does not mean that the man is not affected in other ways.

When someone loses the sensation of pain in a leg—owing to a disorder of the nerve, for example—isn't this a good thing?

No. In such a situation the warning value of pain is lost and the person will not notice minor injuries. Such injuries may then progress to ulcers that can cause serious damage to the limb. Pain is a helpful sign that gives a person warning signals of actual or potential damage to tissues.

Is there any truth in the theory that twins, although they may be separated by many miles, can feel the pain of each other's injuries?

No. There is no real evidence that this happens and no theoretical way in which it could happen.

I have seen TV programs showing religious initiates walking over red-hot coals with no shoes on. Do these people feel any pain?

At the time, probably not. The situation is similar to that of a soldier who may feel no pain from even a severe injury received in battle. If the mind is sufficiently diverted, either by the induction of a religious trance or by the fear and excitement of a battle, the brain does not pay sufficient attention for the painful sensations to reach the person's consciousness.

Another factor is that there is considerable cultural pressure on religious initiates to hide their pain from others. Even if the pain penetrates their personal threshold, their minds may be able to erect a barrier.

▲ *Some cultures make a virtue of pain and of the idea of "mind over matter". In this Thai Pusau ceremony, a celebrant has both cheeks pierced by a metal rod.*

in this complex form of perception. The frontal lobes, especially those parts concerned with the analysis of emotions—that is, the parts of the frontal lobes that connect with the limbic system—seem to be important for the perception of painful stimuli as unpleasant. People who have lost the use of this part of the brain report that although they can feel pain, they are not upset by it. The parietal lobes of the brain seem to be important in the localization of the painful stimulus, but they also participate in the perception of the sensations associated with pain.

Types of pain

Skin pain: This is usually localized. It is a sensation of either pricking or burning or a combination of both, according to whether the fast- or slow-conducting nerve fibers or both are stimulated.
Internal pain: This is more variable—that is, it has different qualities, such as sharp or dull pain—and tends to be poorly localized. It is perceived as deeper and often of a duller quality than skin pain. The stimulation of combinations of different sensory fibers may produce a variety of stabbing, pressing, or constricting pains, and these may be felt coming from the internal organs.
Referred pain: Pain that comes from any internal organ may seem to come from areas of the body some distance from the position of that organ. This is because the nerves from the organs are received, and their messages analyzed, by parts of the spinal cord that also deal with those areas to which the pain seems to be referred. Thus, pain coming from the heart may be felt in the center of the chest and also in the left arm and in the jaw. This is because the pain messages spill over from their spinal analyzing centers into neighboring zones.

By careful questioning of a person in pain, doctors can usually get a clear idea of the organ involved. Not all organs refer their pains to distant sites; however, those that do always do so in characteristic distributions.
Pain from the nervous system: Damage to the peripheral nerves rather than the

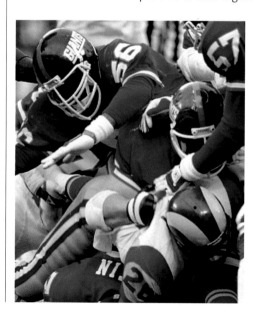

◄ *The threat of injury, and the pain that is associated with it, is common in a contact sport such as football.*

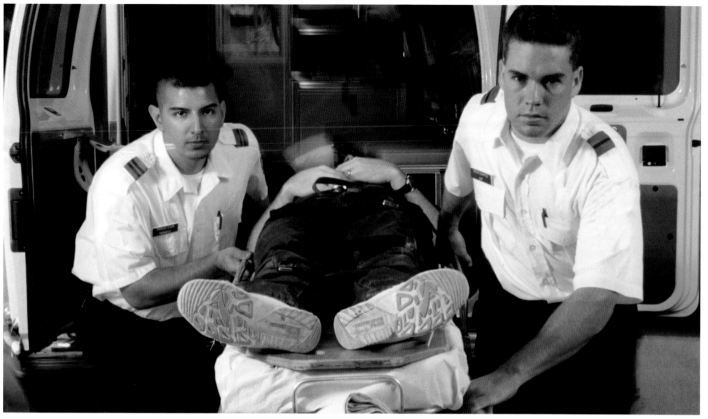

stimulation of these nerves by harmful stimuli may be the cause of pain. For example, pressure on the median nerve in the wrist may cause pain and tingling in the hand. The sensation may spread up the arm to other parts of the body, again because of the connections in the spinal cord.

"Slipped" disks in the spine can cause pressure on the sensory nerves as they enter the spinal cord; since the nerve being pressed carries impulses from the back of the leg, the pain is felt by the sufferer as traveling down the back of the leg (see Slipped Disk).

Damage to the spinal cord itself, from pressure that is due to tumors or inflammations such as multiple sclerosis, also causes pain. This pain may be sent to the part of the body whose sensations are analyzed by the segment of the cord that has been affected.

Damage to other parts of the central nervous system may also cause pain. In particular, damage to the thalamus due to minor strokes may cause very unpleasant sensations and pain, since the nerves that organize the incoming stimuli become disorganized and interpret ordinary sensations as painful (see Stroke).

Phantom pains: When an arm or a leg has been amputated, the nerves remain in the stump. If they are stimulated by the swelling or scarring of the remainder of the limb, the brain actually registers the pain as if it were coming from the lost leg or arm. After a while the brain usually reorganizes its perceptions so that any pain is actually felt in the stump alone; however, initially the site of the pain is perceived according to where the nerves originated.

Psychological aspects of pain

The state of a person's mind is an important factor in his or her perception of pain, because large areas of the nervous system participate in feelings and responses to painful stimuli. This state of mind is strongly influenced by the situation in which a particular

▲ *One person might faint from the pain of an injury that another person perceives as merely uncomfortable.*

painful sensation occurs, and the cultural and social background against which people's attitudes to pain have developed.

In the heat of a battle, soldiers may feel no pain even though they have suffered substantial injuries, partly because the mind is being distracted by the battle itself. Also, in a highly stressful situation such as this, the brain produces morphine-like substances called endorphins that can, for a time, abolish pain totally. Later, however, when a soldier has calmed down, the pain may become unbearable, although the injury itself is no more severe.

During yoga or meditation, the mind may be diverted away from painful stimuli by the deep contemplation of other things, so that what seem to be feats of endurance—such as lying on beds of nails and walking over hot coals—can be achieved. It is likely that people undergoing such an ordeal are not actually feeling the pain in the same way that they normally would. They have managed to distract the mind from the unpleasant significance of the stimuli that are still undoubtedly reaching the brain.

The psychological effect of prolonged pain may be pronounced. Severe pain can begin a cycle in which the mental ability of the sufferer to cope with pain is eroded gradually, and causes a change in the person's personality. The person begins to concentrate unduly on the pain and begins to perceive the pain as more severe than it really is. People who suffer constant and prolonged pain often become depressed. Pain management that is swift and effective is vital once the cause of the pain is known.

See also: **Brain; Mind; Nervous system; Painkillers; Pain management; Spinal cord**

Painkillers

Questions and Answers

Are low doses of aspirin good for the heart and circulation?

Yes. Aspirin taken in very low doses helps to prevent heart attacks, as was proved by long-term studies using doctors as patients.

Is aspirin safe for everyone?

Aspirin should not be taken by anyone with a history of stomach trouble (particularly ulcers). Nor should it be given to children under 12, because it can cause Reye's syndrome to develop when there is a viral illness present.

Can acupuncture really treat pain?

Yes, it does work, although we are not sure why. In China, dentists can drill and fill the teeth of people who have been anesthetized by acupuncture; these procedures are a good test of its effectiveness.

I'm pregnant. Should I use painkillers if I have a headache?

Because pregnant women ingest so many drugs in normal day-to-day life—caffeine in tea and coffee, and nicotine in cigarette smoke, for example—it is often difficult to blame a particular drug for a particular abnormality. Also, a problem may arise from a drug combination rather than any one individual drug. Hence researchers cannot be sure of the effects of many over-the-counter painkillers.

If a pregnant woman takes any substances, many of these will pass to the fetus. This is especially dangerous during the first three months, when fetal abnormalities are most likely to be caused by drugs or other agents. As a general rule, drugs (even mild painkillers) should be avoided during the first three months of pregnancy. Acetaminophen is probably the safest, however.

Most people take or are given painkilling medications at some time or other. How do they work, and which drugs should be used—or avoided—for particular individuals and in particular circumstances?

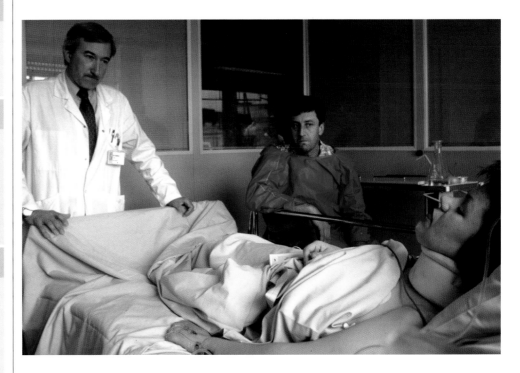

▲ *Narcotic drugs such as morphine are still used in hospitals; addiction to these drugs is unlikely if their use is limited to the relief of fairly short-term severe pain.*

The medical term for a pain-relieving drug is "analgesic." Doctors usually divide painkilling drugs into two categories: narcotics and other painkilling drugs.

Narcotics, such as morphine and heroin—which are derived from opium—together with their synthetic relations, such as pethedine and methadone, act principally on the brain and often produce drug dependence. Narcotic drugs are typically used in highly controlled conditions, such as a hospital environment, to give relief for pain in internal organs.

Other painkilling drugs, such as aspirin, are rarely addictive and act directly on the site of the pain. They are used to control pain felt in the joints, muscles, bones, and skin.

In the past, pain-relieving drugs were obtained only from natural sources. Morphine, for example, comes from the opium poppy. Purified opium preparations are still widely used, but many drugs for medical use are now prepared synthetically.

Most common painkillers

The best-known painkillers are aspirin, acetaminophen, ibuprofen, and morphine. Aspirin and acetaminophen are available in drugstores and are used to relieve headaches or pains such as premenstrual cramps. Painkillers that can be purchased over the counter are different combinations of aspirin, acetaminophen, and ibuprofen, sometimes with the addition of a stimulant such as caffeine. They each produce different effects on the body.

Aspirin

Aspirin is probably the best-known and most widely used drug. Not only does it relieve pain; it also reduces fevers and has an anti-inflammatory effect on the joints. That is why doctors often prescribe aspirin for influenza, not necessarily to kill pain—which in any case is more discomfort

Common painkillers

	USES	DANGERS	LONG-TERM USE	CONTRAINDICATIONS
Aspirin	Mild painkiller; brings down temperature and reduces inflammation. Good for headaches, discomfort from colds and influenza, or pains such as backache.	Irritates stomach lining; can cause ulcers and bleeding. Can cause severe side effects in young children who have a viral illness.	Nonaddictive, but patients should not take aspirin regularly without first seeking a doctor's advice.	Should not be taken by people with stomach problems. Do not take on an empty stomach or without water. Do not give to children under 12.
Acetaminophen	Mild painkiller. Used similarly to aspirin; can also be used for stomachaches.	Can cause fatal liver failure if taken in high doses over a long time.	Large doses can cause liver failure. Use with caution.	Should not be given to patients suffering from liver problems.
Codeine	Painkiller available with prescription; available over the counter in some states in small dosages combined with other ingredients.	Can cause constipation, nausea, and vomiting.	Can be addictive and may cause damage to the kidneys.	Should not be given to patients suffering from liver or kidney problems.
Naproxen, Ibuprofen	Similar to aspirin.	Stomach irritation, but less severe than with aspirin.	Not addictive.	Use with caution in patients with stomach problems or aspirin allergy.

than pain—but in order to reduce the patient's temperature and to help ease the aching joints often experienced in such an illness. Aspirin is prescribed to ease rheumatism, often over extended periods, because of its powerful anti-inflammatory property (see Inflammation).

Dangers of aspirin
Aspirin can be extremely dangerous to some people in certain circumstances. It is an irritant and can cause stomach pain with nausea and vomiting. Much more important, if it is swallowed whole, an aspirin tablet will not just irritate the stomach lining but may even cause bleeding. For this reason, aspirin should never be taken on an empty stomach without a drink of water.

Aspirin can also be dangerous to elderly people on poor diets, especially if diets are low in iron, and to patients who are weak and recovering from an illness.

It is even possible for people to develop superficial stomach ulcers from aspirin without realizing it (see Ulcers); this in turn can lead to blood loss and anemia. Some people are allergic to aspirin.

However, perhaps the greatest danger of aspirin is to children who are suffering from a viral illness. This combination can result in a potentially lethal brain and liver disorder (see Reye's Syndrome).

Since aspirin is present in many drugs, often under its chemical name—acetylsalicylic acid—people should always read the list of ingredients on the label of any medications they buy.

Acetaminophen
If for any reason a patient should not take aspirin, acetaminophen is often prescribed as a good alternative. Acetaminophen is also a mild pain reliever and can reduce the temperature, although it has no effect on inflammation, so it is of little use for treating rheumatism. Acetaminophen does not irritate the stomach lining and so may be taken for abdominal pain. However, it can damage the liver and

should not be taken in high doses over long periods or with other drugs, with alcohol, or by anyone who drinks alcohol heavily.

Someone who attempts suicide by taking an overdose of acetaminophen may appear to have failed for a day or two, only to die soon afterward as a result of liver failure. Any large overdosage must be reported urgently and treated if life is to be saved.

Codeine
Codeine is an opium derivative used in painkilling, antidiarrhea or cough suppressant medications. In addition to being a mild pain reliever, codeine slows down the action of the intestine and

▲ *Some painkillers are made specifically for children. Parents should always check the correct dose for their child's age group.*

Questions and Answers

I occasionally get a blinding headache that makes me feel sick. Two aspirins have no effect. Should I take more?

A blinding headache with nausea is a good description of a migraine. It is often difficult to tell the difference, but the classic symptoms of a migraine are a headache on one side of the head accompanied by nausea and vomiting. There are often visual disturbances and slurred speech. Migraines may respond to aspirin or acetaminophen, but often they do not. Other drugs can help if they are taken as soon as possible after the migraine starts, but a doctor should be consulted first.

In the case of an overdose, is it enough to make the person vomit to get rid of the painkilling drugs?

Immediate action is necessary, but never try to take care of an overdose patient on your own—always call an ambulance.

You may be able to void the drugs before they are absorbed, but after some painkillers have entered the bloodstream—this can take place very quickly—the damage may be widespread. Acetaminophen, for example, can cause liver damage that kills several days after an overdose. The sufferer may show very few signs of damage for many hours before lapsing into a coma.

Never try to induce vomiting if the person is unconscious. This is because the vomit may be inhaled into the lungs, causing choking.

I am an ex-alcoholic and have some liver damage. Is it safe for me to take acetaminophen?

No. Acetaminophen (Tylenol) should never be used as a painkiller if you have any liver damage. Even a small dose could be dangerous. Because your liver is damaged, it cannot perform its normal function of detoxification properly. Therefore, any acetaminophen you take cannot be cleared from your system, so fatal poisoning could result.

Points to watch with painkillers

All analgesics cause a certain amount of drowsiness. It is wise to avoid driving or handling machinery while taking them.

Analgesics can be harmful if they are taken over a long period of time. If you are in constant pain, consult a doctor.

Be careful about taking painkillers if you are already taking other drugs.

All pills, including analgesics, should be kept in childproof containers and locked in a medicine chest.

Do not take painkillers with alcohol.

Always take painkillers with water and, if possible, with or after food.

Check with a pharmacist if you are unsure about how much a child's dose should be.

suppresses the cough center in the brain. Codeine is rarely used on its own, but it is frequently combined with other drugs, most commonly with aspirin and acetaminophen. As well as increasing the effects of these painkillers, codeine has a mild pain-relieving action on the brain; the aspirin and acetaminophen ingredients act on the site of the pain itself. Codeine is available over the counter only in combination with other drugs and in dosages of no more than 30 mg in the United States.

Morphine

Morphine is made from opium. If it is taken repeatedly, it may become addictive; as a result, the painkilling effect lessens as the patient gradually builds up a tolerance to the drug. Despite this serious effect, narcotics such as morphine are still the most effective painkillers available to doctors. They are used to relieve severe pain from many different causes and also act to relieve the stress and anxiety that people in extreme pain are likely to experience.

Function of pain

Pain can be regarded as a warning signal to instigate investigation into why the pain is happening. In most cases the cause of pain, rather than the symptom that is the pain, should be sought after and cured.

Some people may sometimes experience pain for either temporary or passing reasons that do not really require a doctor's attention. In such cases a safe, effective painkiller is both necessary and beneficial.

It is not advisable, however, for people to continue taking over-the-counter painkillers for longer than two or three days. In addition, people should always read instructions carefully and take note of any warnings of side effects. If the pain persists beyond a few days, medical advice should be sought.

See also: Aspirin and analgesics; Birth; Fevers; Liver and liver diseases; Medicines; Morphine; Narcotics; Overdoses; Pain; Pain management

▲ *Raspberry tea is sometimes claimed to be help relieve the pain associated with childbirth and menstruation.*

Pain management

The perception of pain is influenced by the mind and the body. Pain management aims to help sufferers tackle their pain by considering both its physical and mental aspects.

Can surgery deaden pain?

Surgery can relieve pain, but doctors use this method only as a last resort because it can destroy other sensations or it may create new pain elsewhere. Also, the old pain may come back. The most common surgical technique for pain relief involves cutting the nerve fibers on one or both sides of the spinal cord. This procedure, called cordotomy, affects the sense of temperature as well as that of pain because nerve fibers for both sensations travel together along the spinal cord to the brain.

How can severe pain be controlled without medication?

One method of pain relief relies on electrodes implanted in the brain. The electrodes are attached to areas that are rich in cells that produce endorphins, the body's natural painkillers. The patient alters the frequency and voltage of the electrical stimulation until his or her pain disappears. The technique relieves pain well for some patients, while leaving their other senses unaffected. Researchers are studying whether patients who undergo repeated brain stimulation develop tolerance to the stimulation, so that their pain returns.

How does acupuncture work?

An acupuncturist inserts the tips of fine needles at specific points in the body. These points are some distance from the area on which they must act. A needle in the thumb, for example, reduces pain in the abdomen. After insertion, the needles may be rotated to stimulate nerve signals that stop the pain. Exactly why acupuncture works is unclear. It may be that the stimulation of sensory fibers boosts the production of endorphins and blocks the transmission of pain messages to the brain.

According to the American Chronic Pain Association in 2003, about one in three Americans is affected by some degree of chronic (persistent or recurring) pain. Millions suffer so badly that they cannot sleep, work, exercise, or concentrate. People suffering from chronic pain include those with cancer, lumbago, fibromyalgia, and arthritis. Doctors distinguish chronic pain from acute pain, which is intense but relatively brief, and affects patients with short-term injuries, such as broken bones.

Pain warns people that something is wrong with the body. A person feels pain when an injury or disease stimulates special sensory nerve endings called nociceptors and triggers pain messages to travel from the site of the injury to the brain. Nociceptors are found in the skin and other places such as the tendons. Although the cause of pain may begin in another part of the body, the sensation of pain necessarily involves the brain.

Pain comes in many forms, and how an individual reacts to it does not depend only on the pain. A person's perception of pain is influenced by social and cultural factors, such as how he or she has been brought up to handle pain, as well as on his or her state of mind. A ballplayer, for example, may be so caught up in a game that he carries on playing, not realizing that he has torn a ligament. Someone who is feeling worried or depressed, by contrast, may experience pain more intensely. Pain relief should aim to resolve both the physiological and the psychological elements of pain. There are various ways of treating pain other than medication. Cold water can be applied in cases of burns and bruises, massage and heat can soothe aches; and electrical stimulation is also used. Some less common methods of pain management include biofeedback, psychotherapy, acupuncture, hypnosis, meditation, relaxation, and exercise (see Alternative Medicine).

Medication

Drugs that relieve pain are known as analgesics. The most powerful of these are opioid analgesics, such as morphine, heroin, and codeine, which are derived from opium or are synthetic chemicals related to opium. Opioids are narcotics—that is, drugs that act on a person's brain to cause numbness and stupor.

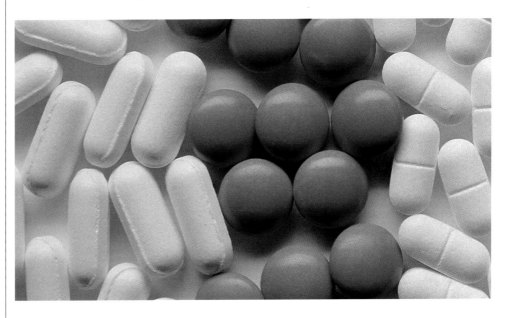

▲ *Acetaminophen, ibuprofen, and aspirin can all be bought in drugstores. Powerful narcotic analgesics, on the other hand, are available only with a prescription.*

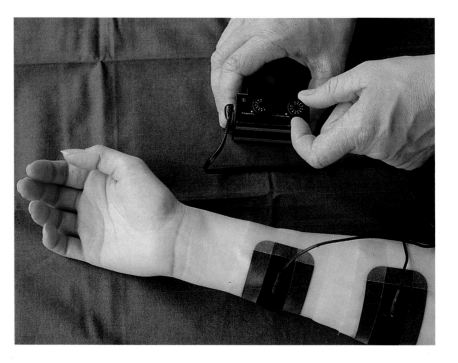

▶ *Electrical stimulation using a TENS machine has many applications in analgesia, particularly for patients with chronic pain. It is both cheaper and safer than using drugs.*

Opium is made from the dried juice of the opium poppy and was used to ease pain as early as 6,000 years ago by the Sumerians. Opiates mimic the effects of endorphins, a group of painkilling proteins that occur naturally in the brain. Like endorphins, opiates block the activation of pain neurons.

Narcotics can be addictive, and opiates can cause side effects such as respiratory depression, nausea, and constipation. As a result, powerful opiates are usually prescribed only for severe pain, such as that experienced with diseases such as cancer. For moderate pain, such as that caused by headaches, patients can take analgesics such as aspirin.

Aspirin is a member of a group of drugs called nonsteroidal anti-inflammatory drugs (NSAIDs), which decrease inflammation, fever, and pain. They work at the site of an inflammation, preventing the body from producing certain prostaglandins, chemicals that trigger pain and inflammation (see Prostaglandins). However, NSAIDs can irritate the stomach lining and may cause ulcers. These drugs can also lead to nausea and vomiting and are toxic to the kidneys.

Another analgesic, acetaminophen, is good for treating mild pain and fever; because it does not irritate the stomach lining, it can also be taken for abdominal pain or when there is a history of ulcers. However, it does not reduce inflammation and is a dangerous liver poison if too many tablets are taken in a short period of time.

How doctors give analgesics

Experts in pain relief now recognize that the almost universal practice of withholding powerful analgesics until a person's pain became severe was a mistake. Today, doctors recognize that when the pattern of pain is known, analgesics should be given at regular intervals in anticipation of pain. Once severe pain has occurred, it is much more difficult to relieve than it would have been to prevent; larger doses of analgesics will also be needed.

Treatment involves repeated small doses of an analgesic at relatively short intervals and is often more effective than larger doses administered three times a day. Many pain relief experts have found that the most effective method is one in which the patient controls the dosage by pressing a button whenever he or she feels pain. This method necessitates an intravenous line with saline running in constantly at a slow rate.

Another important lesson that has been learned from research is that addiction to a powerful opioid analgesic is unlikely if its use is limited to the relief of a reasonably short-term severe pain. Many patients have been unnecessarily denied adequate pain relief because of past fears of causing addiction.

Electrical treatment

Some types of pain can be treated by electrical stimulation. Patients with chronic pain sometimes find effective pain relief with a TENS—transcutaneous electrical nerve stimulation—machine, a device that sends out electrical impulses through the skin to nerve endings. The patient adjusts the frequency and voltage of the electrical stimulation until the pain goes away. The electrical activity of the TENS machine probably works by blocking pain signals on their way to the brain and by stimulating the release of endorphins. Some women find that a TENS machine can be effective during childbirth.

Behavior therapy

If people have felt pain for a long time, they often anticipate it and become tense. Biofeedback training is a type of behavior therapy that aims to control pain by changing the person's responses to it. Some patients are able to treat migraines, muscle tension, and high blood pressure using biofeedback techniques.

In biofeedback training, a patient is linked up to machines that monitor the heartbeat and blood pressure and test the tension in the neck muscles. The patient receives this information by looking at a monitor or by listening to it: a louder sound could mean an increase in heart rate, for instance. Scientists do not understand how people use biofeedback to control their bodies, but patients say that imagery, such as thinking of a hot bath, can help them relax.

Pain clinics

For people whose pain has taken over their lives, the answer may be to visit a pain clinic. There are more than 800 pain clinics in the United States. Such clinics vary in their approach, but a team of specialists will usually read a patient's medical records and arrange tests if required. The patient will then be guided through a personal treatment program. The program may include exercises or a special diet. Other treatments may involve receiving electrical stimulation and analgesic drugs. The patient's thoughts, feelings, and actions can affect the pain, so there may also be psychotherapy.

The ultimate aim of any pain clinic is to reduce the patients' reliance on medication so that they can resume a normal life.

> See also: **Biofeedback; Birth; Narcotics; Nonsteroidal anti-inflammatory drugs; Pain; Painkillers; Psychotherapy**

Palate

Questions and Answers

Will a premature baby always have a cleft palate?

No. In a normal baby, the proper knitting together of the bones that form the palate occurs early in the fetus's life. Being born prematurely will make no difference to the structure of a baby's mouth. A baby destined to have a cleft palate will have one whether or not he or she is born before the due date.

I am 36 and pregnant with my first baby. Because of my age, is my baby more likely to be born with a cleft palate?

Surveys have found a relationship between the age of a mother and the likelihood of a baby's having a cleft palate, but the link is not very strong. About one in 750 babies is born with a cleft palate, and the number rises to one in 20 if someone in the mother's immediate family has the problem. If you have any concerns about this, talk to your doctor.

My daughter speaks with a lisp. Could it indicate that there is something wrong with her palate?

No. A lisp usually results from the faulty movement of the tongue inside the mouth. Although the palate, particularly the hard palate, plays a part in the formation of the sounds of speech, it has a passive role compared with the active influence of the tongue, mouth, and lips. A lisp can be corrected by teaching the correct movements to make. It may be useful for your daughter to see a speech therapist.

What is a "falling palate"?

"Falling palate" is a term used to describe an abnormal enlargement of the uvula, which hangs down from the back of the soft palate. This may cause constant coughing and is usually treated by surgery.

As an integral part of the mouth, the palate helps in breaking up food. It also plays a crucial role in subtly changing the shape of the mouth to create an enormous variety in the sounds and character of speech.

"Palate" is the technical word for the roof of the mouth. It is divided into two parts: the hard palate, toward the front of the mouth, and the soft palate at the back. The palate is involved in many of the functions of the mouth: eating, tasting, swallowing, breathing, and speaking. The palate can be injured, but the most common problem is faulty development, which can lead to the birth of a baby with a split or cleft palate.

Structure

The hard palate is created by the links between the maxillae, the bones of the upper jaw, and the palatine bones on either side of the face that connect with them. The soft palate has no such bony base. Instead it is underlaid with tough fibers and with muscles that allow it to move. At the back of the mouth, behind the tongue, the soft palate splits into two, and the gaps are occupied by the tonsils. Just in front of this divide hangs a fleshy projection called the uvula.

Covering the hard and soft palates, and forming the lining of the mouth, is a layer of mucous membrane that contains mucus-secreting glands. This membrane is subject to a great amount of

▲ *For a child, the feel of food is as important as its taste in determining whether or not it is enjoyable. The texture of food is picked up by nerves in the palate.*

Questions and Answers

My baby has suddenly developed white patches inside his mouth, with some on his palate. What should I do?

It sounds as if your baby has a yeast infection. This is caused by a fungus and needs treatment, so take him to a doctor as soon as possible. The usual treatment is either a topical or an ingestible antifungal medication.

Why is it that eating salty food makes my palate dry?

The sensation of a dry palate is part of the body's natural reaction to thirst. Salty food makes you feel thirsty because it temporarily upsets the body's internal water balance, drawing water out of the blood and into the tissues. The brain monitors this water level and also responds to the sensation of a dry palate. As a result, you are driven to search for a drink and therefore put the blood and body tissues back into their proper equilibrium.

Why is my palate so sensitive to the texture of certain foods? Sometimes the sensation makes me feel physically sick.

Like other parts of the body, the palate is endowed with a rich supply of nerves. When we eat, some of the nerves of the palate send signals to the brain about the nature of the food that is in the mouth. If these nerves send back the message "unpleasant," then the natural reaction of the brain is "reject." One of the most common rejection mechanisms is vomiting, which explains why food that is unpleasant to you produces such a strong physical sensation.

Does a cleft palate always have to be corrected?

Almost always. The only notable exception is if the split or cleft in the palate is very slight and affects only the area of the uvula at the back of the palate.

wear and tear, so it has to be tough and capable of renewing its surface cells constantly. The membrane on the hard palate is stuck tightly to the bony structure beneath to prevent it from becoming dislodged by the movements of the tongue. The ridge of bone which runs along the middle of the palate, and to which the membrane is attached, is called the raphe. Horizontal ridges of tissue called rugae extend from the raphe. These can be felt with the tongue, and are most prominent in childhood. The mucous membrane that covers the soft palate extends backward to join with the lining of the back of the nose. To aid lubrication of the throat during swallowing, it is more richly supplied with mucous glands than the lining of the hard palate.

What the palate does

The soft palate contains a few taste buds, which supplement the more numerous ones of the tongue. When people eat, the hard palate acts as the mortar onto which the pestle of the tongue pushes food to soften and mash it. When food is ready to be swallowed, the muscles of the soft palate contract and pull this part of the palate upward. This action not only helps push the food toward the esophagus but also blocks off the airway at the back of the nose (see Esophagus). By helping to keep breathing separate from the eating process, the movements of the soft palate help to prevent choking.

The texture of food is sensed by nerves in the palate's mucous membrane. Any food that has an unpleasant texture is appropriately described as unpalatable. In extreme cases, unpalatable food may make a person feel sick because it causes "reject" messages to be sent to the brain, which trigger a vomiting reflex (see Vomiting).

During normal breathing, the soft palate is held in a relaxed position to allow the free passage of air in and out of the lungs via the nose. When people speak, air is taken in through the mouth and molded by the tongue and lips as they exhale; movement of the soft palate creates subtle differences in the shape of the mouth's acoustic chamber; and the hard palate acts as a sounding board for the tongue, giving basic sounds the shape of speech.

Development

The palate begins to develop as early as the fifth week of life in the womb. At this stage the face is molded in gristly cartilage; later it hardens into true bone

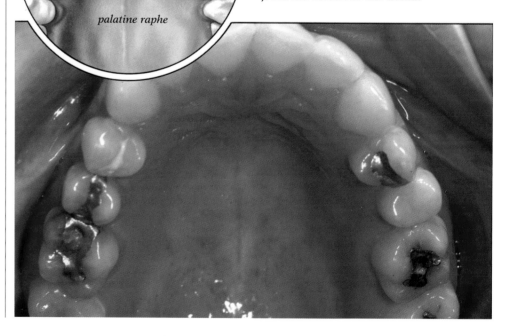

palatine rugae

palatine raphe

▼ *The photograph below shows the normal palate of an adult (the rugae and raphe can be seen more clearly in the insert). The rugae are the horizontal ridges; the raphe is the bone that runs from the mouth to the uvula.*

NORMAL AND ABNORMAL DEVELOPMENT OF THE PALATE

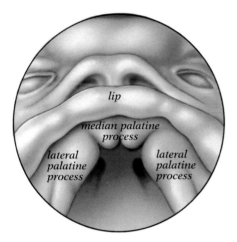

▲ *The palate normally begins to develop when the fetus is about five weeks old; by eight weeks each part has formed.*

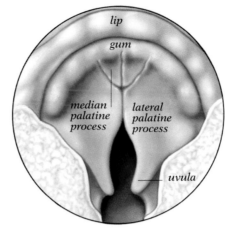

▲ *By nine weeks the lateral processes have grown and fusion of the two sides has begun; a week later it will be complete.*

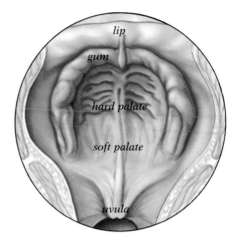

▲ *The palate at birth, showing the prominent ridges of the hard palate; these become less pronounced with age.*

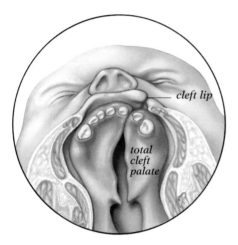

▲ *Incomplete development of both the hard and the soft palate; this type of cleft may be accompanied by a cleft lip.*

▲ *A cleft affecting the whole of the soft palate occurs symmetrically along the midline from the hard palate to the uvula.*

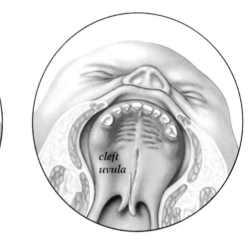

▲ *A cleft uvula; unlike other types of cleft palate, this is not serious and does not usually require surgical treatment.*

(see Cartilage). The palate does not develop from a single bone. Instead a pair of horizontal projections grow from the rudimentary upper jaw, under the eyes, to meet in the center of the skull. At the same time another projection grows down between the eyes to create the nose. The three pieces of cartilage finally fuse, and the fusion creates the palate. The process of growth and fusion demands precise timing and is synchronized with the formation of the outer tissues of the face, including the skin. For a perfect result, each part of the process must take place at the right time and at exactly the right rate (see Fetus).

Problems and treatment

The most serious and common defect of the palate comes from poor synchronization during the growth and fusion of the bones. The result is a split or cleft palate. A baby born with a cleft palate has a gap, usually Y-shaped, in the roof of the mouth (see Cleft Palate). A cleft palate is often associated with a harelip. This second deformity is a puckering of the lip due to the faulty synchronization of cartilage growth with skin growth. Both cleft palate and harelip are believed to result from defects that are hereditary (see Congenital Disorders).

Plastic surgery has made a cleft palate less serious than it used to be, but the necessary operations demand great skill and careful timing. A baby with a cleft palate needs special help to eat properly (see Plastic and Reconstructive Surgery).

Sometimes the hard palate may be excessively concave in shape, impairing breathing. This problem is often associated with enlarged tonsils and tends to improve once the tonsils are removed surgically (see Tonsils). Abnormalities of the soft palate can cause snoring and respiratory problems during sleep.

Any accident that involves a burn in the mouth, or an injury that leads to bleeding, should be treated by sucking on an ice cube. If there is bleeding from a palate injured in an accident, lay the victim on his or her side to prevent him or her from choking on blood.

See also: **Mouth; Mucus; Snoring; Speech; Taste; Tongue**

Pancreas and disorders

Questions and Answers

I have been told that the pancreas is so important that if it is removed or destroyed, the patient's life is in danger. Is this true?

It is true that the pancreas is one of the body's most important organs, but it can be removed by surgery and its function replaced in various ways. The first problem that has to be dealt with is diabetes, since the pancreas is the only source of insulin in the body. This problem is solved relatively easily with insulin injections.

The pancreas is also important in the digestion of food. When it is removed, the patient is usually treated with an extract of pancreatic digestive enzymes from animal sources, which is added to food. The drug cimetidine is used to stop the stomach from producing acids, thus preventing the breakdown of pancreatic enzymes by acid.

Can the pancreas be injured in an accident?

Yes; injuries to the pancreas most commonly occur as a result of car accidents, in which the upper part of the abdomen is struck with force during the crash. It can be difficult to tell if the pancreas is involved, and surgery is always performed if a pancreatic injury is suspected; if it is left untreated, the digestive juices of the pancreas leak into the abdomen.

Does a person who has a diseased pancreas always get diabetes?

No; many pancreatic problems do not cause diabetes. However, if there is inflammation of the entire pancreas as there is in pancreatitis, the insulin-producing cells in the islets are almost bound to be involved, leading to a diabetic tendency that is often less marked than might be expected from the extent of the damage.

The pancreas is one of the most important glands in the human body. It secretes most of the hormones, such as insulin, that are vital to life, as well as the enzymes that make digestion possible.

The pancreas, one of the largest glands in the body, is really two glands in one; almost all of it deals with secretion. It is an endocrine gland that secretes hormones, of which insulin is the most important. It is also an exocrine gland—one that secretes directly into the gut (or another body cavity) rather than into the blood.

The pancreas lies across the upper part of the abdomen in front of the spine and on top of the aorta and the vena cava (the body's main artery and vein). The duodenum is wrapped around the head of the pancreas; the rest consists of the body and tail stretched over the spine to the left. The basic structures in the pancreas are the acini, which are collections of secreting cells around

DUAL ROLE OF THE PANCREAS

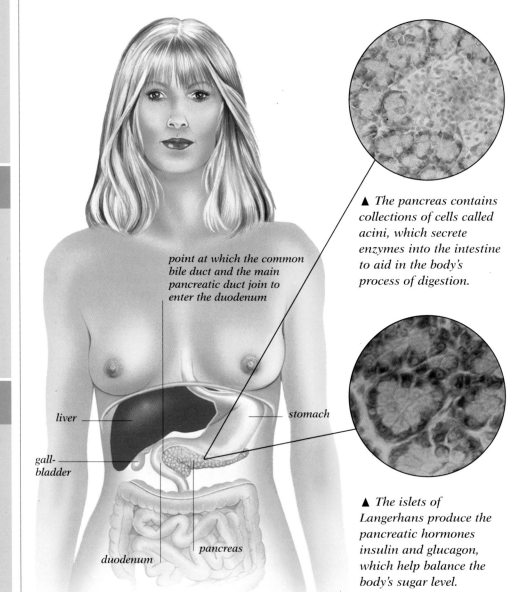

point at which the common bile duct and the main pancreatic duct join to enter the duodenum

liver

stomach

gall-bladder

duodenum

pancreas

▲ *The pancreas contains collections of cells called acini, which secrete enzymes into the intestine to aid in the body's process of digestion.*

▲ *The islets of Langerhans produce the pancreatic hormones insulin and glucagon, which help balance the body's sugar level.*

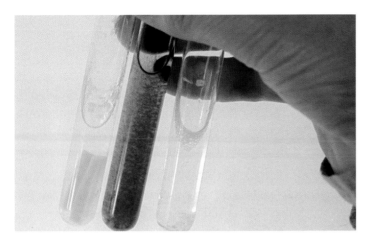

▲ *The enzyme amylase breaks down starch. From left to right: first, a vial filled with amylase; second, a vial that consists of a colored starch solution that has been added to the amylase; third, a vial of the colored starch solution after it has been broken down by the enzyme amylase, causing the colored starch solution to disappear.*

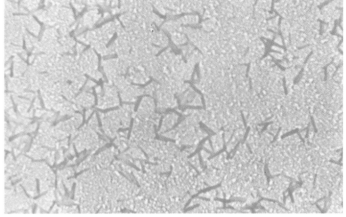

▲ *Crystals of insulin—an extremely important pancreatic hormone—keep the level of blood sugar down in the body by counteracting the effects of certain other hormones, such as adrenaline and cortisone, that raise the level of blood sugar. A deficiency of insulin results in the disease called diabetes, which can be treated with injections of insulin.*

the blind end of a small duct. Each duct joins with ducts from other acini until all of them eventually connect with the main duct that runs down the center of the pancreas.

Among the acini are small groups of cells of endocrine tissue, called the islets of Langerhans. They control glucose concentration in the blood and regulate other pancreatic hormones (see Diabetes).

What the pancreas does

Exocrine pancreas: The pancreas produces essential alkali in the form of sodium bicarbonate to neutralize the heavily acidic contents of the stomach as they enter the duodenum. The pancreas also produces many important enzymes that help to break food down into basic chemical constituents; these are then absorbed by the intestinal wall (see Enzymes).

Most of the main enzymes for the digestion of protein are produced by the pancreas; this creates a problem. The pancreas itself, like the rest of the body, is basically a protein-based structure (see Protein). Therefore, there is a risk that the pancreas might self-digest, but this is avoided because the main protein-digesting enzyme, trypsin, is secreted in an inactive form called trypsinogen, which changes to the active form once the pancreatic juices reach the duodenum. The pancreas also produces amylase and lipase—enzymes that break down starch and fats respectively (see Fats).

The digestive juices are powerful and cannot be released into the intestine safely unless food is present for them to act upon. Therefore, a sophisticated control system acts on pancreatic secretions. The vagus nerve—the main nerve of the parasympathetic system (see Autonomic Nervous System)—stimulates the first small secretion as a result of the thought, taste, or smell of food (see Smell; Taste).

Further secretion is stimulated by distension of the stomach, but most of the secretion takes place when the food finally reaches the duodenum. As this happens, cells in the wall of the duodenum release into the bloodstream two separate hormones —secretin and cholecystokinin—which travel in the blood to the pancreas and speed up secretion.

Endocrine pancreas: Insulin, a substance produced in the islets of Langerhans, lowers blood glucose levels. The islets also produce a hormone called glucagon, which has the effect of raising, rather than lowering, the level of sugar in the blood.

What can go wrong?

Three rare diseases can cause disorders of pancreatic digestive activity. The first is acute pancreatitis, which can cause sudden abdominal pain and collapse. The second is chronic pancreatitis, characterized by recurrent attacks of pain and failure of the pancreas to produce adequate amounts of digestive juice. The third is an inherited disease called cystic fibrosis, in which many glands, including the pancreas, produce abnormally thick secretions (see Cystic Fibrosis). Inadequate secretion of digestive juice causes malabsorption; a common cause is chronic pancreatitis, accompanied by severe pain in the abdomen, sometimes so severe that the pancreas has to be removed. The condition is often associated with alcohol consumption (see Alcoholism). Acute pancreatitis can also be associated with alcohol but may occur without any apparent cause.

Another disease that can affect the pancreas is hemochromatosis, in which the gene that regulates the amount of iron absorbed from food is defective. This can cause an overload of iron in the body, which accumulates in the vital organs, including the pancreas. This causes serious damage to the pancreas and can lead to diabetes.

Finally, cancer can affect the pancreas (see Cancer). Pancreatic cancer is very difficult to treat because it is usually advanced before the cause of its vague pains is apparent. Surgery may be necessary, but it is done only when the cancer has not spread to other organs. If the pancreas has to be removed, the body can still function. Insulin injections can be given, digestive enzymes can be sprinkled on food, or the stomach can be prevented from producing acids with certain drugs.

See also: **Abdomen; Digestive system; Duodenum; Endocrine system; Glands; Glucose; Hemochromatosis; Hormones; Insulin; Starch; Sugars**

Pap smear

Most cases of cancer of the cervix, the neck of the uterus, could be avoided if all women had regular Pap tests. This simple procedure detects precancerous conditions early enough for effective treatment.

The "Pap smear" is named after the American pathologist George Nichola Papanicolaou (1883–1962), who developed the test while working at the Cornell Medical College in New York. The Pap smear can detect the earliest precancerous cell change in the cervix, a condition that is called mild dysplasia. The cell change can return to normal without any treatment, or it may develop into severe dysplasia, or carcinoma in situ in which the cells lining the cervix have some characteristics of cancer cells. Although the cells may remain unchanged for a long time, they can progress to microinvasive cancer. In that case the abnormalities of the lining of the cervix have broken through to some of the underlying tissue. True invasive cancer of the cervix occurs when these abnormalities have totally invaded the underlying tissue. All the abnormal cell changes preceding invasive cancer may be cured by removing the abnormal tissue in a minor operation. Many treatments are available, some of which do not need anesthesia.

How a Pap smear is done

Pap smears are usually performed by gynecologists or nurses as part of a vaginal examination. The cervix is at the top of the vagina, and it can be examined using a speculum that is gently introduced into the vagina. The speculum is usually metal or plastic and is shaped like a duck's

Questions and Answers

I bleed from my vagina after lovemaking. I had a Pap smear six months ago, so should I worry?

You should see your doctor immediately to exclude the rare possibility of cancer of the cervix, or of a precancerous state. Bleeding after sexual intercourse is likely to be caused by a less serious condition, such as cervical polyps. Your gynecologist should be able to put your mind at rest.

Are Pap smears taken when a woman starts taking oral contraceptives because there is a greater risk of getting cancer?

No. Current evidence does not suggest that cervical cancer is likely to be caused by the Pill. It is simply convenient to have a Pap smear done on a visit to a gynecologist's office. Pap smears may also be done at other facilities, and by many family physicians and internists.

At my postnatal visit I was told that I had an erosion on the cervix. Will it develop into cancer?

No. It is fairly common for women to develop an "erosion" after having a baby. The central canal through the cervix is lined with deep red glandular tissue which can pouch outward, making the area appear red and rough. This so-called erosion gradually disappears and is rarely caused by abnormal cell changes, but it is wise to have routine Pap smears.

I have had a hysterectomy. Do I still need Pap smears?

Usually the cervix is removed in a hysterectomy, so it is unnecessary to have further Pap smears. However, the cervix may not be removed, or abnormal cells may remain in the vagina. Your gynecologist will advise you.

▲ *Slides of Pap smears taken from female patients are prepared for microscopic examination. Only 10 percent of such specimens will indicate abnormalities.*

HOW A PAP SMEAR IS DONE

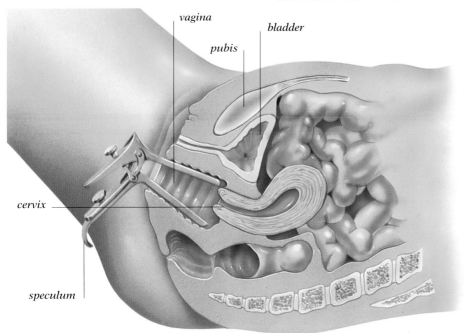

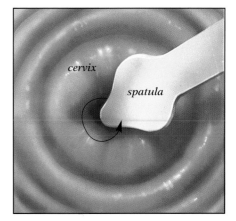

◄▲ *A Pap smear need cause no discomfort or distress. First a speculum is gently inserted into the vagina to enable the gynecologist to view the cervix. The sample of cells is taken by rotating a plastic spatula or brush 360° within the cervix.*

bill. The two blades are about 4 inches (10 cm) long and 1 inch (2.5 cm) wide. When the upper and lower blades are opened the cervix can be viewed. The Pap smear should be done before a bimanual examination so that the diagnostic cells are not inadvertently removed. The speculum may be rinsed in water or saline, or lubricated with K-Y jelly to ease its entry into the vagina. A sample of cells is then taken from the junction between the canal through the cervix and the part of the cervix forming the top of the vagina. This area is most likely to develop the more common type of cervical cancer. The sample is removed with a plastic spatula, spread onto a glass slide, and placed in a fixative medium. The slide is later stained and examined under a microscope. Patients should relax during this examination because tightening of the vaginal muscles causes discomfort and makes it difficult to insert the speculum. Although the procedure can be uncomfortable, it is an important preventive test.

Why have a Pap smear?

Women with precancerous changes of the cervix seldom develop any signs or symptoms. Gynecologists cannot detect any abnormality just by looking at the cervix, so it is vital for women to have regular Pap smears. The earlier an abnormal condition is found, the easier it is to treat. Pap smears can help in the diagnosis of other conditions. For example, cells from cancer of the ovary or cancer of the lining of the uterus (endometrial cancer) may be shown up by a Pap smear. The Pap test is also used to detect vaginal infections that cause a discharge. This method is not totally accurate but may be used in centers where it is impossible to do formal studies of the bacteria in the vagina. Infections diagnosed in this way include herpes, yeast, and trichomonas vaginalis (see Vaginal Discharge).

Having a Pap smear

Pap smears are done in doctors' offices, hospitals, and gynecologic facilities. A woman should have her first Pap smear at 18, or after her first act of intercourse, whichever comes first. The greatest risk factor for cervical cancer is a woman's sexual history, so all sexually active women have a Pap smear each year. About 10 percent of tests are unsatisfactory or unreliable. If a woman has a bloodstained discharge between periods, or bleeding from the vagina during or after intercourse, she should see her gynecologist because such irregularities may, rarely, be due to cancer of the cervix.

If a Pap smear shows abnormalities it may be repeated sooner than usual, but it is unwise to have two tests done within a month as the first may remove all the abnormal cells, and the second may then be incorrectly read as negative since the abnormal cells will not have regrown. If there is a vaginal infection such as yeast or trichomonas, the test results will be slightly abnormal. The doctor will then treat the infection and repeat the test.

Treatment of an abnormality

Treatment can vary. If the changes are due to mild dysplasia, most doctors repeat the Pap smear every six months to see if the cells have returned to normal or progressed to severe dysplasia. If severe dysplasia is detected, the area of abnormal cells is removed. Women who want children have as little surgery as possible to avoid damaging the cervix.

Sometimes the cervix can be viewed under a special microscope called a colposcope. Abnormal cells may be removed with a laser or by freezing or burning them off. In some hospitals a ring or cone biopsy is done under general anesthesia to remove cells where cancer is likely to develop. Such minor operations cure the precancerous condition, but the patient must have regular Pap smears to ensure that the disease does not recur. Similar treatment is used for older women who have completed their families. If they have other gynecological problems, such as heavy periods, they may need a hysterectomy; women with cervical cancer may need radiotherapy as well as a hysterectomy. About 85 percent of cases of cervical cancer that are caught early do not recur after treatment.

See also: **Cervix and cervical smears; Hysterectomy; Lasers**

Paralysis

My cousin's legs have been paralyzed for some time. Is there any hope of recovery for him?

It depends on the cause. If his paralysis followed an injury, there is less hope than if he was suffering from a disease that caused paralysis. However, even if the motor nerves have been badly damaged, there is often some degree of recovery, which may even allow him to walk again and lead an almost normal life.

My father's stroke paralyzed his right side. Has the stroke damaged that side of his brain?

It's the brain damage that causes the stroke. Since the nerves to the muscles cross over at the bottom of the brain stem, damage to one side of the brain causes paralysis of the other side of the body. Your father has suffered damage to the left half of his brain, opposite his right paralyzed side.

Does a stroke victim always recover from the paralysis?

If the patient survives the acute stage, there will be some recovery after a stroke. Recovery depends on the extent of the brain damage and on whether or not any other body functions have been affected. Most people show considerable powers of recovery.

Why do paralyzed people tend to develop bedsores?

When we are asleep, we move around so no part of the body rests in the same place for too long, because the skin cannot cope with the pressure of body weight for long. Paralyzed people cannot relieve this pressure and need to be turned regularly to prevent bedsores. That is why badly paralyzed people are difficult to take care of at home.

There are many different types of paralysis, ranging from a weakness in one muscle to an inability to move at all. However, it is possible that the cause of the paralysis can be corrected and the outlook can be optimistic.

One of the most important functions that enables people to exist independently is the ability to move about and manipulate objects using different parts of the body. In addition to the muscles that are needed for these obvious external movements, other muscles are needed to breathe, eat, and speak (see Muscles). Paralysis causes the temporary or permanent loss of some or all of these muscular activities. A complex motor system controls movements, and it can be attacked on many levels by different diseases and injuries.

What is paralysis?

Paralysis is the loss of normal functioning of the muscles to a part of the body. When this happens a person feels a weakness when he or she tries to use that part of the body. When

▲ *Children with muscular dystrophy meet to take part in outdoor activities. Specially adapted wheelchairs give body support and mobility—keeping them as active as possible.*

▲ *Indulging a passion for sports is one way of adjusting to and overcoming a disability.*

paralysis affects the arm or leg muscles, walking will be difficult or the grip will lose its strength. If the muscles affected are those related to speech, paralysis may cause slurred or incoherent speech. If the eye muscles are affected, double vision may be experienced. The common factor in all these symptoms is that some or all of the muscles are not working properly. The term "paralysis" is also sometimes applied to loss of other functions, especially sensation.

How does paralysis occur?

The muscles are made up of tiny fibers that are grouped together in bundles, which are each connected to the fiber of a single motor nerve cell or motor neuron in the spinal cord. Motor neurons are closely connected with many other nerve networks in the spinal cord, and also with fibers of the nerves that descend from the brain (see Brain; Spinal Cord). Paralysis can happen as a result of damage to, or malfunction of, any part of the neural network. The area that is damaged will dictate the type of weakness experienced.

The muscles

When paralysis is caused by a disease of the muscles, the effect is usually felt on both sides of the body, and it generally affects the shoulder and hip muscles most strongly. Diseases such as muscular dystrophy that affect the muscles and cause paralysis may be present from birth, or the cells of the muscles may become inflamed, a condition called myositis. When these diseases strike, in addition to being weak the muscles often waste away, making the affected part of the body look thin. Walking may be difficult because the hip muscles are involved, and if the disease is severe enough, the leg muscles may become totally paralyzed. Paralysis of the shoulder

muscles will make shaving and hair-brushing more difficult, even if the hands retain their ability to grip things. The diseases of the muscles that cause a degree of paralysis vary enormously in their severity; often the paralysis is only partial. In myositis, there may be pain as well as weakness, since the inflammation causes the muscles to swell.

The muscle-nerve junction

The connection between the surface of the muscle fibers and the nerve fibers is not direct; there is a very short gap across which tiny quantities of chemical transmitters jump when the nerve is activated. In a disease called myasthenia gravis, the receptors on the muscle fibers, to which the transmitter jumps, are reduced in numbers as a result of autoimmune damage, and weakness ensues. This paralysis is progressive; the muscle gets weaker the more it is used but recovers with rest. The first muscles to be affected are usually those that keep the eyelids from drooping, but the shoulder and hip muscles, and muscles affecting the voice, swallowing, and breathing may be involved. Breathing, for example, may become so difficult that artificial help is needed. When the throat muscles are affected, a drink may be regurgitated or go down the wrong way into the lungs and cause the patient to choke.

Damage to the motor nerves

Weakness and paralysis of some groups of muscles can occur as a result of damage to the nerves that serve those muscles. For example, the ulnar nerve, which passes down the arm, is rather exposed at the back of the elbow and may be damaged if the elbow is jarred continually. This jarring will lead to paralysis in the muscles of the hand. The grip will become weaker, because the thumb cannot be brought across to meet the fingers when a person is trying to grasp something in the hand. Individual motor nerves may be damaged by a prolapsed disk in the spine. As the nerves emerge

Questions and Answers

Can a boy who is paralyzed in both legs have sex later in life?

This depends on the cause of the paralysis and its severity. Many men whose legs are paralyzed have an active sex life and produce children. If the spinal cord has been seriously damaged, however, impotence can result. An enjoyable sex life need not include penile penetration.

Why are some paralyzed limbs stiff while others are limp?

When nerve tracts are damaged as in a stroke, a small sensory stimulus such as a passive muscle stretch may be enough to produce tight reflex contraction and hence severe stiffness. This is called an upper motor neuron lesion. Conversely, a lower motor neuron lesion cuts the spinal motor reflex circuit so that the fibers of the brain can't act, and flaccid paralysis results.

If my legs become paralyzed, will I lose all sensation in them?

Not necessarily. In some kinds of paralysis, it is possible for just the nerves to the muscles to be affected, leaving nerves to the sense organs intact. Then, although you may not be able to move your legs, you may still feel sensation in them. Sometimes, both sets of nerves are affected; then sensation will be affected too, and feeling in the legs will be lost.

Can hysterical paralysis be long-term or permanent?

Hysterical paralysis is rare. If the psychological process causing the hysteria continues, paralysis may last some time; but hysterical paralysis is easy to recognize, and treatment of the psychological condition can reverse it. Simply telling the person that he or she is not really paralyzed may bring on other symptoms, so it is important to get to the root of the psychological condition.

SPECIFIC CAUSES AND AREAS OF PARALYSIS

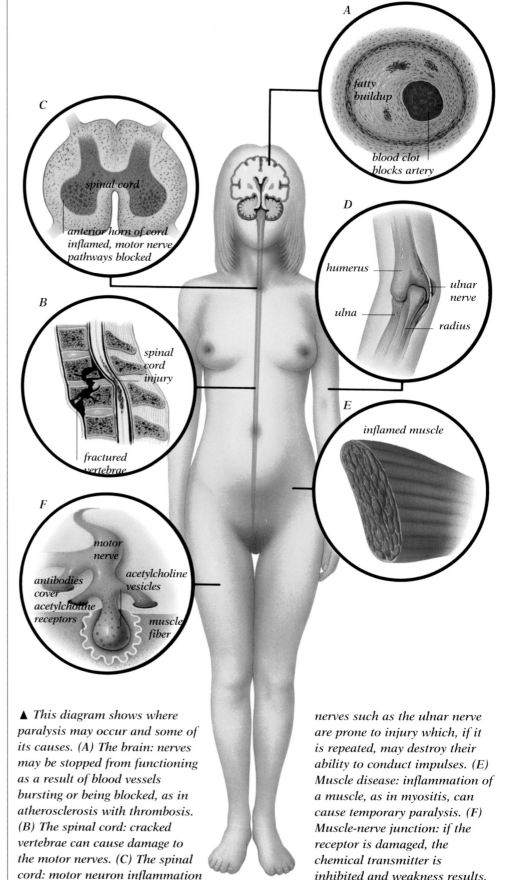

▲ *This diagram shows where paralysis may occur and some of its causes. (A) The brain: nerves may be stopped from functioning as a result of blood vessels bursting or being blocked, as in atherosclerosis with thrombosis. (B) The spinal cord: cracked vertebrae can cause damage to the motor nerves. (C) The spinal cord: motor neuron inflammation occurs in polio. (D) Motor nerve:* *nerves such as the ulnar nerve are prone to injury which, if it is repeated, may destroy their ability to conduct impulses. (E) Muscle disease: inflammation of a muscle, as in myositis, can cause temporary paralysis. (F) Muscle-nerve junction: if the receptor is damaged, the chemical transmitter is inhibited and weakness results, as in myasthenia gravis.*

Workstation

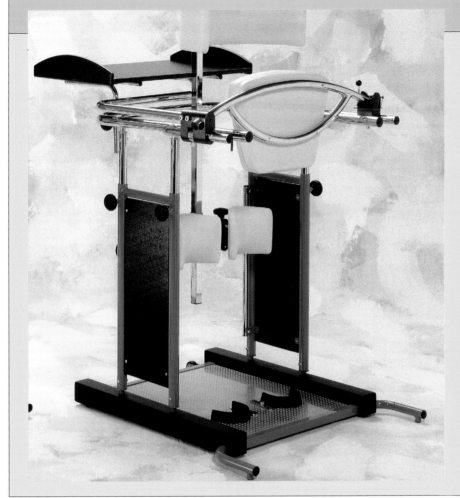

This workstation is an innovative design that can help make life much easier for anyone confined to a wheelchair.

The structure of the station allows the person in the wheelchair to pull himself or herself out of the chair to a standing position by bracing the heels and knees against the supports shown. The backrest is then closed to give support. The person can then position the worktable in a suitable position in front of him or her.

This model is made of metal and has metal tubular framing. It has a nonslip aluminum footboard and transport wheels. The backrest has a safety lock, and the pelvic support unit is adjustable for comfort. The chest support is also adjustable.

A unit such as this enables anyone with a disability to lead a more active live. Standing with mechanical support results in good psychological benefits as well, for even though a person is standing with support, at least he or she is standing.

There are many types of standing units. For information on units available in your state, contact the local disability organization in your town; it will be able to put you in touch with suppliers.

from the spinal cord, the prolapsed disk may put pressure on the nerve or nerves (see Slipped Disk). The paralysis affects only part of the leg or arm, and unless the damage is severe or prolonged, relief of the pressure on the motor nerve will remove the paralysis.

The spinal cord

Damage to the spinal cord usually involves damage to the nerve fibers that carry instructions from the brain down both sides of the body. The area of the spinal cord that has been damaged will determine which parts of the body are paralyzed. Both legs may be paralyzed (paraplegia) or all four limbs may be affected if the damage is in the neck (quadriplegia). The spinal cord may be damaged in an accident in which the backbone or neck is broken or displaced; there may be blood vessel damage due to clots or hemorrhage; or there may be inflammation caused by multiple sclerosis. If the cause of the paralysis can be removed, there may be almost immediate relief. Another cause can be simply a depressed fragment of bone that presses on the spinal cord.

Diseases of the spinal cord can cause paralysis. For example, polio, which used to be a common disease, is a viral infection of the spinal cord. Polio starts with paralysis of an arm or a leg and may progress to involve the entire body.

The nerve fibers that run from the brain to the spinal cord carry instructions to the muscles. The fibers cross over from one side to the other at the bottom of the brain stem as it meets the spinal cord.

Damage to the nerves above this crossover point will cause weakness in the opposite side of the body. A common cause of this type of paralysis is a stroke, which is caused by damage to the brain, usually by a hemorrhage or blocked vessel. If the part of the brain that is supplied by a blocked or burst blood vessel includes the motor nerves, then the opposite side of the body becomes paralyzed. Strokes usually cause paralysis suddenly, and the brain often recovers well. Paralysis caused by a brain tumor develops slowly.

The outlook following paralysis

The cause of the paralysis will determine the recovery time. Some diseases that cause paralysis will resolve without treatment (see Guillain-Barré Syndrome). Similarly, most people who are admitted to the hospital totally paralyzed on one side because of a stroke can later walk out of the hospital, albeit with a limp. Multiple sclerosis can wax and wane, or be progressive. However, treatment is always necessary to maintain the health of the affected limbs. Physical therapy and careful nursing are vital.

During convalescence, occupational therapists will help the paralyzed person to make the most of any remaining abilities so that some independence can be retained. Recent research suggests that the spinal cord might be able to regenerate somewhat after injury.

See also: **Muscular dystrophy; Poliomyelitis; Stroke**

Paraplegia

Questions and Answers

I am now confined to a wheelchair. Should I change my diet?

Yes; you should be eating much less than before. Because you are a lot less active, you will not be able to burn up as many calories; thus you are likely to put on weight, which is not easy to lose when you are confined to a wheelchair.

My son puts on a brave face despite becoming a paraplegic, but I know he hasn't come to terms with it. How long will it take?

You shouldn't expect him to adjust quickly. Remember that different people adjust at different speeds. However, he will come to terms with it eventually, in his own time.

My husband has been diagnosed as a paraplegic. I'm embarrassed to ask the doctors this, but are his sexual feelings dead, too?

No, his sexual feelings are not dead. You may be able to have a sexual relationship and this will be important in his rehabilitation. However, his sexual performance may be impaired, depending on how much of his spinal cord is affected. Some paraplegics can have erections and reach orgasm. However, remember that neither is vital for a satisfying sex life.

I know paraplegics are prone to bedsores. How can I prevent them?

Bedsores result from blood being prevented, by body weight, from properly circulating. This causes the skin and underlying tissue to die and leads to gangrene. The cure is simple: lift the body regularly so that the pressure is relieved and the blood can flow freely. In the wheelchair, lift yourself off your buttocks every 15 minutes for at least 20 seconds. If you are bedridden, you need to turn over every four hours.

No one should underestimate the extreme difficulty of this type of paralysis; however, a willingness to adapt, and a flexible attitude on the part of carers can do much to overcome many of the resultant disabilities.

To be told that one has lost the use of the legs, that the trunk is paralyzed, and that one will be confined to a wheelchair for the rest of one's life may seem like a death sentence. Following such a blow, many people would feel that life is not worth living, yet with the support of relatives and friends, most people do go on to live fulfilling lives.

Causes

The spinal cord is a cylinder of nerve tissue with 31 pairs of nerves connected to its length. Each of these nerves carries information to and from particular parts of the body, including the legs and the intestines. If this central highway of the nervous system is damaged, the associated parts of the body may be put out of action.

Paraplegia is a result of either direct damage to the nerves in the spinal cord or brain, or a disease, typically of the nervous system, which spreads to or involves the spinal cord. The

▲ *Paraplegics who enjoy sports can join the Special Olympics, which organizes international competitions along the lines of the Olympic Games.*

▶ *One of the most important aspects of a paraplegic's rehabilitation is warmth, support, and encouragement from family and friends.*

condition is often caused by automobile accidents and sports injuries, or gunshot wounds to the spine; the incidence is highest in young men between the age of 19 and 35.

Coping in the hospital
"Why me?" is the unanswerable question that is often asked; it is usually accompanied by emotional outbursts of crying, swearing, or aggression.

Close relatives will bear the brunt of abuse, as will the medical staff. However, the paraplegic is just lashing out at his or her own paralysis. Although this can be extremely distressing for relatives, they should be reassured that it is the healthiest reaction to paralysis. It often signals a better recovery than resignation.

Aggressive outbursts are usually followed by depression, particularly since some of the routine of a disabled person's life feels humiliating (see Depression). For example, the patient spends a lot of time naked to facilitate washing, and there has to be urine collection, as well as other undignified procedures.

How others can help
Relatives and friends will be upset, too. Their initial reaction will be shock and disbelief, and they will also need help in coming to terms with the crisis. They should spend as much time as they can encouraging the patient. They should not, however, be overprotective, since protectiveness only highlights the paraplegic's awareness of his or her own helplessness. It is sensible to ask the hospital social worker at this stage for help with domestic and financial worries. When the patient starts to ask about the future, relatives and friends can then put him or her at ease.

Going home again
Even if the patient seems to have adjusted well in the hospital, going home can be a setback; the hospital routine is comforting, and the trained staff can cope with the problems of the paraplegic.

The quickest adjustment to the new circumstances are made by those who keep themselves occupied when they return home, possibly by retraining for a job.

Relationships
When one partner becomes disabled, a huge strain is put on close relationships. Many couples overcome this and become closer than before, although inevitably some couples break up. Some paraplegics meet new partners after they have become disabled.

The paraplegic usually needs much more care from a partner than an able-bodied person. However, both the patient and the partner can eventually develop a new daily routine.

Sex is often as important to a disabled person as it is to an able-bodied person. While most male paraplegics are unable to maintain an erection or to ejaculate, this inability does not rule out other sorts of sexual contact (see Erection and Ejaculation). Both male and female paraplegics have claimed that sensitivity in other areas

increases when part of the body is paralyzed, and a form of orgasm may be experienced (see Orgasm).

Most female paraplegics will continue to ovulate and have periods, and with special management, they can bear children. A spinal specialist should be consulted before pregnancy is decided upon.

It is more difficult for the couple to produce their own children when the man is a paraplegic. However, in some cases a spinal specialist may be able to stimulate the prostate gland to ejaculate by electrotherapy. Sperm produced in this way can sometimes be used to artificially inseminate the woman, or intracytoplasmic sperm transfer may be possible. If a couple cannot have their own children, it may be possible for them to adopt.

Urinary problems
An able-bodied person receives warning signals when the bladder is full and can empty it more or less at will. A paraplegic may receive no such signals and instead must rely on a urine collecting system.

For a male, this is usually a type of condom fitted to the penis, which drains into a bag that is changed every 24 hours. A female paraplegic has to rely on regular visits to the lavatory, absorbent pads, and plastic underwear. Self-catheterization is also a possibility.

Wheelchairs
A wheelchair is a paraplegic's most important aid, and it has to be chosen carefully. Any paraplegic who can afford to buy a spare wheelchair should do so because wheelchairs do malfunction from time to time. Wheelchairs should be kept in perfect working order. The more severely disabled should use a powered wheelchair.

Going back to work
Some paraplegics can continue working in their old professions after they have been confined to a wheelchair. For others, further education and training will be necessary.

It is easy to feel that getting a job is impossible. However, a surprisingly wide range of jobs are available for paraplegics, and the Americans with Disabilities Act prohibits discrimination against the disabled. For those who cannot find a job, and even those who can,

LIVING SPACE DESIGNED FOR A PARAPLEGIC

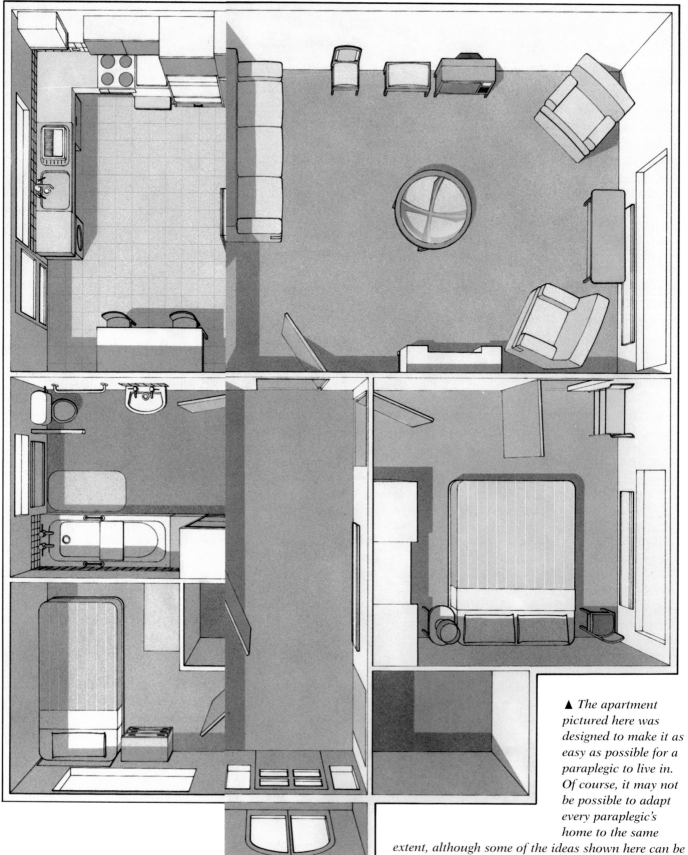

▲ *The apartment pictured here was designed to make it as easy as possible for a paraplegic to live in. Of course, it may not be possible to adapt every paraplegic's home to the same extent, although some of the ideas shown here can be incorporated. In many areas, financial assistance may be available through local or state grants.*

▲ Large, open spaces with minimal clutter and furniture, as well as easy access to all rooms and outdoor areas, provide a suitable environment for wheelchair users. Couches and chairs should be easy to get in and out of, and fireplaces must be screened to prevent the legs of a paraplegic from getting burned.

▲ In the kitchen, all the work surfaces and appliances can be adjusted for the convenience of the paraplegic. The cupboards are the push-open type.

▲ This workspace is built so that the wheelchair user has easy access to a computer, desk, and bookshelves.

▶ A pneumatic chair offering a full range of height adjustment will allow a paraplegic to be raised or lowered to various levels.

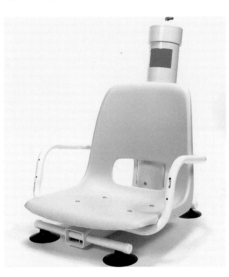

Bathrooms and bedrooms

The bathroom should be accessible directly from the bedroom, and, if there is enough space, it should have a special shower stall. If there is a bath, a hoist should be used to lift the disabled person in and out of the bath safely. A paraplegic's bed needs the most careful consideration, and the hospital will be able to give advice on the various types that are currently available. Adequate heating is also important. Many paraplegics suffer from a dangerous loss of body heat (see Hypothermia) because their blood flow tends to be more sluggish than normal. Central heating is best, because direct heat from a fireplace or electric heater can burn a paraplegic's legs without his or her noticing. Windows should be able to be opened and shut by winding a handle.

hobbies and recreational activities will play an important part. Opportunities to take part in sedentary activities are plentiful, and for those who like sports, there is a paraplegics' sports movement.

Adapting the home

Everyone recognizes the need to adapt a paraplegic's home for ease of living, and grants are available to help those who cannot afford to do so. If it is possible, the house or apartment should be adapted before the paraplegic comes home from the hospital. A ground floor apartment or room is ideal.

The wheelchair user should be able to leave home without help. This ability usually requires the construction of ramps to and from the building. Doors should be wide enough to give access. Light switches and thermostats should be lowered and sockets raised.

Getting around

Invalid vehicles are the best way of getting around for most disabled people, but ordinary cars can also be converted to hand controls. Many clubs and associations cater exclusively to disabled drivers and passengers.

It is not impossible for a disabled person to travel by public transportation, just more difficult. Many transport systems provide ramps and lifts for disabled passengers.

See also: **Bedsores; Bladder and bladder problems; Brain; Handicaps; Hydrotherapy; Incontinence; Nervous system; Occupational therapy; Paralysis; Spinal cord**

Parasites

Some kinds of viruses, bacteria, fungi, protozoa, worms, flukes, ticks, lice, bugs, flies, and leeches are the cause of hundreds of human diseases. Hygienic practices and better sanitation can help to prevent such diseases.

Questions and Answers

Can humans be vaccinated against diseases caused by parasites?

Parasites have evolved many ways of escaping our immune defense mechanism. Diseases like malaria persist because mosquitoes develop a resistance to specific antimalarial drugs. So far, there is no totally effective vaccine against such diseases, but scientists are working to improve prevention.

Are parasites especially harmful during pregnancy?

Many parasitic diseases can increase the risk of miscarriage. They also increase the possibility of anemia, various vitamin deficiencies, and malnutrition, all of which could endanger the lives of a mother and unborn baby.

Do parasites do any good in the human body?

Some bacteria help us digest food and protect us from infection, but most parasites are not welcome. The most harmful bacteria cause hundreds of human diseases.

Is it true that tapeworm eggs could help me lose weight?

You would certainly lose weight if you had a tapeworm, but it would be dangerous. Eating tapeworm larvae causes a disease known as cysticercosis. The outcome could be fatal.

Does freezing food kill parasites?

Storing food in a home freezer helps to destroy nearly all of the harmful parasites that might be present. Remember that frozen meat must be adequately thawed before cooking. This helps to ensure that any remaining parasites will be destroyed by the cooking process.

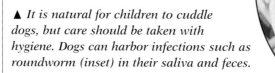

▲ *It is natural for children to cuddle dogs, but care should be taken with hygiene. Dogs can harbor infections such as roundworm (inset) in their saliva and feces.*

Parasites live in or on their hosts and depend totally upon the host for survival. People and animals are troubled by numerous types of parasites, which can be as small as one cell (like the malarial parasite) or up to 65 feet (20 m) long, like a fish tapeworm (see Worms).

Parasites can damage hosts in different ways. Some feed directly upon tissues; for example, the liver fluke feeds on liver cells (see Liver Fluke). There is also the hookworm, which lives on its host's blood (see Hookworms).

Many parasites are more common in poorer, tropical countries. The better the sanitation and living conditions in richer countries, along with easier access to medical care and a cooler climate, the less likely it is for parasitic diseases to be transmitted (see Public Health).

Threadworms are perhaps the most common disease-causing parasites in countries like the United States. They inhabit the large intestine and lay eggs around the anal skin during the night. The eggs cause intense itching. Disadvantaged children in families where hygienic practices are lacking are most commonly affected by threadworms.

Fleas, head and body lice, and mites are also relatively common (see Fleas; Lice). They differ from parasites that infest the liver or the intestines because they live outside the body and feed exclusively on their hosts' blood.

The parasitic lifestyle

Parasites have adapted and modified their way of life to the lifestyles of their hosts. They can overcome immune defenses, so the body can do very little to fight the parasite (see Immune System).

Parasites have voracious appetites. For example, each tiny hookworm consumes 8,000 times its own weight in human blood each day. Parasites produce eggs or larvae at such a colossal rate to ensure that reproduction takes place and that their new hosts are infected. Ascaris is a common type of parasitic worm, infesting at least one billion people around the world. Transmission takes place when the host eats food that has been contaminated with infected feces. Once it is established in the body, the parasite lives in the small intestine. Parasites living in tissues or in the bloodstream depend on mosquitoes or other biting insects (called vectors) for transmission. Their larvae or reproductive cells are microscopic. They have to be produced in massive quantities to ensure that an insect becomes infected each time it bites the host.

How parasites are spread

The eggs, cysts, or larvae of many parasites are found in the feces of human or animal hosts. In some countries, human feces are still an

▲ *The surrender of Singapore to Japan in February 1942 and other conflicts resulted in years of captivity for some Allied servicemen. Many of those who survived Japanese prisoner of war camps returned with serious parasitic diseases.*

important source of fertilizer and are spread over the land. In poorer countries, generally, the facilities for disposal of sewage are not always adequate.

Flies and cockroaches spread eggs directly from the feces of one host to the food of another. Transmission can also take place when dirty hands touch food. Water from wells and rivers is easily contaminated by unhygienic disposal of feces and sewage.

Soil that has been contaminated with feces often harbors larvae that are able to penetrate the bare feet of the next host. Hookworm is transmitted in this way. Feces may also contain eggs or cysts that infect secondary hosts like cows or pigs (in cases of tapeworm) and freshwater snails (in cases of bilharzia). In this way, parasites multiply and are spread farther afield.

Obviously, better sanitation and more careful disposal of feces would interrupt the life cycles of all these parasites, helping to bring the diseases that they cause under control. Better hygiene and more care when handling food are also essential to prevent parasitic diseases (see Hygiene).

Meat infestation can be a serious problem, for developed countries as well as developing nations. For example, pork can contain one million larvae of the parasite *Trichinella* in a small fraction of an ounce (a single gram). Eating even a very small quantity of such infected meat can be potentially dangerous. Careful, thorough cooking is necessary to make all meats safe.

Another transmission route for parasites is by insect vectors. A vector becomes infected when it bites the host. The parasite multiplies within it, and the infected vector is soon able to pass the disease on to new hosts with each bite. In this way, flies can spread amebic dysentery, and anopheles mosquitoes can spread malaria (see Malaria). One way of controlling such diseases is by attacking the insect vector. Breeding grounds can be destroyed by draining mosquito-ridden swamps and spraying them with insecticides.

▲ *Workers who plant rice in watery fields in Asia are likely to become infested by schistosomiasis, which is carried by larvae of the freshwater snail (inset).*

Questions and Answers

Can a parasite live in a human without revealing its presence?

Yes. Many intestinal worms cause no symptoms at all in well-nourished people. The parasite will not cause too much harm, for if the host dies, so does the parasite. A check on the health of ex-soldiers who had been prisoners in Asia during World War II showed that many still had parasitic infestations. Some of these had been present without symptoms for decades.

I have been losing weight since returning from Pakistan. Could the weight loss be the result of a parasitic disease?

Parasitic diseases may cause weight loss, as can many other illnesses. You should consult your doctor, who can carry out tests to discover the cause.

Is it true that dogs carry parasites that can be transmitted to humans?

Dogs can harbor around 40 different infections harmful to humans, including several types of parasite. The most dangerous parasite is a small tapeworm, which lives in the dog's intestines. Eggs are discharged with the feces. Contamination of food leads to a severe infestation of larval cysts that can develop in the liver and lungs. This condition is called hydatid disease.

Toxocariasis is another common and serious infestation that can cause blindness in young children. It is caused by a small worm that wanders around the human body. Fecal contamination of food is the source of infestation.

Can parasites be spread to humans through blood transfusions?

Malaria may be spread by transfusion if medical facilities are poor. Donated blood is usually checked thoroughly for diseases before it is given in a transfusion.

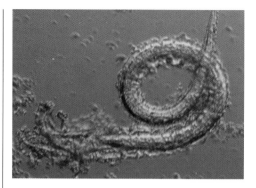

▲ *An ancylostoma larva, which causes hookworm infestation in the intestines.*

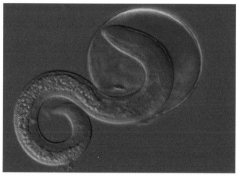

▲ *The hatching of the ascaris larva, which infects the intestines and stomach.*

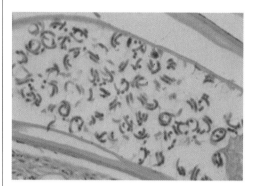

▲ *Onchocerca parasites, which cause river blindness, live in the skin nodules.*

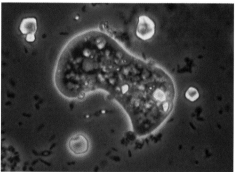

▲ *Entamebae in contaminated food and water cause amebic dysentery.*

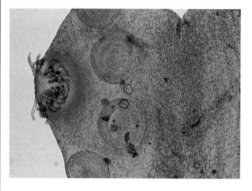

▲ *A tapeworm (taenia) attaches itself with its hooks and suckers to the intestine.*

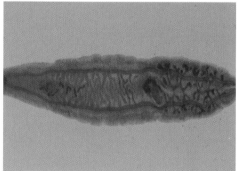

▲ *The liver fluke (clonorchis) infects the liver and bile duct.*

▲ *The anopheles mosquito is an insect that transmits malaria through a bite.*

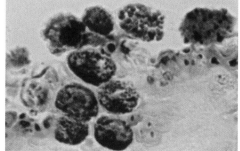

▲ *Malaria parasites (plasmodium) line a mosquito's stomach.*

The most common parasitic diseases

INFESTATION	PROPER NAME	WHERE PARASITE LIVES IN BODY	HOW TRANSMITTED	HARMFUL EFFECTS	PEOPLE AFFECTED	PLACES WHERE MOST COMMON
Malaria	*Plasmodium vivax, P. falciparum, P. ovale*	Bloodstream; liver	Mosquito bite	Recurrent fever; anemia; ill health; miscarriages; often causes death	Over 300 million each year	Africa; Latin and South America; India; Southeast Asia; Asia
Amebic dysentery	*Entameba histolytica*	Large intestine	Flies spread cysts from feces; these contaminate food and water	Diarrhea; dysentery; liver abscesses	About 500 million at any time	All parts of the world, but Africa, Latin America, Asia especially
Hookworm	*Ancylostoma duodenale* and *Necator americanus*	Intestines	Eggs passed in the feces hatch in the soil; larvae burrow into bare feet	Weight loss; anemia; malnutrition	About 1 billion	Africa; Asia; Latin America and South America
Bilharzia	*Schistosoma mansoni*	Veins around intestines and bladder	Larvae live in fresh water and burrow through human skin; they develop into snails	Damage to the liver and bladder; often fatal	About 200 million	Africa (Egypt especially); China; Latin and South America; Asia
Filariasis	*Wuchereria bancrofti; Brugia timori*	Lymph vessels	Mosquito bites	Elephantiasis	Over 120 million	Asia; Africa; parts of Latin and South America
Ascariasis	*Ascaris lumbricoides*	Intestines and stomach	Eggs from feces spread by flies; found in contaminated food and water	No symptoms with a light infestation; heavy infestation causes malnutrition with obstruction of the intestine	Over 1 billion	All parts of the world; especially Africa, Asia, and Latin America
River blindness	*Onchocerca volvulus*	Adults live in nodules beneath the skin; larvae live in the tissues and eyes	Bites from blackflies (*Simulium damnosum*), which live only in rapid-flowing rivers	Blindness; skin damage	About 18 million	Africa; parts of South America
Guinea worm	*Dracunculus medinensis*	Beneath the skin of feet and legs	Larvae live in water fleas, which contaminate drinking water	Increased risk of foot and leg ulcers	About 80,000	Africa; Asia
Tapeworms	*Taenia solium* and *T. saginata* (beef and pork tapeworms); *Diphyllobothrium lata* (fish tapeworm)	Intestines	Cysts and larvae infest meat and fish; these mature into adult tapeworms if meat is not properly cooked; smoked and cured meats are common sources	Malnutrition and anemia; the pork tapeworm can kill if cysts form in the brain; tapeworms may not produce symptoms	Over 100 million	Many parts of the world, especially Africa, South America, Asia, Scandinavia (fish tapeworm)
Liver fluke	*Clonorchis sinensis*	Liver and bile duct	Cysts are present in raw fish	Liver damage and obstruction	Over 20 million	Asia
Threadworms (pinworms)	*Enterobius vermicularis*	Large intestine and anus	Contamination of bedding; clothing; dirty hands; fingernails	Itching; can cause secondary infection through irritation	Over 400 million	Worldwide

Prevention of a parasitic disease

If you live in or visit a country where parasitic diseases are a problem, these rules will help you to stay healthy.

Check that drinking water is safe to use. If you are in doubt, drink only boiled water or use purifying tablets that contain chlorine.

Never eat food that has been left in the open or exposed to flies. Eat food that has been cooked recently and thoroughly. Wash hands and maintain hygiene when handling food.

Wash all fruit and vegetables in clean water before eating. If possible, use detergent.

Avoid exposure to insects. Wear sensible clothing and use insect repellent sprays and gels containing DEET. Use mosquito nets, or burn pyrethrum mosquito coils at night.

In malarial regions, take antimalarial pills. Seek your doctor's advice well before going on your trip.

Do not swim in canals or rivers.

Do not walk around with bare feet.

Detection of a parasitic disease

Your doctor will perform the following tests if you report feeling unwell after returning from an area where parasitic diseases are common.

Blood tests: Blood is first examined under the microscope for signs of any of the nonspecific changes found in parasitic infestations—for example, disordered white blood cell counts and anemia. Blood is then checked carefully. Malarial parasites, trypanosomes (which cause sleeping sickness), and the larvae of some filarial worms can all be seen under a microscope.

Stool tests: A fresh stool sample is examined under the microscope for the eggs, cysts, and larvae of parasites. Almost all of the parasites produce eggs with a characteristic size and shape. Finding and recognizing them requires skill. Several stool samples may be necessary if the infestation is not a heavy one.

Urine tests: In diseases such as bilharzia the urine may contain eggs. These eggs may be detected by using a technique of centrifugation or filtration. The resulting sediment is then examined under a microscope.

Effects of parasites

Parasites can cause considerable harm, but the damage to the host may not appear for a long time. Infestation with ascaris or tapeworms, which live in the intestines and feed on partly digested food, may not be noticed by a healthy host. In developing countries, where many people do not have the food they need for good health, such parasites contribute to the widespread problem of malnutrition. Sometimes the damage done to the host is so severe that whole populations have chosen to move away from villages rather than remain exposed to a debilitating disease.

Treatment

Drugs are available to treat most parasitic diseases, and treatment is usually simple. However, when the host suffers damage over a period of many years, treatment to kill the parasite may come too late. Drugs cannot undo the liver damage that occurs in schistosomiasis or the deformity caused by elephantiasis. Drug treatment is not always practical for dealing with large communities. Some drugs are too toxic for use on a large scale and have to be carefully supervised. Whatever the treatment, it is vital to focus on prevention, too, so that reinfection becomes less likely.

Outlook

Many parasitic diseases have proved difficult to eradicate completely, and preventive programs can be costly. Poorer countries that have the worst problems with parasites often have inadequate resources to deal with the problems. There have, however, been advances in recent decades. As basic hygiene, sanitation, and health improve throughout much of the world, the parasitic diseases of poverty are becoming less inevitable.

See also: Protozoal infections

▲ *Cooking pork thoroughly —for example, sausages and bacon—helps ensure that any parasitic larvae contained in the meat are completely destroyed.*

Parathyroid glands

The tiny parathyroids are among the most important glands in the body. They produce parathyroid hormone (PTH), which is vital for maintaining the delicately balanced quantities of calcium in the bloodstream.

I heard that years ago when the thyroid was removed during surgery, the parathyroids were often accidentally removed too. What happened in cases like these?

The patient would develop a very low level of calcium in the blood, which led first to tetany (an uncontrolled muscular spasm that occurs particularly in the hands and feet) and eventually to the loss of respiration, unless the problem was corrected. Once the condition was recognized, it was treated by giving the patient intravenous injections of calcium. The parathyroids may be removed if there is cancer in the thyroid region, but the patient would be treated with calcium supplements and possibly vitamin D, and would have regular blood tests to monitor the level of calcium.

My sister has an overactive thyroid gland. Is there any chance that her parathyroids will be affected?

No. Although the thyroid and parathyroid glands are close together, the disease processes that affect each are separate, and so her parathyroids should be normal. It is possible to develop a raised level of calcium in the blood simply as a result of a severely overactive thyroid gland.

My father recently underwent surgery on his parathyroids, and he was injected with blue dye. What was the reason for this?

The parathyroid glands are very small organs, so it is not surprising that they are difficult for a surgeon to find during surgery. For some unknown reason, the parathyroid glands are able to absorb a dye called Evan's Blue. This coloring allows the surgeon to see them more easily and to distinguish them from the rest of the tissues. Many surgeons use this technique to help with the operation.

The parathyroids are four tiny glands found behind the thyroid glands, which in turn are found just below the larynx in the throat. They play a major part in controlling the levels of calcium in the body. Calcium is a vital mineral, not only because it is a major structural element in the formation of bones and teeth, but also because it plays a central role in the workings of the muscles and nerve cells. The calcium levels in the body have to be kept within fairly constant boundaries, otherwise the muscles stop working and fits may occur (see Muscles). The parathyroid glands keep the calcium levels in balance.

The absorption of dietary calcium into the bloodstream is controlled by vitamin D, which people get from sunlight and some foods, and by an important hormone produced by the

PARATHYROID GLANDS

▲ This hip X ray shows a prominent bone cyst (center) in the head and neck of the femur, which was later operated upon. A parathyroid tumor was discovered and removed in the operation.

thyroid cartilage

thyroid gland

superior parathyroid glands

trachea

inferior parathyroid glands

◀▲ The tiny parathyroid glands are usually situated near the thyroid gland at the back of the larynx in the throat. The upper two, the superior parathyroids, are behind the thyroid. In this illustration, the inferior parathyroids are inside the thyroid.

Questions and Answers

How are the parathyroids affected if the diet is deficient in calcium?

A low level of calcium in the diet will certainly tend to raise the output of parathyroid hormone from the parathyroids. In fact, it is more common for the diet to be deficient in vitamin D than in calcium. However, this, too, will result in a low blood calcium level, since vitamin D is essential for the absorption of calcium from the intestine into the bloodstream.

My brother has had to have his parathyroids removed because of kidney trouble. Why was this done?

The kidney contains an enzyme that activates vitamin D. If there is a lack of the enzyme, low vitamin D levels cause blood calcium levels to fall, and the parathyroids may enlarge to compensate.

If you start having muscular spasms, do they necessarily mean that your parathyroids have failed?

There are many types of muscle spasm, and anything from an epileptic fit to abdominal cramps can be responsible. However, if you have tetany—an uncontrollable contraction of the muscles, usually starting in the hands and feet—a lack of PTH may be responsible. However, the most common cause of this is hysterical overbreathing (hyperventilation). Loss of too much carbon dioxide changes the blood's acidity, and the calcium level drops. The treatment is to rebreathe for a time into a small plastic bag.

Can PTH arise from any area aside from the parathyroid glands?

Yes. A number of different hormones can be manufactured by various types of cancer, and PTH is one of these. PTH can be produced by cancers of the lung and kidney. It used to be injected into patients to correct calcium levels, but this practice has been discontinued because of its uncertain biological effects on the body.

What can go wrong?

SYMPTOMS	CAUSES	TREATMENT
Overactive parathyroids (hyperparathyroidism): Thirst; increased urination. Pain in the stomach; loss of appetite; vomiting; kidney stones; fatigue; general feeling of ill health. Bone pain; spontaneous fractures.	Benign tumor of one or more glands. Hyperplasia (enlargement) of the glands, often due to kidney disease.	Surgical removal of the affected gland or glands. The outlook is good, but in kidney disease it depends on the kidney problem.
Underactive parathyroids (hypoparathyroidism): Tetany; cramps; uncontrollable muscle spasms; seizures. Tiredness, irritability, depression, psychosis.	Idiopathic (this means "cause unknown"). There may be yeast infection of the nails. Surgical removal of the gland.	Vitamin D by mouth is very effective, but the level of calcium in the blood has to be monitored carefully.

parathyroids called parathyroid hormone, or PTH. If the level of calcium is too low, the parathyroids secrete an increased quantity of the hormone, which has the effect of releasing calcium from the bones to raise the level in the bloodstream. Conversely, if there is too much calcium, the parathyroids reduce or halt the production of PTH, thus bringing the level down.

The parathyroids are so small that they can be difficult to find. The upper two are situated behind the thyroid gland; the lower two, however, can actually be inside the thyroid or occasionally down inside the chest.

Like most endocrine hormone glands, the parathyroids can cause two main problems. They can be overactive, leading to a high level of calcium in the blood; or they can be underactive, leading to a dangerously low level.

INTERACTION BETWEEN BLOOD CALCIUM AND PTH

vitamin D enables calcium to be absorbed into the bloodstream (normal calcium level)

blood calcium level increased as a result of high PTH level

calcium level falls; PTH is produced

calcium level normal, PTH production is reduced

▲ *This diagram shows how, as the level of calcium in the blood drops, the parathyroids increase production of PTH; once the blood calcium level returns to normal, the production of PTH is reduced.*

▲ *Vitamin D, which is essential for the absorption of calcium, is found in fish oils and is synthesized from sunlight.*

Overactive parathyroids

Hyperparathyroiditis, or overactive parathyroids, is a common problem. Doctors now measure the level of calcium in the blood as a routine part of the biochemical screening test that is carried out on practically all hospital patients, and also on many patients by their own doctors (see Screening). As a result, more instances of unexpectedly high blood calcium levels have been found in patients, whereas in the past the level of calcium in the blood was measured only when an abnormality was suspected. It is now thought that as many as one person in a thousand may show some degree of parathyroid overactivity.

Symptoms

A raised blood calcium level may be caused by hyperparathyroidism. However, it is important to realize that there could be other causes. For example, a common cause of a high level of blood calcium is a cancer that leads to secondary deposits of cancer tissue in the bones. This causes the bones to be eaten away and an excess of calcium to be released into the bloodstream. An excessive intake of vitamin D can also cause a raised calcium level.

The two main symptoms of a raised calcium level are thirst and increased urination. There may also be fatigue, poor concentration, loss of appetite, and vomiting. When overactive parathyroids are the cause of a high blood calcium, many patients develop kidney stones. In this disease, the urine contains an excess of calcium, which tends to settle in the kidneys.

People with overactive parathyroids may suffer from indigestion. In about 10 percent of cases, the amount of calcium that is released from the bones as a result of the high level of PTH is so great that the bones themselves begin to show signs of strain—there may be bone pain, some loss of height, and even spontaneous fractures. X rays show a characteristic picture of cysts in the bones, particularly the bones of the hands (see Cyst). The combination of bone problems, kidney stones, and indigestion has led to an old saying among doctors that the disease causes problems with "bones, stones, and abdominal groans."

Treatment

The only effective treatment for an overactive parathyroid is surgical removal of the overactive gland. In most cases all the glands are larger than normal (hypertrophied), and the standard surgical procedure is to identify all four glands and then to remove all but one half of the gland. The remaining half-gland provides enough PTH to keep the calcium level under control.

In the remainder of cases there is a tumor. Usually this affects only one gland, and only a tiny minority of patients will be found to have a tumor that is malignant (see Tumors).

It is not certain what the best treatment is for those people with a slightly higher blood calcium level but no symptoms. In general, most younger patients are advised to have an operation, since a high level of calcium in the blood may eventually damage the kidneys. The outlook following treatment is usually good.

Underactive parathyroids

In contrast, underactivity (hypoparathyroidism) is rare, unless, of course, the parathyroids are removed during surgery on the thyroid. People suffering from this disease are often tired. They may start having seizures and there may be signs of tetany—muscular spasm that initially affects the hands and feet.

There can also be marked psychological problems. Many patients will have depression, but a large number show irrational overactivity. People who have hypoparathyroidism are susceptible to candida infection of the nails, as well as all the symptoms of low blood calcium (see Yeast Infections).

This disease can be combated effectively by taking vitamin D by mouth. Even though a careful eye has to be kept on the patient's calcium level, the outlook after treatment is very good.

Another condition is called pseudohypoparathyroidism: the parathyroids are normal, but the body does not respond in a normal way to parathyroid hormone.

> *See also:* Bones; Calcium; Cancer; Endocrine system; Glands; Hormones; Kidneys and kidney diseases; Surgery; Thyroid; Vitamin D

Parkinson's disease

Parkinson's disease is a common illness of older people. It causes the limbs to shake and makes simple movement difficult. Modern medication has done much to prolong the active years and slow the progression of disability.

The former names for Parkinson's disease, "paralysis agitans" and "shaking palsy," describe one of its most common symptoms. A person who suffers from this disease (named after an 18th-century English physician, James Parkinson) experiences shaking or tremor of the limbs (especially the hands), stiff limbs, and difficulty in carrying out certain types of movement (see Tremor). In advanced stages of the disease, there are associated problems with control of circulation and perspiration.

Parkinson's disease is a common disorder of middle-aged and elderly people, but treatment can, to a great extent, postpone for many years the onset of any disability.

▲ *Muhammed Ali, the former Olympic and world heavyweight boxing champion, is living with Parkinson's disease.*

Causes

Most cases of Parkinson's disease are caused by premature aging of deep-seated brain cells in an area called the basal ganglia. The cells in the basal ganglia normally form a complex control system to coordinate muscle activity, the function of which is to allow smoothness of muscle movements. These movements include swinging the arms when walking, making facial expressions, and positioning the limbs before standing up or walking (see Coordination). Difficulties occur when the brain cells that allow the body to perform these tasks die off prematurely (see Brain).

Symptoms

The symptoms of Parkinson's disease usually develop very slowly and are often assumed to be part of the normal process of aging. At the onset of the disease, they appear to occur on one side of the body only. Ultimately, however, both sides are usually affected. The most noticeable symptom is trembling of the hands, which shake in a "pill-rolling" tremor as if the person were rolling something between his or her fingers and thumb. It is most noticeable when the arms are inactive; the shaking usually stops as soon as movement begins, for example, in reaching for a cup.

The muscles of people afflicted with the disease become unusually stiff. In the early stages there are symptoms of aching shoulders and

◀ *A shuffling, unbalanced walk, rigid posture, and slow tremor are typical symptoms of Parkinson's disease; therefore, many sufferers cannot walk unaided.*

POSITION OF THE BASAL GANGLIA

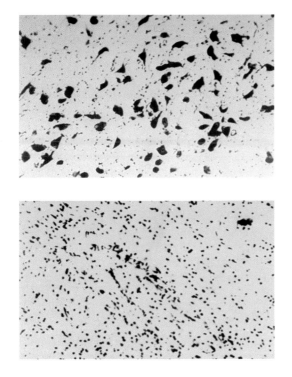

▲ *Dopamine produced by cells (top) in the basal ganglia is severely lacking in patients with Parkinson's disease (above).*

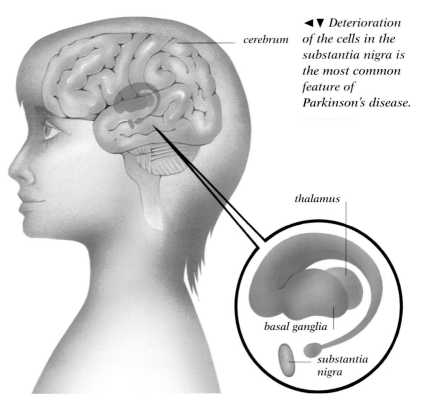

cerebrum

◀▼ *Deterioration of the cells in the substantia nigra is the most common feature of Parkinson's disease.*

thalamus

basal ganglia

substantia nigra

discomfort first thing in the morning, after hours of rest (see Stiffness). The face is also less mobile than usual, giving the person an expressionless or masklike face.

Walking is also very difficult for someone with Parkinson's disease. After a hesitant start, a person will move forward quickly in a shuffling manner. He or she takes small steps and leans forward in a stoop. This instability creates difficulty in walking and can sometimes lead to severe falls because the usual automatic reaction of using the hands to break a fall is no longer automatic.

Speech becomes slow and halting and swallowing may become difficult. In the early stages, the intellect is not affected, but after some years about 30 percent of patients gradually develop dementia. In the advanced stage of the disease every physical movement becomes increasingly difficult.

The disease is accompanied by a drop in blood pressure when the patient stands up, which results in episodes of fainting, and by slurred and distorted speech, as a result of muscle damage.

Treatment

The usual treatment for Parkinson's disease is a drug called L-dopa, which is given in tablet form. It replenishes the brain's supply of dopamine, the chemical transmitter produced by cells in the basal ganglia, and it alleviates many symptoms of the disease. Transplantation of dopamine-secreting fetal adrenal gland tissue into the brain has helped in some cases, but this surgical treatment is still in the experimental stage. Physical therapy and speech therapy can help with mobility problems and speech and swallowing difficulties.

Outlook

Although degeneration of the brain cells cannot be reversed, medication, regular exercise, and proper nourishment will allow the patient to lead a full life for at least 10 years from the onset of the disease. After this period it becomes more difficult to control the symptoms, but drugs that mimic dopamine may help to treat the symptoms and improve quality of life.

Progressive symptoms
Limbs become stiff, causing aching joints
Face becomes immobile
Limbs stiffen further, making it difficult to initiate movements
Gait becomes stooping and only small steps can be taken
Reduction in sweating or increased occurrence of a greasy face, due to abnormal activity of sweat glands
Feelings of faintness accompany standing
Walking is difficult because of stiffness
Hands tremble almost constantly when the person is inactive
Fingers are increasingly affected by slight tremor

See also: **Muscles; Posture**

Pathogen

Questions and Answers

My son is a medical student and tries to impress me by using technical language. He never talks about germs but seems to call them pathogens. What exactly does the word "pathogen" mean?

The Greek word *pathos* means "suffering" and the suffix "-gen" comes from the Greek word *genes,* meaning "to be born" or "to have origin in." A pathogen is any factor, object, or influence that can cause a disease to start. It is correct to refer to germs as pathogens, but as diseases can be caused by agents other than germs, those agents may also be called pathogens.

My uncle went to a hospital for a hernia operation and nearly died two weeks later from an MRSA infection. What does MRSA mean?

MRSA is an abbreviation of "methicillin-resistant *Staphylococcus aureus*." *S. aureus* is a common germ that causes a range of infections, but it can change rapidly by natural selection so as to resist destruction by the common antibiotics. Strains of *S. aureus* that are not killed by the powerful antibiotic methicillin are also resistant to many other antibiotics, so MRSA requires treatment with unusual antibiotics. To limit this dangerous process of evolution, methicillin was withdrawn from clinical use and is now used only in laboratories to test for MRSA.

Is genetics or the environment more likely to cause illness?

Many disorders, such as sickle-cell disease, hemophilia, and muscular dystrophy, are purely genetic in origin; many others, such as breast cancer, atherosclerosis, Alzheimer's disease, diabetes, and osteoporosis, have a partially genetic cause. The environmental element is also very important, however; many diseases result from an interaction of genetics and environment.

A pathogen is an agent that is capable of causing disease. This can happen in many different ways, and the range of pathogens is very wide. The action of pathogens in causing disease is often very complicated.

Pathology is the scientific study of disease; here, the term "disease" means any local or general ailment, abnormality, or damage to the body. The word "pathology" is also used as a general term to refer to any area of disease or damage in the body. Pathogenesis is the development of disease, and a pathogen is anything that can cause disease. Among the many agencies capable of causing disease, one of the most important, and certainly the most common, is the group of microorganisms commonly known as "germs." These are so important as a cause of disease that the term "pathogen" has sometimes been limited to germs. The current tendency, however, is to refer to all disease-causing agencies as pathogens.

The range and effect of pathogens

In considering the causes of disease, it is not sufficient simply to list the immediate and most obvious causes, such as genetic factors, germs (viruses, bacteria, fungi, parasites, and prions), chemical agents (poisons), mechanical injury, heat and cold, and radiation. Environmental factors such as malnutrition, atmospheric pollution, low-grade housing, inadequate hygienic facilities, and so on greatly influence whether pathogens will bring about disease (see Hygiene; Malnutrition; Pollution). In this context, the term "environmental" is taken to have a much wider

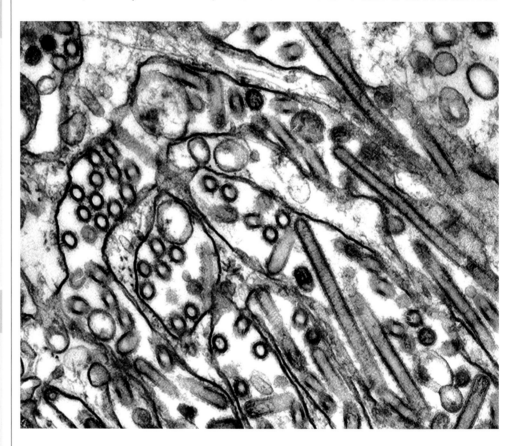

▲ *The influenza A H5N1 virus (gold) is shown in Maudin Darby canine kidney (MDCK) cells (green). This virus affected only birds, including chickens and ducks, until a mutation allowed it to infect the human immune system, causing an epidemic in Hong Kong in 1997 that resulted in the deaths of six people.*

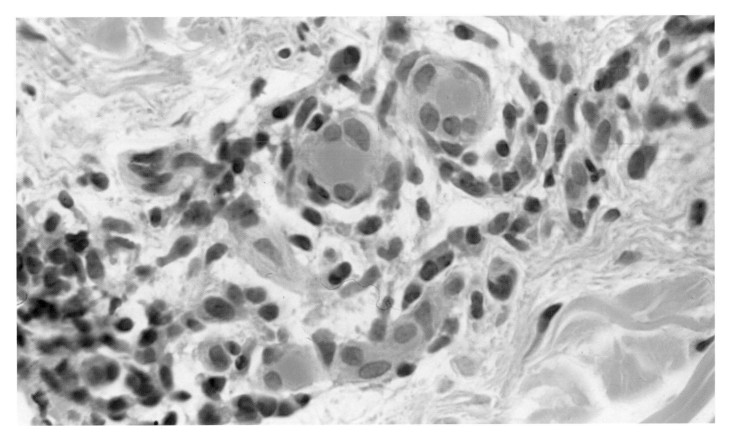

▲ *The histopathology of an inflammatory skin reaction to the* Schistosoma mansoni *parasite is shown here in a monkey infected with* Mycobacterium tuberculosis *bacteria. In humans, this parasite can cause a skin disease called "swimmer's itch."*

sense than is usually understood. It describes anything that encroaches in any way on the individual and that can, in any way, modify the individual. It includes sources of information, such as newspapers and TV, that may modify a person's behavior or opinion.

The case of infection illustrates this interaction well. People are exposed to varying numbers of germs all the time, but they do not all necessarily succumb to these germs. To some extent, this is a matter of the dose of germs to which they are exposed. Whether or not an infection occurs is a result of the outcome of the shifting balance between the size of the attack on the person and the strength of the body's resistance to the attack—the health and efficiency of the immune system. Therefore, the establishment of disease caused by an infection may be the result of an unusually large dose of germs that is able to overcome a healthy immune system, or a moderate dose that overcomes a defective immune system.

The ability of the immune system to resist infection can be influenced by a variety of environmental factors such as diet, abnormal stress, cigarette smoking, and so on, and these may be affected by incoming information. Similarly, the ability of the body to react positively, and in a healing manner, to what doctors call insults of any kind is a variable that depends on other health factors. Healthy living that promotes the efficiency of the heart, circulation, and respiratory system, and that maintains unclogged arteries so that every part of the body receives an adequate supply of well-oxygenated blood, has a major bearing on the ability of the body to overcome the effects of any such attacks.

Genetic pathogenesis

A great deal can be done to minimize the damaging effect of most pathogens. However, since people are unable to choose their own parents, there is not much they can do about the genes they inherit. Genes are lengths of DNA; local lengths of DNA that differ from the normal sequences are called mutations. Mutations can be inherited through many generations, and new inheritable mutations can arise if changes occur, as, for instance, from radiation in the cells that produce sperm and eggs. Mutations in the general body cells cannot be inherited, but can cause disease, especially cancer (see Mutation).

The pathogenesis of many diseases is known to be the result of the interaction of genetic and environmental factors. Because several different genes and several different environmental factors may be involved, this kind of causation is called multifactorial. More obvious genetic pathogenesis arises from major genetic abnormalities involving single genes—as in the case of cystic fibrosis, phenylketonuria, neurofibromatosis, and Huntington's disease—or whole chromosomes, as in Down syndrome and Turner's syndrome (see Down Syndrome).

Germs

Germs are called microorganisms because most of them are so small that they can be seen only with the aid of a microscope. A few, however, such as the amoebas that cause amebic dysentery, are larger and can be seen with the naked eye (see Dysentery). Germ pathogens cover a wide spectrum of sizes and types. Prions are the smallest and are at one extreme of the spectrum. These are protein molecules (see Protein) that are not actually living organisms, but they can still infect humans to bring about the inevitably fatal Creutzfeldt-Jacob disease (CJD), a disease that also occurs in cattle, where it is called bovine spongiform encephalopathy (BSE).

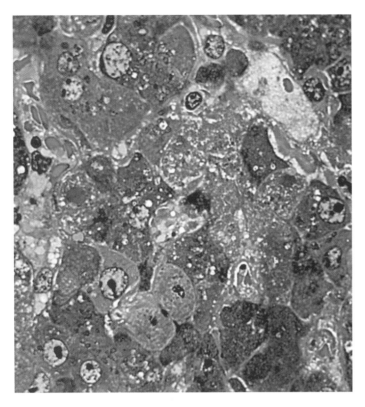

▲ *This photomicrograph, stained with blue dye, shows the liver inflammation of hepatitis caused by the Lassa virus.*

Next in size are the viruses, which are still far too small to be seen even by the most powerful optical microscopes. They can, however, be seen using electron microscopes. It is arguable whether or not viruses are living organisms. Although they are of different shapes and sizes, they consist of little more than a length of genetic material packed into a protein envelope. They are incapable of reproducing unless they can invade living cells. Viruses have already been made in the laboratory. There are many hundreds of different kinds of infective viruses all capable of causing disease. Some of the many diseases caused by viruses are AIDS, influenza, the common cold, measles, hepatitis, herpes, shingles, polio, yellow fever, rabies, meningitis, and warts.

Bacteria are all larger than viruses and can be seen with regular optical microscopes. They take various physical forms. Cocci are small, spherical organisms. Streptococci form chains and cause sore throats, spreading skin inflammation (cellulitis) and, as a secondary effect, rheumatic fever, and kidney disease (see Streptococcus). Staphylococci form clusters and cause boils, abscesses, impetigo, osteomyelitis, food poisoning, and a dangerous form of pneumonia (see Staphylococcus). Diplococci collect in pairs, often in cells, and cause gonorrhea and meningitis. Bacilli are rod-shaped organisms and are often able to move about, driven by lashing hairs called flagella. They cause many diseases, including bronchitis, pneumonia, typhoid, food poisoning, dysentery, cholera, diphtheria, Legionnaires' disease, and tuberculosis. Spirochaetes are slender, spirally coiled organisms that cause syphilis, Lyme disease, and leptospirosis.

Fungi cause only minor infections, generally confined to the skin, in healthy people. These diseases include tinea and thrush. Tinea (epidermophytosis) includes athlete's foot, jock itch, tinea corporis, and tinea capitis. Thrush (candidiasis) is usually confined to the mouth and genital area (see Thrush). When the immune system is defective, however, fungi may be much more dangerous.

Amoebas and other protozoal organisms are the largest of the microorganisms. They cause diseases such as malaria, amebic dysentery, trichomonal vaginitis, giardial infections, leishmaniasis, and toxoplasmosis (see Protozoal Infections).

Physical and chemical pathogens

Injuries from accidents and assaults are obvious causes of pathology, such as bone fractures, wounds of all kinds, secondary infection, scarring, disfigurement and disability. Burns are an important and serious cause of bodily damage. The danger is related to their extent and depth. If a large area of the body is burned, the outcome is commonly fatal (see Burns). Cold injuries commonly lead to death of tissue (see Gangrene), especially in the extremities. This is the effect of the loss of blood supply to these tissues (see Frostbite).

Chemical pathogens include poisons and corrosive substances, both of which can severely damage or destroy tissue. Poisons often act by interfering with essential enzyme systems of the body or by damaging the important actions and functions of cell membranes (see Poisoning). Chemical agents can be pathogens by acting directly on the early development of the fetus so as to produce congenital malformations, or by damaging DNA so as to cause cells to become cancerous (see Cancer; Congenital Disorders).

Among the most dangerous chemical pathogens are those contained in the tars of tobacco smoke. Ironically, the nicotine content offers little or no risk. Tobacco tar contains many polycyclic aromatic hydrocarbon cancer-causing substances (carcinogens) capable of causing cancer of the lung, larynx, bladder, and cervix. It also contains pathogenic substances that promote stomach ulcers, chronic bronchitis, emphysema, and arterial disease leading to angina pectoris, heart attacks, and strokes. It is no exaggeration to state that cigarette smoking is probably the most dangerous avoidable pathogen (see Smoking).

Another important chemical pathogen is ethyl alcohol taken in excess of one or two units per day. Excessive alcohol intake is directly implicated in the development of cirrhosis of the liver, chronic inflammation of the pancreas (pancreatitis), stomach inflammation (gastritis), heart muscle damage (cardiomyopathy), and brain damage (encephalopathy). Alcohol also acts as a pathogen because it is a factor in accidents on the road and other dangerous accidents (see Alcoholism).

Ionizing radiation, from X rays, natural radiation, radioactive isotopes, and cosmic rays, is a less obvious but still very real pathogen. In this case the risk is to DNA and to the primitive cells forming the embryo or young fetus. Abdominal X-ray examination is avoided in women who might recently have become pregnant (see Fetus; Pregnancy; X Rays). Routine chest and orthopedic X rays are not thought to offer a significant risk of causing cancer, but unnecessary exposure to any form of ionizing radiation should certainly be avoided (see Radiation Sickness).

See also: **Bacteria; Environmental hazards; Genetic diseases and disorders; Genetics; Immune system; Infection and infectious diseases; Opportunistic infection; Parasites; Pathology; Viruses**

Pathology

Questions and Answers

Recently I had a mole removed for cosmetic reasons, and my doctor sent it to a pathologist. Does she suspect cancer?

Probably not. Virtually anything that is removed from the body is examined by a pathologist, to guard against the very small chance that a spot, mole, or lump may be cancerous.

A friend of mine died suddenly at the age of 43 and an autopsy was done. Was foul play suspected?

An autopsy rarely implies that foul play is suspected. Two types of autopsy are usually carried out. The first is performed when the doctor has no idea of the cause of death. The second is performed when doctors feel it would further their knowledge of a disease.

Is pathology a dangerous job?

It can be. All doctors run the risk of catching diseases, but certain branches of pathology are especially risky. In particular, microbiologists handle dangerous, infectious material in their daily work. Each year, there are cases of serious infections in doctors and laboratory personnel.

When I was pregnant, I had to give blood samples. Why?

Pregnant women are susceptible to certain disorders. The most common of these disorders is anemia, so a blood test for anemia is done routinely. Often a test is performed to see if the mother has been exposed to German measles (rubella). If she hasn't and she is infected during pregnancy, rubella can be harmful to the baby. Also, screening tests allow problems to be anticipated and treated. Blood tests such as alpha fetoprotein (AFP) can help in diagnosing birth defects.

People often think of a pathologist as someone who dissects corpses or as someone who works in the medical examiner's office to investigate violent deaths. In reality the scope of pathology is far wider than this.

Every patient in a hospital and many patients who go to their doctor's office make use of pathology services. A treatment clinician is responsible for the care and treatment of patients, but the final, definitive diagnosis often rests with a pathologist.

Pathology is the medical specialty that deals with the causes and changes produced in the body by disease. Because the field is now so wide, it is subdivided into seven main areas: histopathology, forensic pathology, hematology, chemical pathology, microbiology, cytology, and immunology. Each attempts to give a definite answer to what is often an educated clinical guess.

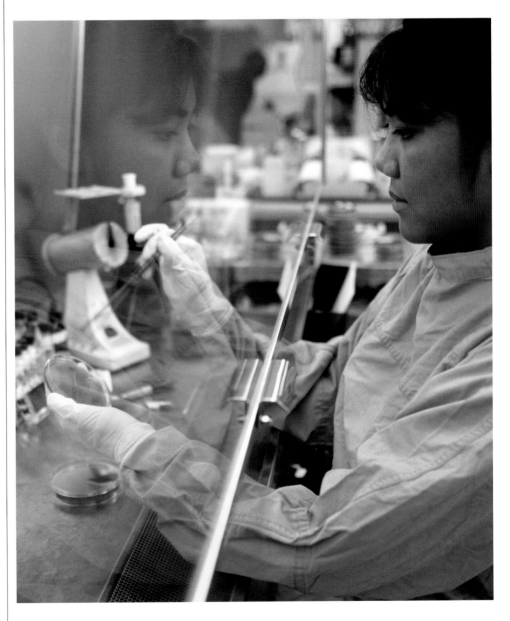

▲ *Some pathologists look for signs of disease in samples of blood, tissues, and organs. Others use specimens to identify particular microorganisms that cause infection.*

▲ *Medical examiners perform autopsies on people who have died in suspicious circumstances to obtain vital clues.*

For instance, although appendicitis is one of the most common emergencies needing surgery, it can be a very difficult diagnosis to make. After the appendix has been removed, the surgeon sends the tissue to the pathologist to assess if it really was inflamed. If the inflammation is in fact someplace else in the patient's abdomen, different treatment will probably be required.

Pathologists are doctors who, in addition to having the same four-year training as every other doctor, must spend one year working in clinical medicine—that is, with patients—and a further five years training in pathology. Early on in his or her training, a pathologist will specialize in one particular branch of pathology, because the work of each branch is very different.

The different specialties

Histopathology: This is what many people mean when they use the term "pathology." A histopathology department does both biopsy and autopsy work—examining tissues removed during surgery and those removed after a person's death.

There are two reasons for carrying out an autopsy. Deaths that occur in suspicious circumstances are referred automatically to a medical examiner, as are those that occur soon after surgery or following trauma, or those caused by alcohol. The medical examiner then decides if an autopsy is needed.

Another reason for an autopsy is that a doctor believes the treatment of a disease was correct; however, for educational purposes he or she may still wish to explore the extent of the disease, or determine whether or not another disease was present. In such cases, the doctor will ask the dead person's closest relative to give permission before an autopsy can be carried out.

Such examinations often turn up the unexpected. One study showed that in a third to half of cases, either the patient had been misdiagnosed or there was significant disease present in addition to the one diagnosed and treated. In many instances, then, autopsy results can further the progress of medical science.

However, most of the work of a histopathology department concerns specimens removed by a surgeon in the operating room. Virtually everything that is removed is sent for examination, because a histopathologist is the only person who can give a definite diagnosis by examining a specimen under a microscope. A harmless-looking mole may turn out to be a skin cancer; lifesaving treatment can be given because of the pathologist's diagnosis.

When a specimen is received, it is left to fix in a preservative for about 12 hours, depending on its size, then processed and finally embedded in wax. This takes 24 hours. The specimen is fixed in a wax block so that fine slivers (about one-millionth of an inch thick) can be cut on a machine, called a microtome. The thin sections are then transferred to slides and stained different colors before being examined under a microscope.

For urgent specimens, a frozen section can be done. This is what happens in a suspected case of breast cancer. The patient is warned

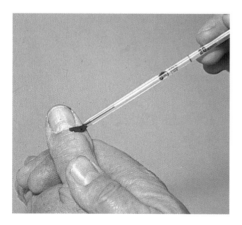

▲ *A blood sample is drawn to be used for laboratory tests.*

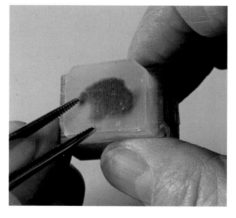

▲ *Tissue from a liver is embedded in wax, then sliced and stained for testing.*

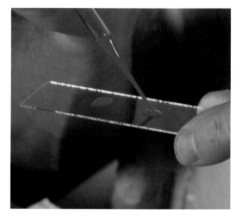

▲ *A blood sample is spread on a slide for examination under a microscope.*

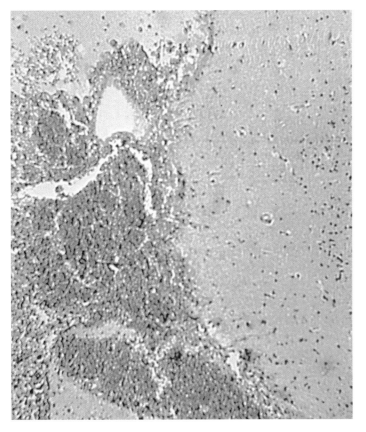

▲ *This sample of brain tissue shows acute inflammatory encephalitis due to infection by* **Salmonella typhi** *bacteria.*

that she may have cancer, and she will usually give consent for removal of the breast if the cancer is confirmed. Initially, the surgeon removes the suspicious lump only and sends it to histopathology immediately. Here a small piece is taken off, deep-frozen, cut very thin, stained, and examined under a microscope. If the lump is benign, the patient is left with a small scar on her breast. If it is cancerous, the surgeon removes enough tissue to include the whole cancer.

Although it is quick, this procedure is not used for all specimens, as it gives less than perfect results. If there is any doubt at all, the pathologist recommends halting surgery until a specimen that has been prepared routinely can be examined two days later.

Cytology: This department is closely linked with histopathology. However, a cytologist looks at the individual cells that make up the human body. Pap smears, for instance, are examined here in an attempt to detect cancer in its earliest stages.

Smears are mostly painless and involve scraping the outside of the cervix (where the womb joins the upper part of the vagina) and smearing the tissue onto a glass slide. If any of the smear cells look cancerous, a gynecologist takes a larger specimen and sends it to a histopathologist. If cancer is confirmed and is still at an early stage, surgery is carried out to remove the cancerous part of the cervix.

A cytologist will also examine a variety of other cells for potential cancer; for instance, cells from a lung cancer may be found in sputum, and those from bladder cancer in the urine.

Forensic pathology: This department deals with the effects that violence, criminal or other, has on the human body. Although many people find forensics fascinating, only in the last 70 years or so has it acquired respectability as an independent branch of pathology.

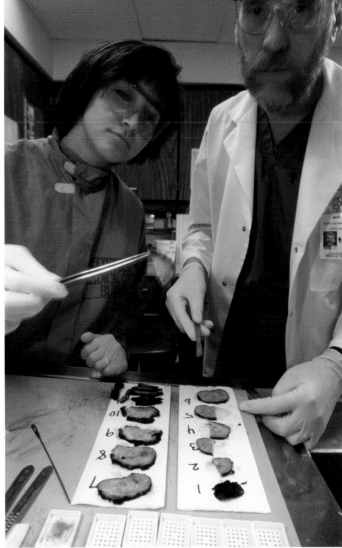

▲ *In some cases, the cause of a person's death will become clear only after examination of organ and tissue samples.*

People may be aware of some forensic techniques from watching television programs. For example, a forensic scientist can judge the time of death from the temperature of the corpse and the degree of rigor mortis—that is, the stiffening of the muscles which occurs after death but which then disappears.

Pathologists can give dramatic assistance to the police. In one example, a man lured women to his farm, killed them, and dissolved their bodies in sulfuric acid. A forensic pathologist who was at the scene picked up an object and recognized it instantly as a human gallstone. The police soon found the false teeth of a victim, from which she was later identified.

Hematology: This department investigates blood disorders. About half the volume of blood consists of cells and half of plasma, a fluid containing many different chemicals (see Plasma). Hematology is concerned mainly with the red blood cells that carry oxygen, the white blood cells that fight infection, and the cell fragments—the platelets—that make the blood clot. Most people who go to a hospital have a routine hematology screen, in which the red and white cells and the platelets are counted by a machine.

▲ During an autopsy the pathologist takes a tissue sample from the infected organ to examine it microscopically.

Extra information can be found if the hematologist examines a blood film on a glass slide under a microscope. If the red blood cells are small and pale, they suggest anemia due to iron deficiency. If they are large and reduced in number, they suggest pernicious anemia. A reduced number of platelets could indicate that the patient has a tendency to bleed a lot. Abnormal white blood cells may indicate blood cancer. The presence of immature red and white blood cells may suggest cancer elsewhere in the body. Other specialized tests exist, such as measuring the amount of hemoglobin in the blood or carrying out very detailed clotting tests.

Another test performed by the hematology department is examination of bone marrow, which is where the blood cells are manufactured (see Marrow and Transplants). A needle must be pushed through the bone to collect a specimen; marrow is then withdrawn and spread quickly on a slide. This test is used to confirm a diagnosis, in particular, of leukemia.

The hematology department also looks after blood transfusions. Anyone who requires a blood donation has first to give a small sample so that his or her blood group can be cross-matched. Giving the wrong blood to a patient can cause death, and it is the job of skilled technicians to prevent this (see Blood Groups).

Chemical pathology: This department measures a wide range of chemicals in blood, urine, feces, and stomach fluid. Routine tests include measuring the amount of urea or sodium or potassium in the blood; however, the possibilities for chemical tests are almost endless. Many hormones can also be measured in this department.

Some drugs in the blood can be measured to ensure that a patient is receiving the correct amount of a prescribed medication. In the case of drug overdosage, it is vital to test the blood level, as this will determine how vigorously the patient should be treated. The treatment for certain overdoses is in itself dangerous and justified only if the patient's life is in danger.

Diabetics make a great deal of use of the chemical pathology department. In diabetes there is a deficiency of the hormone insulin, which allows cells to take up sugar from the blood so that it can be used as fuel. Normally diabetics can test their own sugar level at home by measuring the sugar in their blood. However, if the condition gets out of control, then more accurate measurements are needed in a hospital (see Diabetes).

Microbiology: This department identifies which microorganism is causing a particular infection. Microbiology departments usually study the relatively small group of pathogenic (disease-causing) microorganisms. These include bacteria, which cause many disorders including pneumonia and typhoid; viruses, which cause many infections including AIDS, influenza, and the common cold; protozoa, which cause diseases such as malaria and amebic dysentery; and fungi, which cause disorders such as thrush.

Identifying microorganisms is a skilled job. A specimen is taken from the patient without touching anything else, to avoid contamination. The sample is then smeared over a growth plate containing a special jelly substance, and this is kept at body temperature. In about 24 hours the bacteria, viruses, or any other types of microorganism grow enough to be identified. Once an organism is identified, it can be tested in the laboratory against a range of antibiotics to determine the best treatment.

There is definite risk to workers in this department. Although strict safety precautions are taken, several cases of infections acquired from samples occur each year.

Immunology: This department looks at how diseases progress and the role of the body's immune system. As a result of research into AIDS and cancer, many discoveries have been made in this area in the last 10 to 15 years. Immunotherapy, in which drugs are used to enhance the immune system, is also increasingly successful. Progress in immunology has also undoubtedly helped to combat many cases of cancer in recent years.

The future

Vigorous research is going on in all departments of pathology. One goal is to find a cure for some forms of leukemia. Great strides have been made with immunosuppressive drugs and gene therapy to help solve the problem of the body's rejection of bone marrow tissue. New research suggests that stem cells taken from the blood of newborn babies' placentas may serve as an alternative to bone marrow. Also, new computer technology and software has been specially designed to enhance the efficiency of genetic analysis of tissues in both medical and forensic pathology.

See also: **Biopsy; Blood; Cancer; Laboratory tests; Lumpectomy; Medical research; Pap smear**

Pediatric medicine

The branch of medicine that is concerned with the health and illnesses of children is called pediatrics. From the time a child is born, a pediatrician will do his or her utmost to prevent, alleviate, and cure any diseases or conditions that children are prey to and safeguard the child's well-being.

A pediatrician is a doctor who cares for children from the moment they are born until they reach puberty. These age limits are not fixed; the pediatrician may already have been involved during the pregnancy along with the obstetrician (the doctor concerned with pregnancy and childbirth) if a problem was anticipated (see Pregnancy).

In the hospital the pediatrician works together with other specialists to care for children. He or she also works with other pediatricians at centers specializing in rare problems. Some pediatricians, called neonatologists, specialize in the problems of newborn babies.

The birth of a baby

The vast majority of babies are entirely normal at birth and start to breathe spontaneously a few seconds after delivery. However, in some cases, such as a forceps delivery or a premature birth, a baby is more likely to have difficulty breathing. Because of this, there is usually a pediatrician in the delivery room at such times to help the baby. Because it is not always possible to predict which babies will have problems, a pediatrician is available at the hospital 24 hours a day. However, even if a baby needs some encouragement to start breathing, once this is established almost all babies have no more trouble and are returned to their mothers.

▲ *Thanks to advances in medicine, most babies are not only born healthy but, with pediatric care, they also remain that way.*

Questions and Answers

I am due to give birth soon and feel anxious about the first few weeks of caring for my baby. Is there anyone I can talk to about this before leaving the hospital?

Yes. Any worries can be discussed with the pediatrician who examines your baby before you leave the hospital. He or she can answer your questions and refer you to other reliable sources.

Is it true that newborn babies cannot see?

No; babies can see as soon as they are born and are instinctively interested in the human face. They focus best at about 12 in. (30 cm) —about the distance a breast-feeding mother is from her baby.

My teenage daughter had her belly button pierced six months ago and it is still producing pus. She says this is normal and refuses to see a doctor, but could it be infected?

Yes, it is likely that it is infected. However, pierced belly buttons can take months to heal because the skin there is constantly being bent and stretched as the person moves. To prevent infection, the jewelry in the piercing should be of the best quality metal. You must take her to a doctor to verify whether the piercing is infected; if it is, the jewelry should be removed.

I got so angry with my two-month-old baby recently when he was crying that I shook him vigorously. I am frightened I might harm him in the future. What should I do?

Shaking babies hard can be very harmful, especially when they are so young. The blood vessels around the brain can be damaged, causing a clot to form between the brain and skull. If you fear that you may injure your baby, seek expert help immediately through your doctor.

Guidelines for young children in the hospital

Children are naturally anxious about their first visit to the hospital, so it is best to prepare them beforehand so that they know what to expect. Fears can then be dealt with, and their stay made more enjoyable.

Explain what a hospital is. Try to take the child on a tour of the children's floor before he or she is admitted.

Explain what is going to be done, and be honest if something will be painful. Don't be an alarmist.

When you are packing the child's bag, let him or her choose some favorite items, like a toy or a pillow.

Try to stay with the child in the hospital if possible; otherwise, visit frequently and bring along other members of the family. Children are welcome too.

Be prepared for tears, which are normal and healthy. In most cases, the child will soon stop crying and begin to get interested in the activities on the floor. If problems persist, speak to the play therapist.

Ask the staff members on the floor any questions, however busy they seem. If you feel reassured you will give your child more confidence.

Discharge means only that the child is well enough to be home, so don't expect him or her to be entirely fit.

Expect a difficult period following the child's stay in the hospital: dependence and bed-wetting are common afterward, but these problems will normally resolve themselves within a short while.

▲ *The doctor will often measure a child's weight and height during a checkup to see whether the rate of growth is normal.*

Child development

Children are continually growing, physically, mentally, and emotionally. It is an important part of pediatrics to observe these changes, identify problems if they occur, and advise on how best to deal with them (see Growth).

The routine surveillance of most children is carried out by pediatricians and family doctors. The time of the examinations should be spaced so that children are seen at key points of their development, especially in the first two years of their life.

The first major check on babies is in the first week of life before leaving the hospital. The primary concern here is to look for any congenital abnormalities, such as hip dislocation or heart disorders (see Congenital Disorders). There is a similar review at six weeks to ensure that the baby is growing well, and that there are still no congenital problems. Again, the hips and heart are looked at closely. This is a good opportunity for the mother to discuss with the pediatrician any problems she may have with feeding or sleeping, and generally in coping with her new baby. At about eight months the emphasis is on general development. By this time babies should be smiling, babbling, and aware of what is happening around them. At this stage, many are sitting up and beginning to crawl. Hearing tests and a test for strabismus (cross-eye) should be done around this age (see Hearing).

The next examination is at about 18 months, when most children are walking and starting to talk (see Coordination; Speech). At two

Preventive pediatrics

AGE OF CHILD	6 WEEKS	2 MONTHS	4 MONTHS	6 MONTHS	6–18 MONTHS	12–15 MONTHS	15–18 MONTHS	1–12 YEARS
Immunization		H. Influenza type B (hib); Hepatitis B; diphtheria, tetanus, pertussis/ whooping cough (DTP); polio	Hepatitis B; polio; DTP; hib	DTP; hib	Hepatitis B; polio	Measles, mumps, rubella (MMR); hib; polio; varicella (chicken pox)	DTP	Tetanus-diptheria booster
Checkups	For congenital defects; growth, feeding problems			Hearing, sight, overall develop-ment (at 6–12 months)			Overall development, especially walking, language, behavior (repeated at 2 years)	Preschool assessment (at 4 to 5 years)

▲ *During a normal physical examination by a pediatrician or family doctor, a child's reflexes are routinely tested by quick, gentle taps with a piece of equipment called a reflex hammer.*

years of age, language skills, vision, and behavior are assessed; at five years readiness for school is assessed. This method is designed to discover abnormalities as soon as they arise. However, parents should not feel that they have to wait for the next appointment if they are worried, particularly about their child's vision and hearing. There are a great many specialists and resources available, and the most appropriate help must be chosen in each case. For example, a child with a physical disorder, such as a heart murmur, may be referred to a pediatric cardiologist, and severe behavioral problems may require psychiatric help at a child guidance center or at the hospital.

A child whose overall development is giving cause for concern may be referred to a local assessment center. Here a whole team of experts can meet and examine the child. Such experts often include pediatricians, specialists in hearing and vision, orthopedic surgeons, physical therapists, psychologists, teachers, and speech therapists. They may be able to assess a child immediately or may need to admit him or her briefly to the hospital for tests and closer observation. A plan for any further therapy can then be made.

Preventive medicine is important too, and includes immunization of children (see Preventive Medicine). Immunizations are done as a matter of routine at the doctor's office. They are very important and should not be missed (for more detailed information on when children should receive immunizations and checkups, see the chart above). As well as having checkups, babies may attend frequently for weighing when they are small. These visits are usually arranged individually with the doctor's office.

Preschool assessment

Before a child starts to attend kindergarten or a day care center, a program of regular physical examinations is arranged. Nowadays, most babies are born healthy, and, with pediatric care, remain so.

See also: Birth; Child development; Hospitals; Immunization; Lazy eye; Neonatal intensive care unit; Obstetrics; Physical examination; Premature babies; Whooping cough

Pelvic inflammatory disease

Pelvic inflammatory disease (PID) is inflammation of the female reproductive organs, usually as a result of infection. If the condition is left untreated, it can cause infertility and the risk of ectopic pregnancy.

"Pelvic inflammatory disease" (PID) refers to any inflammatory condition affecting a woman's pelvic organs, but it is a term most commonly used to refer to bacterial infections of the pelvic organs. PID affects the cervix (the neck of the uterus where it protrudes into the vagina), the ovaries, the uterus, the fallopian tubes, and other parts of the pelvis. It is one of the main causes of infertility in women, usually because the delicate fallopian tubes, which connect the ovaries to the uterus, become damaged by scar tissue or develop adhesions that cause an obstruction.

To be effective, treatment should be carried out as soon as possible. However, doctors can have difficulty recognizing and diagnosing the disease and identifying infections. Once someone has had an attack, he or she should take precautionary measures to stop the condition from recurring; the measures include barrier contraception and good hygiene.

Symptoms

When PID has reached an acute stage, there may be severe pelvic pain, a high temperature, and possibly vomiting and diarrhea. If acute PID is left untreated, it can lead to death through septicemia (blood poisoning). To avoid septicemia in severe cases, a hysterectomy may be necessary (see Hysterectomy).

PID can also be subacute, with symptoms similar to those of acute PID but less severe; it can be chronic, so that there is a constant condition of PID of varying severity over long periods of time; or it can be recurrent, so that periods of health are interspersed with attacks of PID. All varieties of the disease need to be taken seriously and require prompt treatment.

Other symptoms include an abnormal vaginal discharge, (a common symptom); lower abdominal pain, which may be on one side only and becomes worse during sex or

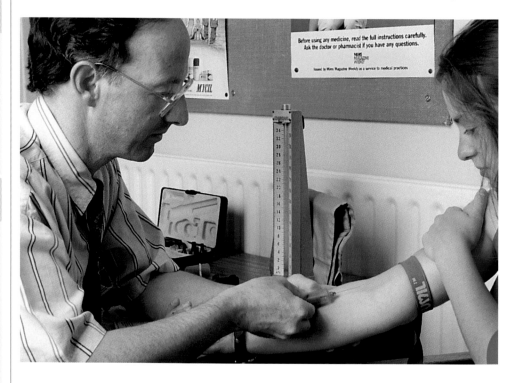

▲ *The doctor usually takes vaginal swabs to assess the presence of PID. However, the infection can be difficult to spot; further tests may be performed to confirm the diagnosis.*

▲ *Tenderness and swelling of the abdomen can be a sign of PID. The doctor may palpate the abdomen to look for these symptoms during a pelvic examination.*

menstruation, during urination or defecation, or when the woman moves around; lower-back pain; nausea; dizziness; and irregular or heavy bleeding.

Causes

As with all infections, PID can develop when a woman is exposed to an infecting agent. Women are most susceptible when their immune system is low. Around 80 percent of cases of PID are caused by sexually transmitted chlamydial infection or by gonorrhea. Other possible causes include herpes, HIV, syphilis, and genital warts (see Sexually Transmitted Diseases); the insertion or the removal of a contraceptive IUD; a termination of pregnancy (see Abortion); a miscarriage (see Miscarriage); giving birth; and abdominal surgery, for example, having an appendix removed.

Tests

If a woman experiences any of the symptoms listed above, she should visit her doctor or a hospital genitourinary (GU) clinic as soon as possible. To test for infection, a doctor will take swabs from the vagina and possibly from the cervix. The procedure is similar to a Pap smear (see Pap Smear). A pelvic examination may be given in which the doctor inserts two fingers into the vagina, while feeling the abdomen for any tenderness or swelling.

Further tests might include swabs from the urethra and from the rectum, as well as blood and urine tests. Less commonly, a doctor might perform an ultrasound scan or an endometrial biopsy. In some cases, although this is quite rare, a laparoscopy is performed (see Laparoscopy). During an ultrasound scan, a transducer that transmits sound waves is passed over the abdomen so that a picture of the internal organs appears on a screen. It is a completely painless

procedure and does not appear to be harmful (see Ultrasound). An endometrial biopsy involves passing a small tube into the uterus so that a sample of tissue can be taken. Although the procedure is uncomfortable, it is not painful.

Laparoscopy is the only sure way to diagnose PID, and this is usually done under a general anesthetic, although occasionally only a local anesthetic is administered (see Anesthetics).

Treatment

Treatment is with antibiotics—usually with several kinds, because different infections have to be treated with different drugs. This is why it is so important to identify the infections correctly.

If a woman has acute PID, she may be admitted to the hospital so that the antibiotics can be administered intravenously and her condition, and reaction to the drugs, more carefully monitored.

Some women require bed rest; some do not. If a woman is in extreme pain, walking may exacerbate it. Resting in bed can be beneficial because it stops the infection from spreading and stops the organs from moving around and becoming further inflamed.

Fast treatment is vital to prevent future problems. In one study, women who received treatment within two days had no complications, whereas 30 percent of women who did not receive any treatment for a week or more had reduced fertility as a result (see Infertility).

It is important that a woman makes sure her partner is tested and treated for the infection, and that she does not have sexual intercourse until she and her partner have completed a course of antibiotics and recover from the infection. Sometimes, a woman may be offered surgery, particularly if she has chronic symptoms. However, surgery does not always help, and if any organs are removed it it is possible she will never be able to conceive.

A fallopian tube may be removed if it is damaged, because if it is not removed there will always be a risk of ectopic pregnancy. This condition occurs when a fertilized egg is unable to travel to the uterus and starts to grow in the fallopian tube instead. Ectopic pregnancy can be very dangerous for the mother (see Ectopic Pregnancy).

Self-help

Antibiotics can destroy the body's beneficial bacteria as well as the harmful ones, and so upset the body's natural balance. Drinking probiotic preparations and taking acidophilus pills (available from health food stores) will help put back the beneficial bacteria.

Once a woman has had an attack of PID she is more likely to develop it again, so it is very important for her to pay attention to personal hygiene (see Hygiene). To prevent PID, or any other STD, a barrier contraceptive such as a condom should always be used, especially if the partner's sexual history is unknown.

Checkups are essential at least twice a year at a genitourinary (GU) clinic if a woman is having sex in any relationship other than one that is monogamous and long-term.

If a woman is pregnant, she should be tested for infection and treated if necessary. This also applies to any treatment that opens up the cervix (having an IUD fitted, for example), or if a woman is about to have an abortion.

Many women find vitamin supplements beneficial, and they may help the immune system to fight disease.

See also: Antibiotics; Biopsy; Internal examination

Pelvis

Questions and Answers

Are women who have had babies more likely to get pelvic problems later in life?

Yes. The main reason is that some of the joints in the pelvis (especially those at the back called the sacroiliac joints) and their ligaments become loose during pregnancy to make the birth easier. In most women they never again become as firm as they were before the birth. The abnormal movement of bones at these joints causes backache; good posture and regular pelvic exercises, especially during pregnancy, should give at least a degree of relief.

My elderly mother will not believe me when I say that walking with a stick will help take the strain off her weak pelvis. Who is right?

You are correct in saying that a walking stick will help take the strain off her pelvis. Your mother may feel that using a stick is a sign that she has given in to the fact that she is getting a little unsteady on her legs. Instead of arguing with her, get a close family friend or your family doctor to talk with her. Or try tactfully to tell her that by helping herself she will in fact prolong her active life.

I have heard that the size of a woman's feet will give her an indication as to whether her pelvis is wide enough to allow the natural birth of her child. Is this true?

No. There is no rule relating foot length to pelvis width. Anyway, babies as well as their mothers vary in size. At a prenatal clinic all women have the size of the pelvis checked in relation to the size of their baby to see whether they will be able to give birth easily. In general, tall mothers usually have a large enough pelvis for this, but mothers who are less than 5 ft. (1.5 m) tall are more likely to have a problem giving birth.

Like a large bony hoop, the pelvis forms a complete ring around the lower part of the human body. It protects the organs within, forms a framework for muscles, and is the base to which the legs are hinged.

The pelvis is designed to bear the weight of the human body when it is running, walking, standing, or sitting. In women, the pelvis is relatively wide to help accommodate the presence of the growing fetus during pregnancy, and at the same time to partially protect it. The width of the pelvis gives a woman's hips a characteristic shape. Pelvic problems are most usually the result of damage or deformity of the bones and the muscles and ligaments connected to them (see Ligaments). Many such problems manifest themselves as backache and associated pains.

The bones and joints

The pelvis is constructed from a group of immensely strong bones. The back of the pelvis is made up of the sacrum, a triangular structure that forms the base of the spine, and consists of five individual bones or vertebrae fused together to form a solid structure. No movement is possible between these bones. Attached to the base of the sacrum is a small projection of bone, the rudimentary human tail or coccyx, made from four fused vertebrae. The joint between the sacrum and the coccyx is padded with a disk of fiber-impregnated cartilage. In young people, some movement is possible at this joint, but it becomes rigid later in life. In young people, too, there are true joints between the bones of the coccyx, although this is more pronounced in girls.

Joined to each side of the sacrum is a massive hipbone or ilium; its curved top can easily be felt through the skin. The ilium is filled with marrow and is one of the major sites of blood cell

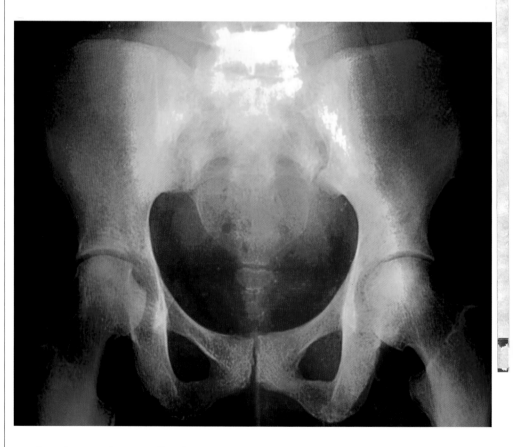

▲ *The pelvis is a large girdle of bone that protects many of the interior organs. Attached to the pelvis by ball-and-socket joints are the thighbones.*

PELVIC MUSCLES (FEMALE, FRONT VIEW)

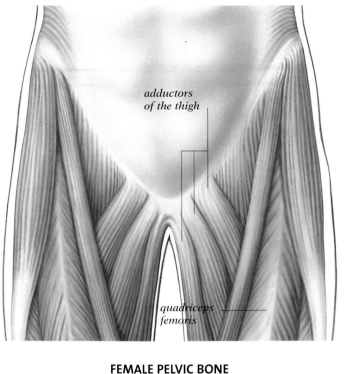

adductors of the thigh

quadriceps femoris

PELVIC MUSCLES (MALE, REAR VIEW)

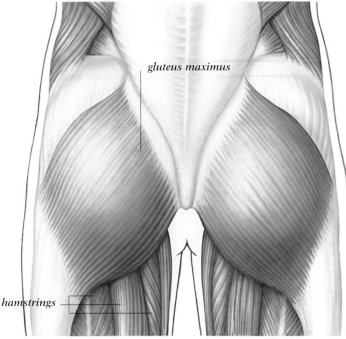

gluteus maximus

hamstrings

FEMALE PELVIC BONE

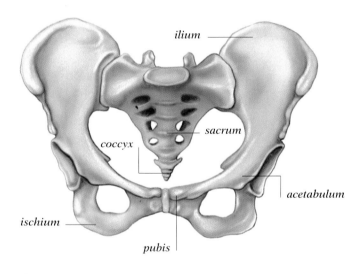

ilium

sacrum

coccyx

acetabulum

ischium

pubis

MALE PELVIC BONE

ilium

sacrum

coccyx

acetabulum

ischium

pubis

production. The vertical sacroiliac joints between the sacrum and ilium are toughened with fibers and bound with a crisscross series of ligaments. The surfaces of the bones are slightly notched, so they fit together like a loosely connected jigsaw, to give extra stability.

About two-thirds of the way down each ilium is a deep socket, the acetabulum, which is perfectly shaped to accommodate the ball at the end of the femur or thighbone. Below this socket, the hip bone curves around toward the front of the body. This part of the pelvis is the pubis and it is supplemented by a loop of bone known as the ischium, which forms the basis of the buttock. At the front of the body, the two pubic bones come together at a joint called the pubic symphysis. Padding the junction between the two bones is a disk of cartilage called the interpubic disk (see Cartilage). More ligaments bind this joint together and also run from the top of it to the ilium to help keep the pelvis stable.

Sexual differences

Of all the bones in the body those of the pelvis show the most difference between male and female, for the simple reason that the female pelvis has to provide more space inside the body to allow for the development of the fetus. The pelvis of a man is relatively much longer and narrower than that of a woman, and because it has to bear a greater weight, consists of bone that is much less delicately molded. Thus the cavity created by a woman's pelvic bones is boat-shaped, and that of a man heart-shaped.

Because of the shape of her hip bones, and the shape and angle of placement of their sockets or acetabula, a woman stands with her feet relatively wider apart than a man, and with her legs at a different angle to her pelvis. The joints of a woman's pelvis also change during pregnancy to allow for expansion during the process of birth (see Birth).

Questions and Answers

Why do women swing their hips more than men when they walk?

The reason for this lies in the shape and positioning of the pelvis. In women, the pelvis is, comparatively speaking, much wider than in men and more tilted, and the bones of the thighs join the female pelvis at a different angle. Therefore, a woman thrusts her legs out at a wider angle as she walks and this, in turn, makes her hips swing more than a man's.

I had a sneezing fit recently and felt weak in the pelvis afterward. Can sneezing strain your pelvis?

Yes, both sneezing and coughing can strain the internal muscles of the pelvic region because both actions lead to a large buildup of pressure inside the abdomen, and, as they expel air at high speed from the body, demand powerful contractions of the pelvic muscles. The reason the pelvic floor muscles contract strongly during a sneeze or cough is to ensure that bowel contents are retained.

I had my first baby normally, but I am much larger this time. Does this mean my pelvis may not be able to accommodate the birth?

Only your obstetrician can answer this question by doing an internal pelvic examination. However, often women seem much larger in their second pregnancies than in their first because their abdominal muscles are not so tight.

Can some exercises actually damage your pelvis?

If you are careful, you should have no problems. However, one exercise can damage the pelvic muscles: the one in which you lie on your back and lift both legs in the air, keeping the knees straight. If you have any hint of pelvic trouble, avoid this exercise. It can be particularly damaging for a mother who has recently given birth, and should never be attempted as a postnatal exercise.

Balance and movement

When a person is standing upright, his or her center of gravity lies near the middle of the pelvis and acts vertically downward. When the person moves his or her pelvis or feet, the center of gravity will readily move outside the supporting base of the feet. Unless the person makes appropriate correcting movements, he or she will fall over (see Balance). Thus throughout each moment of a person's everyday life, except when he or she is lying down, the pelvis bears the weight of all the upper part of the body (the head, arms, and trunk).

The human skeleton is constructed in such a way that it is possible for the body to stay upright, on two legs, without falling over. As part of this design, the pelvis is not absolutely vertical but positioned at a tilt. This tilt, which is more pronounced in women than in men, makes it possible for a person to swing the hips and bear the weight on alternate legs as he

EXERCISES FOR THE PELVIS

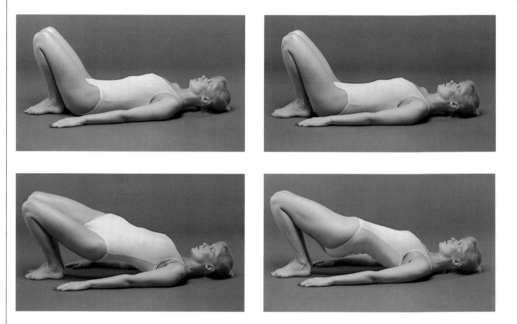

▲ *This exercise, called pelvic rotation, helps loosen the back, pelvis, and hips. Lie on your back with your arms to your sides and your knees bent. Put your feet flat on the floor or as near to the buttocks as possible. Raise your hips off the ground and rotate your pelvis 10–20 times. Rest and repeat the rotation exercise.*

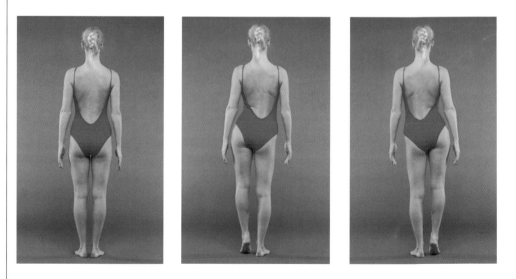

▲ *The pelvic side lift: standing, lift the left side of the pelvis toward the shoulder, but keep your shoulders in a straight line. Repeat with the right side.*

STRUCTURE OF THE MALE AND FEMALE PELVIS

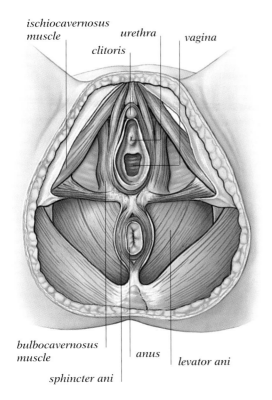

ischiocavernosus muscle

clitoris

urethra

vagina

bulbocavernosus muscle

anus

sphincter ani

levator ani

◄ *The boat-shaped female pelvis houses all the female reproductive organs and provides enough space inside the body to allow for the development of the fetus. The pelvic diaphragm protects the internal organs.*

► *The heart-shaped pelvis of a man is much longer and narrower than that of a woman's, and because a man's pelvis has to bear more weight, it consists of less delicately molded bone. The pelvis of a man also contains glands that act as lubricants for the external sex organs of the man.*

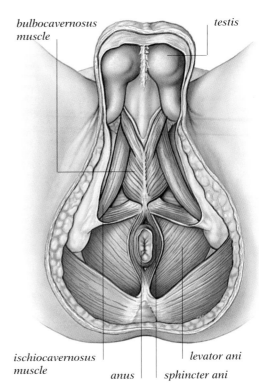

bulbocavernosus muscle

testis

ischiocavernosus muscle

anus

levator ani

sphincter ani

or she walks. Without the tilt, the hips would be too vertical and the person would fall flat on his or her face. At every footfall, the pelvis and particularly the hip joints act as living shock absorbers for the stress energy that passes up the legs, and, in the course of a lifetime, prevent the whole skeleton from crumbling under too much stress.

The pelvis muscles

The muscles of the pelvis do two very separate jobs. One is to make body movements possible; the other is to hold in the contents of the abdomen, and, quite literally, prevent them from falling out of the body.

The pelvic muscles used for movement are the piriformis, which run under the main muscles of the buttock; and the gluteus maximus and gluteus minimus, which join the top of the thighbone with the front of the sacrum. Contractions of the piriformis make it possible to move the thigh out sideways, as a person does when he or she is taking a step with the toes turned out to the sides (see Movement).

The other main muscle used for movement in the pelvis is the obdurator internis. Fanned out so that it is attached at several places within the bony pelvic ring, the muscle forms two large triangular sheets that join up with a tough tendon. This, in turn, is connected to the femur (leg bone). The main job of the obdurator internis is not to move the body from place to place but to keep the body stable when it is standing still. This muscle makes the continual adjustments that are needed in order to keep the stationary body balanced.

The other category of pelvic muscles are grouped together to form an elastic sheet of tissue called the pelvic diaphragm or pelvic floor. The two main muscles in this diaphragm are the levator ani, which forms most of the lower margin of the pelvic cavity and can

be felt working if a person pulls in at the anus; and the coccygeus, which supports the coccyx, particularly during the act of defecation and while a baby is being born.

The layers of tissue, including ligaments and small muscles, that lie over the pelvic diaphragm, together form the perineum. In women, however, the word "perineum" is often used to describe only the tissues between the anus and the opening of the vagina (see Anus; Vagina).

Internal organs

The pelvic diaphragm does not form a complete seal over the base of the pelvis. Inevitably, there must be gaps to allow for the passage of urine and feces out of the body and, in women, to make both sexual intercourse and childbirth possible (see Intercourse). These functions, affected by muscles, give a clue to the vital body organs that the pelvis protects—in both sexes, the bladder and the tube, the urethra, through which urine passes to the outside of the body; the lower part of the gastrointestinal tract; and the rectum and its exit, the anus (see Rectum). These exits are guarded by rings of muscle called sphincters which, in adults, can be relaxed by conscious control to allow urination and defecation.

In men, essential glands that act as lubricants for the externally placed sex organs are found within the pelvis, among them the prostate and seminal vesicles (see Prostate Gland). In women, all the reproductive organs are housed within the pelvis—the ovaries, fallopian tubes, uterus (womb), and vagina (see Ovaries; Uterus). The vagina also has a sphincter muscle, which contracts powerfully during intercourse (see Orgasm).

Like all parts of the body the pelvis has a supply of blood vessels and nerves, and the main ones lie near the bones. Passing in front of the pelvis are the femoral nerve and femoral blood vessel supplying the thigh. Beneath the sacroiliac joint, through a gap

◄ During pregnancy, there is additional strain on the muscles of the back, which can lead to backache if the correct posture is not maintained.

In both women and men, it is important that the pelvis is strong enough to support the body's weight and to take the strain of movement. Rickets, a disease that retards bone growth and may weaken bone, is caused by a lack of vitamin D and is a significant cause not only of poor pelvic development but also of pelvic weakness (see Rickets).

The tilt of the pelvis that makes an upright, two-legged stance possible in the human body also leads to problems, the most common of which is backache. This arises from many causes, including, most commonly, strain of the muscles which are joined to the sacrum and whose contractions help move the pelvis, and problems with the sacroiliac joints. These joints often have such problems because they have little muscular support. The softening of the ligaments that bind the joint at the end of pregnancy results in a characteristic lower-back pain which may persist after the baby is born. A similar sort of pain arises from any trouble experienced at this joint (see Lower-Back Pain).

Accidents that lead to pelvic injuries are uncommon, but they can happen. Falls from heights and crushing blows may break any of the bones in the pelvis. If this happens, the great risk is that the broken ends of bone may pierce one of the internal organs, particularly the bladder. For this reason, and because this sort of accident may well involve spinal injuries, the victim should never be moved. The paramedics who are called to the scene will most likely bind the person's legs and feet together just enough to restrict movement. If possible, they will try to prevent the victim from urinating. If the bladder or ureter has been ruptured, the urine will leak into the internal tissues during urination and cause irritation. With sufficient bed rest and prompt treatment a fractured pelvis usually heals in a couple of months.

Apart from tears that occur during labor, the most common problem affecting the muscles of the pelvic diaphragm is weakness leading to dropping or prolapse of the pelvic organs. This is especially the case following childbirth. One symptom of such weakness is so-called stress incontinence, that is, leakage of urine or feces when a person puts stress on the muscles.

Preventive measures

To avoid back pain resulting from strained pelvic muscles and ligaments, a person should attempt to adopt a good posture with the abdomen held well in and the back straight; lift things sensibly using the muscles of the arms and legs, and keeping the back straight so that excess strain is not put on the pelvic muscles and ligaments; and sit in a chair that provides support in the correct places (see Posture).

The best preventive measure for the pelvic weakness that can lead to the prolapse of the pelvic organs following childbirth is a series of exercises that a woman can do to strengthen her pelvic floor muscles during her pregnancy and afterward. If necessary, a repair operation can be done to strengthen the pelvic diaphragm.

between the ilium and the sacrum, runs the sciatic nerve, which extends up the back (see Sciatica).

Causes and treatment

Each of the separate organs within the pelvis can have specific things go wrong with it, and such problems may lead to pain either in the pelvis itself or in the back, legs, or abdomen. Some problems of the bony pelvis arise from disease of the bones that form the framework of the pelvis, or from conditions affecting the muscles that complete its base.

See also: **Back and backache; Bones; Fetus; Hip; Joints; Muscles; Pregnancy; Rectum; Skeleton; Spinal cord**

Penicillin

The power of penicillin—the first antibiotic ever to be invented—to destroy bacteria and combat potentially fatal infections has made it one of the most valuable drugs used in modern medicine.

Questions and Answers

Can the body build up a resistance to penicillin if you take too much of it?

The body itself does not build up a resistance to penicillin, although it will produce antibodies that attack penicillin. However, the bacteria that the penicillin attacks can become resistant, and some are capable of producing an enzyme (penicillinase) that renders penicillin inactive.

Whenever I take penicillin my urine smells very strong. Is this normal?

Yes, this distinctive smell is quite normal. Sixty percent of an injected dose of penicillin passes through the body very quickly and is excreted in the urine, making the urine smell of penicillin.

I have heard that some people have died after taking penicillin. Is this true?

Death is rare, but it has occurred in patients who are allergic to penicillin. The recorded cases of death were almost all due to misadministration of penicillin when the fact that the patient was allergic to it was overlooked. To avoid such errors (which are not always fatal but will make the patient feel very ill) people who are allergic to penicillin (or any other drugs) should wear a bracelet, or a tag around the neck, to inform others of their allergy in case of an emergency.

After I took penicillin I suffered from diarrhea. Why?

This depends on how the penicillin was administered. If you took the penicillin orally, that could be the reason. Mild diarrhea results if the penicillin kills off some of the resident and balanced population of bacteria that are naturally present in the human gut.

A discovery that was to revolutionize medicine was made in 1928 when a British bacteriologist, Alexander Fleming (1881–1955), noticed that one of his experimental culture plates of bacteria had been contaminated by spores from a mold. Later, he realized that the colonies of bacteria that were growing on the plate were beginning to die. He identified the mold as belonging to the Penicillium family, and he isolated the bacteria-killing substance secreted by the mold and named it penicillin. It was not until 10 years later, however, that clinical trials were performed, the curative properties were established, and the commercial production of the drug began. Penicillin was the first antibiotic to be developed, and it has since become one of the most

▲ *Penicillin is one of the most effective bacteria-killing drugs available today. Certain types of penicillin can be taken orally and are therefore very easy to use.*

Questions and Answers

Why is penicillin sometimes injected rather than taken orally?

The way penicillin is administered depends on the type of infection and the type of penicillin prescribed. Some penicillins are destroyed by the acid juices of the stomach and are only effective if they are given by injection. Other types of penicillin can withstand the acidity of the stomach and can be taken in pill or liquid form.

I keep hearing about different penicillins. Why are there so many?

The wide range of penicillins available allows the doctor to select the correct one for you. The decision is based on the nature of the infection (some bacteria have built up a tolerance to particular kinds of penicillin) and the patient's reaction to drugs.

I am allergic to penicillin. Does this mean that I have less defense against diseases? If I should need an antibiotic, are there any alternatives that I could take?

Penicillin allergy can be very dangerous and you should be aware that a number of penicillins have names that might not identify them as penicillin. There are now many other antibiotics that can be used instead of penicillin. In most, but not all, cases, they do not produce an allergic response in people who are allergic to penicillin.

I keep getting colds and bouts of the flu. My friend told me that next time I get ill I should go to my doctor for penicillin. Will it really help?

No. Your friend, like so many other people, believes that penicillin is a cure-all. However, neither penicillin nor any other antibiotic will have any effect on viruses and will do absolutely nothing to cure the common cold. In fact, if penicillin is overused, there is a danger that resistant strains of bacteria will develop.

◄ *Alexander Fleming is the man who revolutionized modern medicine when he discovered penicillin.*

valuable drugs available for the treatment of a wide range of bacterial infections (see Infection and Infectious Diseases).

How penicillin is made

The original extracts of the fermentation of the mold contained a mixture of many different penicillins. Penicillin is still made by growing the mold on a broth in large vats, but the addition of various chemicals has allowed a number of naturally produced penicillins, such as benzylpenicillin and phenoxymethlypenicillin, to be isolated and developed independently. Several semi-synthetic penicillins have also been produced. These are called semisynthetic because although the chemical structure of the penicillin has been altered, the basic structure of the drug is still produced by a process of fermentation.

How penicillin works

Penicillin works by destroying the cell walls of the bacteria that are multiplying, causing the bacteria to literally explode from internal pressure. It is not effective, however, against resting organisms that are not making new cell walls.

The great advantage of penicillin over the antiseptics that were in use before its discovery is that it does not affect human cells; the traditional antiseptic drugs were often more toxic than the bacteria themselves.

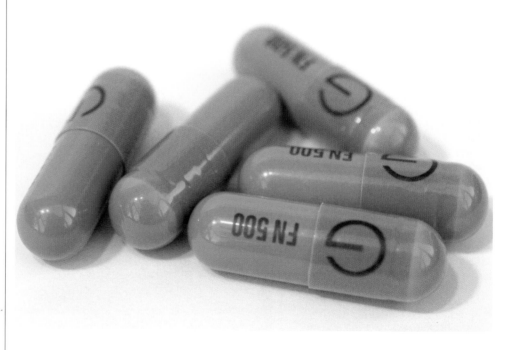

▲ *Flucloxacillin is a type of penicillin that is resistant to attacks by penicillinase, an enzyme that renders penicillin inactive. The drug is often used to treat skin infections.*

▲ *Penicillin is extracted from the mold* Penicillium notatum, *which is shown here growing as a fungus colony.*

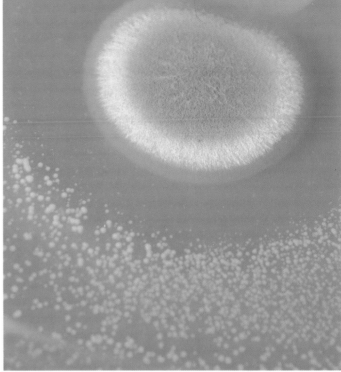

▲ *The penicillin from this mold form a barrier against the spread of bacteria.*

Some of the other antibiotics, such as the tetracyclines, work quite differently; they interfere with bacterial growth. Tetracycline and penicillin are less effective prescribed together than prescribed separately.

Uses

Penicillin can treat a wide range of bacterial infections, such as pneumonia, syphilis, gonorrhea, septic wounds, and sometimes tonsillitis (see Tonsils).

Depending on the type of infection, the severity of the condition, and the type of penicillin prescribed, dosages may be administered either by injection or orally (see Injections). To be effective when it is taken orally, the penicillin must be of a type that is resistant to the acid juices of the stomach.

Penicillin is distributed throughout the body, except to the nervous tissue and bone. Concentrations can vary, and sometimes it may be necessary to inject penicillin locally if high concentrations are required to treat specific infections in particular organs or parts of the body.

Dealing with possible problems

Penicillin is a very useful, effective, and safe drug if it is administered with care. In reality, there are only two dangers associated with its use: overuse, which leads to the development of resistant strains of bacteria and is the reason why penicillin should not be taken for trivial infections; and misuse when it is prescribed to patients who exhibit allergic responses.

Bacteria can become resistant to penicillin in two ways: they can develop a tolerance to the drug and become resistant; or they can produce an enzyme called penicillinase that breaks down the penicillin molecule, rendering it inactive (see Enzymes). Some of the semisynthetic penicillins have been produced specifically to be resistant to attack by penicillinase. Although this enzyme attacks the central ring of molecules that are common to all penicillins, the altered chemical structure of the semisynthetic variety (the addition of different side branches), reduces accessibility to the central ring and therefore increases its resistance to attack. Penicillins are sometimes given together with specific inhibitors of the enzymes that break down penicillins.

About 10 percent of people have allergic reactions to penicillin. A cross-allergy can also occur, so that a person who is allergic to one kind of penicillin may also be allergic to the others. The main symptoms are itching and rashes (see Eczema), swelling of the throat and face, swollen joints, and fevers. Other adverse symptoms that occur when penicillin is taken orally include sickness, diarrhea, heartburn, and itching in and around the anus.

There is no simple test to show a potential allergy to penicillin, so if there is a suspicion that a patient may be allergic to the drug, it is generally advisable to prescribe another kind of antibiotic.

However, if penicillin must be used, it is possible to perform some skin tests. These tests are not completely reliable, because the allergic reaction may actually be caused by breakdown products of penicillin in the body, or other products that are developed during the manufacturing process; but the tests do identify people who are likely to have a serious reaction to the medication, a reaction that, in extreme cases, could be fatal.

See also: **Allergies; Antibiotic-resistant bacteria; Antibiotics; Bacteria; Gonorrhea; Itches; Medicines; Pneumonia; Syphilis; Tetracyclines**

Penis and disorders

Questions and Answers

I have a growth on my penis that has steadily become larger over the last three months. I'm worried that it's cancer, but I'm too terrified to go to my doctor to find out.

Cancer of the penis is rare, and it is usually a persistent, slowly enlarging sore or ulcer rather than a growth. It sounds as though you have a genital wart. This is caused by a virus that is usually picked up during intercourse with someone who already has one. Warts are not dangerous, but they do become unsightly as they grow and multiply. You should go to your doctor or to a clinic to confirm the diagnosis and to be treated. The wart will usually disappear quickly after the treatment has been completed.

I have a slight discharge from the end of my penis when I get up in the morning. Should I see my doctor about it?

Yes, you would be wise to have some tests done. It sounds like a mild attack of a sexually transmitted disease, but it won't be certain until a sample of the discharge is looked at under a microscope. Some sexually transmitted conditions look mild but can develop with seriously permanent consequences for you and any sexual partners you have.

Is there a connection between the overall size of the penis and virility?

Length of penis varies from one person to another. The idea that a long penis makes a man a better lover is a myth. Someone with a penis that is shorter than average is still very capable of giving real pleasure to his partners. It is also true that a penis's dimensions when it is in a flaccid state have no bearing on its size when it is erect. A small organ may well be larger than expected when a full erection has been achieved.

The penis performs two distinct and unrelated vital functions. It penetrates the vagina so that sperm can pass from the man to fertilize the women, and it is an outlet for urine to pass out of the body.

The penis consists of a central tube called the urethra through which urine passes when a man urinates. This is also the track through which semen passes during sexual intercourse.

The urethra connects the bladder, where urine is stored, to an opening at the tip of the penis (the meatus). Semen enters the urethra during intercourse through a pair of tubes called the seminal ducts, or vas deferens, which join it shortly after it leaves the bladder. A tight ring of muscle at the opening from the bladder into the urethra keeps the passage closed. Urine emerges only when this is intended.

The penis usually hangs down in front of the scrotum, which is a wrinkled bag containing the testes in a slack or flaccid state. Penis length varies from 2½ to 5 inches (6 to 12 cm). When the penis is sexually stimulated, it becomes stiff and erect, usually pointing slightly upward. It is then 4 to 8 inches (10 to 20 cm) long. The tip of the penis, called the glans, is the most sensitive area. The valley behind the glans is the coronal sulcus; the main length of the penis is the body or shaft; and the area of the penis where it joins the lower abdomen is called the root.

CROSS SECTION OF THE PENIS AND ASSOCIATED ORGANS

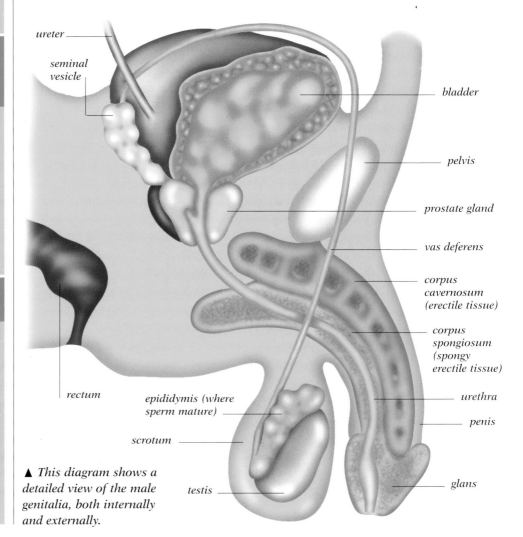

▲ *This diagram shows a detailed view of the male genitalia, both internally and externally.*

ANATOMY OF THE PENIS

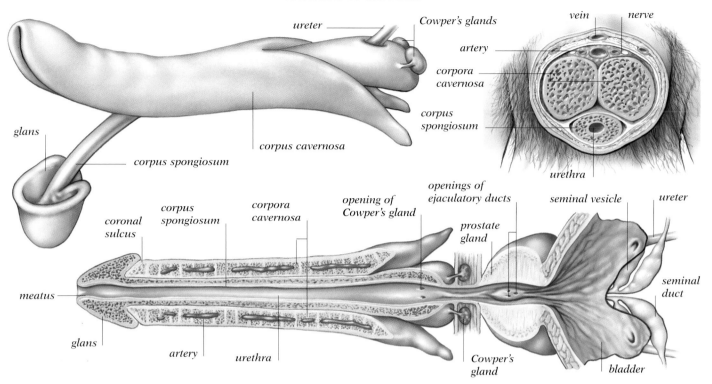

▲ *Above left is a detailed view of the penis, showing all of its parts. The section through the shaft of the penis (above right) shows the three groups of tissue responsible for erections. The longitudinal section of the penis (above) shows the path of the urethra.*

Erection

The largest part of the penis consists of three columns of spongy tissue that are responsible for erection. These areas are supplied with a rich network of blood vessels. When a man is sexually excited, the amount of blood that flows into these areas increases enormously. Engorgement with blood makes the penis longer, thicker, and rigid. It also rises as internal pressure increases. After ejaculation and after excitement subsides, blood flow diminishes and the penis returns to its flaccid state as the extra blood drains away (see Erection and Ejaculation).

The foreskin and the glans

The delicate glans is protected by a loose fold of skin called the foreskin or prepuce. As the penis becomes engorged with blood and enlarges during erection, the foreskin peels back to leave the glans exposed to the stimulation that eventually leads to orgasm.

Skin on the glans and foreskin produces a greasy substance called smegma that acts as a lubricant facilitating the movement of the foreskin over the glans. It is important to wash this away regularly. Failure to do so can result in soreness or inflammation of the foreskin and a condition called balanitis. Repeated or persistent balanitis is sometimes a medical reason for performing a circumcision, if it has not been performed at birth or for religious reasons (see Circumcision).

Infections

The chief hazard to which the penis is exposed is infection, particularly sexually transmitted infections called sexually transmitted diseases (STDs). An inflammation of the urethra, when it discharges pus, is usually accompanied by discomfort or pain in passing urine. This condition is called urethritis. It can be caused by gonorrhea, when the discharge is copious and yellow (see Gonorrhea); or by chlamydial conditions, when the discharge is likely to be less, as well as more mucuslike in appearance. These conditions are potentially dangerous, both to the patient and to his sexual partners, and they should be treated as soon as possible.

A more serious, but less common, disease that makes its initial attack on the penis is syphilis. This normally shows itself as a single ulcer near the head of the penis (see Ulcers). This is a shallow, punched-out ulcer with a base like wet leather that is teeming with the spirochaetes of syphilis. It will heal in a few days, but this is only the first stage. If it is left untreated, syphilis will continue to develop and may eventually become fatal (see Syphilis).

Another condition that may affect the penis is phimosis, in which the foreskin is too tight to peel back during an erection or sticks to the glans. In paraphimosis, the foreskin forms a band around the coronal sulcus and causes the tip of the penis to swell up. Herpes genitalis causes small ulcers similar to cold sores to appear on the penis. Except for herpes genitalis, which is persistent, these conditions respond well to treatment (see Herpes).

Other problems

Severe problems to do with impotence can be treated effectively with the drug Viagra, which works by increasing the blood flow to the penis; or, if necessary, by surgically implantable devices (see Impotence).

See also: **Bladder and bladder problems; Genitals; Intercourse; Prostate gland; Semen; Sexually transmitted diseases; Sperm; Testes; Urethra; Urinary tract and disorders**

Peritoneum

The peritoneum lines the abdominal cavity and covers all the organs inside the abdomen, allowing them to move freely. However, if it becomes inflamed, the patient can become very sick with peritonitis.

The peritoneum is a thin membrane that lines the abdominal cavity. It also covers each of the organs contained within the abdomen.

The liver, stomach, and intestines are all covered with peritoneum, as are the spleen, gallbladder, pancreas, uterus (in women), and appendix. The peritoneum is so thin that if it was separated from the organs that it covers, it would be transparent. Despite this, it is also very strong. The way it is attached inside the abdominal cavity creates various spaces where fluid could collect in the event of leaking from one of the intra-abdominal organs.

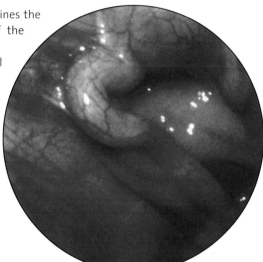

▲ *The peritoneum is the shiny membrane that covers this inflamed appendix; if the appendix ruptures, the peritoneum will become infected.*

The function of the peritoneum

The main function of the peritoneum in a healthy person is to allow the various bodily organs inside the abdomen to move freely. For example, when a person eats a meal, the stomach and the intestines become mobile and the muscles in the organ walls contract. This allows the food that has just been eaten to be mixed up and then propelled along on its journey through the digestive system (alimentary canal). During this process, both the stomach and the intestines are able to slide over one another largely because they are both covered with peritoneum; the two are also separated by a thin layer of lubricating fluid.

The peritoneum that covers the intra-abdominal organs, such as the stomach, pancreas, and so on, is called the visceral peritoneum. However, the peritoneum also lines the abdominal cavity, and where it does so, it is called the parietal peritoneum.

The parietal peritoneum has an extremely sensitive nerve supply, so that any injury or inflammation that occurs in this layer is felt by the patient as an acute localized pain. The visceral peritoneum, on the other hand, is not so sensitive and pain is experienced only if, for example, the intestine becomes stretched or distended. Even then, the pain is not very localized and is felt by the person as a dull ache, usually in the center of the abdomen. These differences in how pain is felt in the abdomen have an important bearing on the symptoms of various disorders of the intra-abdominal contents. In effect, differences in pain can often indicate the type of illness a person is suffering from (see Pain).

The omentum

One structure that should be mentioned in connection with the peritoneum is an extension of it called the omentum. Shaped a little like an apron, the omentum consists of fat with a rich blood supply and is itself covered with peritoneum. The omentum hangs down from the stomach and the large intestine, and its lower part is free to move about in the space between the intra-abdominal organs and the abdominal wall. Hence, the omentum can be found between the visceral and parietal peritoneum, outside the intestines.

The role of the omentum is to act as a fat store and to help limit infections in the abdominal cavity by sticking to whatever area may be affected and so isolating the area to some degree.

Ascites and adhesions

Two of the ways in which the peritoneum can be affected by disease are by ascites and adhesions. In ascites, there is an excess amount of the lubricating fluid that is normally present between the parietal and visceral layers. Either it is caused by an imbalance between the production and absorption of the amount of fluid—such as occurs when a person is suffering from liver disease—or it happens when the peritoneum is irritated to a minor degree over a long period of

POSITIONS OF THE PERITONEUM AND OMENTUM

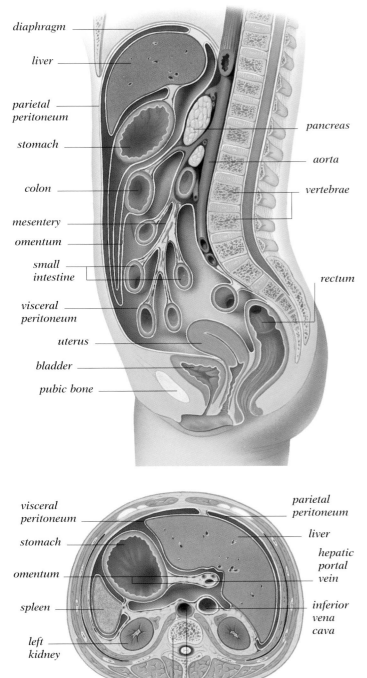

Cross section (above) and longitudinal section (top) of the abdomen, showing the parietal and visceral peritoneum.

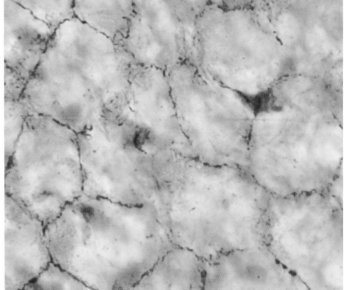

▲ *Mesothelium, the layer of flat cells of that gives rise to the squamous cells of the peritoneum. The membranes that surround the heart and lungs are made up of similar cells.*

time, as can happen with a slow-growing tumor. A person with ascites usually has a very distended abdomen, although often the distention is not accompanied by any sort of pain.

Normally, the intra-abdominal organs, such as the stomach and intestines, are attached to, or suspended from, the peritoneal cavity by mesenteries, fused double layers of peritoneal membrane. The mesentery, which contains a series of branching arteries, veins, lymph vessels, and nerves, is the lifeline of the organ to which it is attached. The organs have a certain amount of movement other than the action of the mesenteries. However, adhesions occur where a part of one of these organs becomes stuck to the abdominal wall or to another organ. This can happen after a person has an abdominal operation or after he or she has had peritonitis.

The effect of adhesions is twofold. First, the mobility of the organ involved is impaired, and this in turn may lead to obstruction of the large intestine. Second, the large intestine may twist around an adhesion, cutting off its blood supply; this could eventually lead to gangrene of the large intestine.

The symptoms of adhesions vary a great deal. They can range from recurrent attacks of abdominal pain to complete obstruction of the large intestine, which causes pain, constipation, and abdominal distention. Bowel obstruction as a result of an adhesion sometimes corrects itself without surgery. However, if it continues for more than a few hours, surgery is needed to divide the adhesion and to check that the bowel has not become gangrenous (see Gangrene). Adhesions that occur after an abdominal operation cannot be prevented. Some people are prone to recurrent adhesions.

Peritonitis

A third disease that can affect the peritoneum is peritonitis. In this, the peritoneum becomes inflamed owing to infection, irritation by harmful substances, or injury. The main symptom is pain, which differs from other pain in that it is constant and may be highly localized. A patient with peritonitis usually lies still, because any

PERITONEUM

Questions and Answers

Is a hole in the peritoneum likely to be a serious problem?

A puncture of just the peritoneum is usually of little consequence. Much more worrying would be a puncture of the intestines, the stomach, or other organs, which could cause peritonitis. Also serious would be a puncture of a main blood vessel in the abdomen, which would cause hemorrhage into the peritoneal cavity.

Does peritonitis always lead to the formation of adhesions?

Yes. However, in many cases these adhesions disappear after a short time. The initial adhesions are made of a sticky substance secreted by the peritoneum. This may or may not eventually be converted into fibrous tissue.

If a person receives a knife wound to the abdomen, does peritonitis always result?

No. A knife can penetrate all the muscle layers and the peritoneum, enter the abdominal cavity some considerable distance, and still fail to puncture the intestine or a blood vessel. The intestine, which is covered with slippery peritoneum, often slides to one side of the knife blade.

I have a duodenal ulcer. How would I know if it had perforated?

You would experience severe pain all over the abdomen, quite unlike the indigestion-type pain you probably get now. It would be so severe that you would be unable to work or do anything else.

I have just had peritonitis from a burst appendix. How long will it be before I am back to normal?

If there are no complications, it usually takes about three months from the operation before you are completely back to normal. After this time, there shouldn't be any restrictions on what you can do.

movement of the abdomen is extremely painful. Even coughing and breathing may cause severe pain in the abdomen. However, patients who take narcotics or steroids may have peritonitis but because of the drugs would feel none of the usual pain.

With abdominal pain that is due to causes other than peritonitis, such as an obstruction with adhesions, the patient experiences waves of pain. When this pain reaches a peak, a person may roll around in agony, changing positions frequently. It is very unusual for someone with peritonitis to move around in this way.

When the peritonitis has been present for some hours, the peritoneum on the outside of the intestine becomes inflamed and the normal movements of the intestines (peristalsis) cease altogether. This state is known as paralytic ileus. Eventually, because nothing is passing through the alimentary canal, the stomach fills up with fluid, and this will cause the patient to vomit.

The spread of peritonitis can be prevented by the omentum, because it has the property of being able to stick to areas of inflammation, block infection, and so prevent the infection from spreading to the rest of the abdominal cavity.

When a doctor examines a patient for possible peritonitis, he or she will look for lack of movement of the abdominal wall, a feeling of rigidity when the abdomen is pressed, and an absence of intestinal sounds. The patient may show signs of shock—a fast pulse, low blood pressure, and pale and clammy skin (see Shock).

Causes of peritonitis

Peritonitis can be caused by various diseases, including acute appendicitis. In this condition, the appendix becomes inflamed and may eventually rupture, releasing pus into the peritoneal cavity. The initial symptom of appendicitis is sharp pain below the navel on the right side of the body, which is caused by the stretching of the appendix wall. However, when the pus is released, the parietal peritoneum becomes inflamed. As a result, the pain becomes localized in the area where the pus is—often the lower right side of the abdomen.

▲ *Boxers risk serious injuries, including blows to the abdomen. Such blows can in turn damage internal organs and lead to peritonitis.*

▲ *Although he had survived many death-defying stunts, the famous escapologist Harry Houdini died of peritonitis after being punched in the stomach.*

Symptoms of appendicitis
EARLY SYMPTOMS
Acute pain in the stomach that comes and goes.
Loss of appetite.
Constipation.
In children, a respiratory infection may have symptoms that imitate appendicitis; these could also be genuine symptoms.
LATER SYMPTOMS (GET MEDICAL HELP AT ONCE)
More pain in the appendix area (right lower abdomen).
Pain may move up or down from umbilicus (navel).
Slightly raised temperature: for example, 99.5°F (37.5°C).
Slight increase in pulse rate.
In children, peritonitis can follow rapidly when the appendix ruptures, usually in a matter of hours after the first onset of pain. Peritonitis is particularly serious in a young child because the omentum—the abdominal "policeman"—is not well developed, so the infection can spread rapidly.

If appendicitis is allowed to progress beyond this stage, it may become blocked off by the omentum and loops of small intestine, leading to the formation of a lump known as an appendix mass; alternatively, it may develop into widespread peritonitis. The latter situation is more common in young children, probably because the omentum is not yet fully developed. Peritonitis can have severe and sometimes fatal consequences.

Another cause of peritonitis is a perforated duodenal ulcer. In this case, a tiny hole is made by the ulcer through the wall of the duodenum, and this allows bile, pancreatic juice, and gastric juice to flood out into the space between the visceral and parietal peritoneum. These digestive juices have a corrosive effect, and if the resulting peritonitis is not treated at an early stage, a widespread infection will result and the patient will become extremely ill with bacterial peritonitis. Once again, this type of peritonitis can have fatal consequences.

Among the other causes of peritonitis is a condition called perforated diverticulitis. In this case a diverticulum—a blind-ended sac on the side of the large intestine—ruptures, with consequences similar to those of a ruptured appendix.

Peritonitis can also be caused by an injury to the stomach, such as a stabbing; as a result of a kick or heavy blow; or from an automobile accident. Peritonitis can be caused by infected fallopian tubes in women, and it can also be a complication of pancreatitis (see Pancreas and Disorders).

Treatment

The treatment of peritonitis obviously depends on the underlying cause. Most causes require an operation, but there is one cause—pancreatitis, which is diagnosed by a special blood test—in which surgery is considered unnecessary and even dangerous.

Because any person with peritonitis will have been vomiting constantly, he or she will be given fluid through an intravenous needle. If an infection is present, antibiotics will be given. A tube is usually passed into the stomach to drain off excess fluid.

The type of surgery (if it is to take place) will also depend on the cause of peritonitis. If it is caused by appendicitis, the appendix will be removed; if it is caused by a perforated ulcer, the perforation (hole) will be repaired. After the cause has been dealt with, the abdominal cavity is washed out with warm saline (salt) water.

Outlook

Most people make a complete recovery from peritonitis, and within a few months their health is generally back to normal. Occasionally a patient can be troubled by recurrent adhesions that may require further surgery. In cases of peritonitis that involve the peritoneum in the pelvis, a woman may be left with fertility problems, as the fallopian tubes sometimes become blocked.

See also: Abdomen; Alimentary canal; Appendicitis; Diverticulitis; Pus; Stomach; Tumors; Ulcers; Vomiting

Pernicious anemia

Questions and Answers

My mother looks very pale. Could she have pernicious anemia?

Although all types of anemia make people look pale, people with pernicious anemia often have other symptoms, including prematurely gray hair and yellow skin. If your mother's paleness persists, make sure that she sees her doctor, who can diagnose the cause and decide on a treatment.

Does pernicious anemia run in families?

Pernicious anemia is one of several diseases in which the body's immune system turns against a normal part of the body. Problems with the immune system do run in families but may vary among family members.

My aunt is receiving injections for pernicious anemia. Will the condition correct itself, or will she have to continue treatment?

Pernicious anemia can be treated with lifelong injections of vitamin B12, which are usually given monthly. The injections will protect your aunt from the effects of the disease, but the underlying cause will not go away, so she will always need treatment.

I need a bone marrow examination for suspected pernicious anemia. How is this carried out, and is it really necessary?

The usual way of examining the bone marrow is to extract it through a needle from a pelvic bone or the breastbone. This is done under a local anesthetic. A blood film should indicate the disease, but bone marrow may be needed to confirm the diagnosis. The Schilling test may also be used to measure the body's absorption of vitamin B12.

This severe form of megaloblastic anemia is caused by an absence or lack of intrinsic factor in the stomach. It is characterized by a progressive decrease in the number of red blood cells, and can be controlled by vitamin B12 injections.

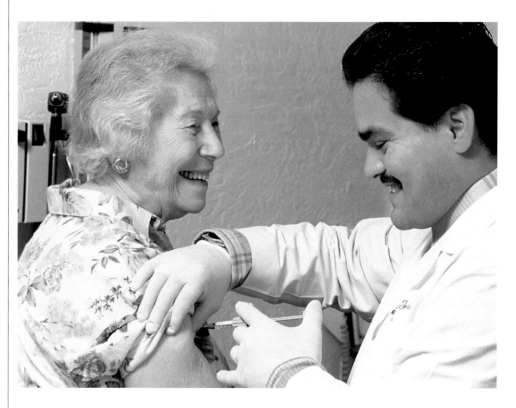

▲ *Regular injections of vitamin B12 help keep patients with pernicious anemia healthy.*

Anemia occurs when red blood cells fail to provide enough oxygen to the body, either because of a reduction in the number of red blood cells or because of a lack of hemoglobin, the oxygen-carrying substance within the cells (see Anemia). There are various types.

Pernicious anemia is a specific form of megaloblastic anemia: an anemia caused by a lack of either vitamin B12 or folic acid. These two vitamins are both necessary for the bone marrow to make an adequate number of healthy red blood cells. When either is deficient, the number of red blood cells is reduced; those that are released into the circulation are larger and more irregular than normal and fail to function effectively. Decreased numbers and immaturity of white (infection-fighting) blood cells and blood platelets may also occur (see Blood; Vitamins).

Causes

Pernicious anemia results when the body lacks intrinsic factor—a protein produced by the parietal cells of the stomach lining. Without it, vitamin B12 cannot be properly absorbed in the ileum (the last part of the small intestine; see Alimentary Canal).

An inability to make intrinsic factor is the most common cause of the disease. In adults this may be a result of chronic gastritis (inflammation of the stomach lining) or of surgery to remove the stomach. Rarely, infants are born with congenital pernicious anemia, a recessive inherited disorder (both parents must pass on the defective gene) in which the intrinsic factor produced is ineffective (see Heredity).

Other causes of pernicious anemia include autoimmune (defense) malfunctions in which the body produces antibodies that destroy either the stomach lining or the intrinsic factor (see Immune System); this may occur in association with autoimmune disorders that affect the

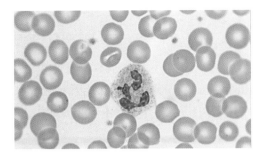

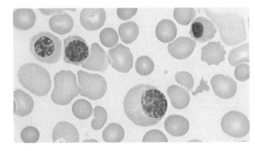

▲▼ *Compared with normal blood (above), the red blood cells in pernicious anemia (below) are large and irregular; the white blood cells are more segmented.*

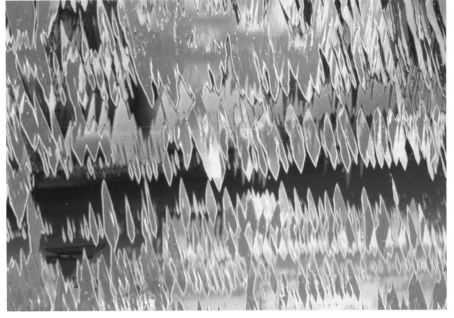

▲ *A photomicrograph of vitamin B12, a complex vitamin that plays a part in the synthesis of DNA. Without an adequate supply, the young red blood cells in the bone marrow fail to mature properly and many are destroyed.*

endocrine system, including type I diabetes, hypoparathyroidism, myasthenia gravis, and vitiligo (see Endocrine System; Parathyroid Glands). Pernicious anemia may also occur if there is any atrophy (wasting) of the stomach lining.

Risk factors
Pernicious anemia usually occurs only in people over age 35. Those of Scandinavian or northern European descent, or with a family history of pernicious anemia or autoimmune disorders of the endocrine system, are also more at risk of developing the disease.

Other causes of B12 deficiency
There may be other reasons for vitamin B12 deficiency, apart from pernicious anemia. These include certain diseases of the intestine, such as Crohn's disease and celiac disease (especially if the ileum is involved); intestinal infestation by parasites, or infection caused by bacterial overgrowth; inadequate nutrition during pregnancy or in strict vegetarians (vitamin B12 is found only in food of animal origin); some metabolic disorders; and certain drugs.

Signs and symptoms
Pernicious anemia takes a long time to develop because a B12 deficiency develops gradually, so the average age of diagnosis is 60. As well as inhibiting blood cell production, the disease affects other types of cell—including the sensory and motor cells—and the gastrointestinal system and the cardiovascular system.

The lack of red blood cells causes the typical symptoms of anemia: paleness, fatigue, breathlessness on mild exertion, and a rapid heart rate as the heart struggles to pump enough oxygen around the body. In severe cases, heart failure can occur.

Gastrointestinal disturbances such as loss of appetite and diarrhea may also occur; and since the cells lining the stomach are affected, there is a loss of normal hydrochloric acid production

(achlorhydia). Those affected may develop gastric polyps, and their risk of developing gastric cancer is doubled.

Other signs may include a smooth shiny tongue, bleeding gums, an impaired sense of smell, prematurely gray hair, and yellow skin due to jaundice. Epithelial changes may also cause a woman to have a falsely positive Pap smear (see Pap Smear).

The most serious complications are in the nervous system. Degeneration of the spinal cord may lead to tingling and numbness in the feet and hands, followed by weakness and difficulties in balancing. There may also be a deterioration in the person's mental state, a condition known as "megaloblastic madness." Neurological affects may be noticed before the anemia is diagnosed.

Treatment and outlook
At one time, pernicious anemia was usually fatal. In 1926, however, the American physicians George Minot and William Murphy found that patients rapidly improved if fed a diet rich in liver. Extracts for injection were soon developed, and in 1949 chemists in the United States and England identified vitamin B12 as the essential factor.

Today, vitamin B12 is given by injection into a muscle. Initially, several injections are given over a short period; this usually starts to have an effect within 48 to 72 hours, so blood transfusions are rarely necessary. After this, the injections are given on a regular basis either monthly or every three months; the defect in the stomach lining is permanent, so the treatment lasts for life. Occasionally, doctors may also recommend vitamin B12 pills, or a nasal spray. Patients will also be advised to eat enough folic acid, iron, and vitamin C for healthy blood development. Most of the complications caused by pernicious anemia are easily controlled, but if treatment is not given early enough, any neurological damage may not be fully reversible.

See also: Congenital disorders; Polyps; Spinal cord; Vitamin B

Personality

Personality is what makes someone an individual, different from everyone else. What each person inherits and what he or she experiences in life are factors that influence the development of the personality.

Is it true that the first five years of a child's life are critical in terms of the formation of personality?

Yes. A baby not only is absorbing information all the time but is more sensitive to his or her environment during this time than at any other time in the future. A child who has been overprotected in the first five years, for example, will tend to be hesitant about making contact with other people later in life; or if a child was not given enough affection in the first two years, his or her emotional responsiveness is likely to be stunted.

Studies have revealed patterns of behavior (which often repeat themselves over generations) that illustrate this. For example, girls who were cared for in a sensitive and intelligent way find it easier to give this sort of mothering to their children, who will, in turn, develop the same sensitivity.

Parents who physically damage their children also tend to pass on similar patterns of behavior: their children may become the same sort of parents. It seems that such parents have a lower sense of their own worth and find it hard to make their own children feel valued.

What is meant by a criminal personality? Are there certain characteristics that make a person more likely to turn to crime?

There is a school of thought that maintains that certain personality traits are more prevalent among criminals of both sexes than among noncriminals. The criminal type tends to be antisocial and impulsive, and cares little for the feelings of other people. This type of person also tends to be highly extroverted and emotional. These qualities may add up to a criminal personality, if such a term can be defined. However, in personality there really are no hard and fast rules.

Personality is often defined as the more or less constant pattern of behavior and way of thinking and feeling that characterizes an individual. Generally, an individual's personality remains much the same throughout his or her life. This means that a happy-go-lucky child will usually develop into an optimistic adult. Similarly, timid young people will generally maintain their nervousness and reserve as they get older, unless powerful influences combine to alter their apprehensions. This is not to say that individuals cannot modify their personality type if they really want to, but the process can take considerable effort over a long period of time.

Traits of personality

Perhaps the most easily noticed parts of personality are character traits, which are qualities that a person exhibits in certain situations. Honesty, meanness, perseverance, laziness, kindness, stubbornness, patience, courage, and modesty are all examples of character traits. Although a person may be said to possess a given trait, he or she will not, and is not expected to, display that trait in all circumstances. For example, a man may be scrupulously honest in all his business deals yet may take office stationery home without a second thought. A woman may be generous to her neighbors and friends yet could be thrifty to the point of meanness with her own family.

▲ *In any family it is normal for the children to have different personalities: the boisterous and outgoing child is quite normal, and so is her quiet, reflective sister.*

A child may be highly willful and aggressive at school, yet meek and mild at home. In spite of such variability, however, character traits are usually regarded as being part of the permanent personality if they occur regularly in a person.

Roles

The roles that people play in life are not attributes of personality in themselves, but they very much affect when and where people display various traits of their personality. For instance, in order to be successful, a man may find that, in his role of sales manager at work, he has to be aggressive, dominating, and quick to make firm decisions without consultation. At home, on the other hand, these qualities might be almost absent. His sales team would regard him as dominant in personality, whereas his wife may even think of him as quite submissive. The different roles he plays all appear to be very real parts of his personality.

Society encourages people to play roles by supporting them when they fit the stereotype for a particular role. Similarly, society tends to reject those people who do not fit a particular stereotype. A politician who admitted in public that he believed the opposing party had made a good decision or had a good policy on something would soon lose his job, whatever the facts of the matter. A mother who confessed that she felt no affection for her newborn child would probably be branded as cruel and inhuman.

Counselors not infrequently have to deal with clients whose personality lies more in the role that society has given them than in traits that they possess themselves (see Therapy).

Personality types

Since the display of a wide range of different traits is a matter of occasion and circumstances, many scientists have looked for broader classifications that describe a person better and more consistently. Perhaps the simplest classification is that developed by the English psychologist Hans Eysenck, who has reduced the variables to three: extroversion (as opposed to introversion), emotionality (versus stability), and tough-mindedness (as against tender-mindedness).

Everyone has these qualities to some extent, but the usefulness of Eysenck's system is that, instead of saying a person is or is not an introvert, for example, the three qualities can be estimated on a rating scale, giving an idea of just how extroverted, emotional, or tough-minded a person actually is.

It is also possible to show that these qualities are related to a person's speed of learning and various other phenomena that, on the surface, seem to have little to do with personality itself. The evidence implies that these three personality factors are real in themselves, rather than something observed by one person in one situation, as can happen with traits such as courage and honesty. Therefore, the three qualities could be built-in, and can be likened to continuous pressures that move a person to act in a certain way. Even when there may be circumstances in which, say, an emotional person finds it better to go against his or her natural inclination, the pressure to act emotionally will still be there.

Inherited or acquired?

Anyone who has brought up more than one child will be aware that children from the same family can show very different personalities almost from the moment they are born. This implies that some

▲ *Some actors and actresses can submerge themselves totally in the parts they play to project a different personality in every film. Robert De Niro has this ability. TV stars, such as Oprah Winfrey, project a particular personality on screen, which may be very different from their off-screen personality.*

aspects of personality are probably innate and may be determined genetically. However, since parents can, unknowingly, bring up successive children in very different ways, researchers have studied to what extent identical twins—who develop from a single egg and therefore have an identical genetic program—raised together have similar personalities. Results from the research show that identical twins are much more similar than fraternal twins—who develop from separate eggs and so have a different genetic makeup—or nontwin siblings (also different genetically) in their measures of emotionality, sociability, and tough-mindedness.

This suggests that in some respects personality is a matter of inheritance, but inheritance should not be thought of as the only factor, or even the most important factor, determining an individual's personality. Rather, many facets of the personality are influenced heavily by a person's experiences in life. For example,

Questions and Answers

I have often heard the term "split personality." Is there such a thing?

Yes, but it is rare. People with this condition behave in radically different ways at different times, almost as if more than one person inhabited the same body. Strictly speaking, the condition is known as "multiple personality."

Although it may be confused with schizophrenia—which means "split mind"—split personality has nothing to do with that condition. In schizophrenia, the patient's speech and thought processes are often split up and confused, whereas in multiple personality each personality within the same body is lucid and coherent.

Why do some people become so violent when they are drunk? My boyfriend seems to turn into a different person when he's had a lot to drink, and I become very afraid of him.

Aggression is a powerful element in every personality. It shows itself more in some people than in others, and most people succeed in keeping it in check. However, alcohol seems to release, or relax, the control mechanisms, and latent aggression may emerge.

Alcohol in large quantities also clouds judgment and acts as a depressant, which may put the drinker in a bad mood. These three effects combine to produce a cocktail, which can—as you say—make your boyfriend seem to be a different person.

Are twins likely to have the same personality or similar personalities?

Identical twins develop from the same egg, are of the same sex, and resemble each other closely, suggesting an identical genetic program. Fraternal twins develop from two separate eggs, are not necessarily of the same sex, and may not resemble each other physically. It does seem that identical twins are far more similar in personality than fraternal twins, who may have completely different personalities.

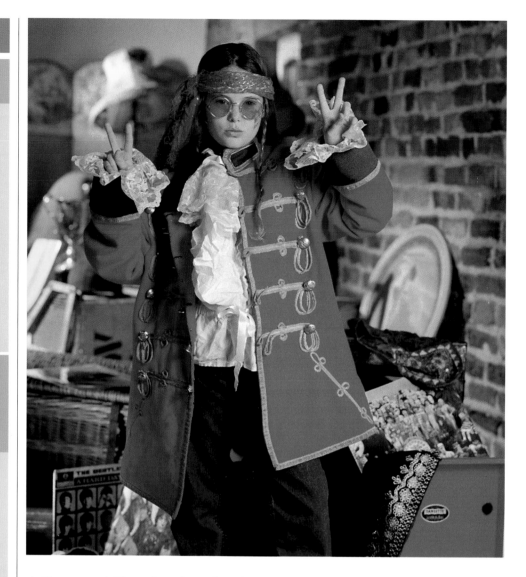

▲ *The games children play often reflect their personalities. When dressing up, an extroverted child will usually choose flamboyant clothes that attract attention.*

similarities in personality between fraternal twins, who generally have much the same upbringing but different genetic influences, show clearly the powerful influence of a person's upbringing. At the same time, the different ways in which an individual can behave in various circumstances—a timid, introverted person finding the courage to address a meeting on an issue about which he or she feels strongly, for instance—shows that people can change certain aspects of their personalities if they have to.

Abnormal personalities

One of the most significant consequences of measuring individuals' degrees of extroversion, emotionality, and tough-mindedness is the discovery that many of the mental illnesses and conditions dealt with by psychiatrists are associated with extremes of one or more of the personality characteristics described by Eysenck's tests.

Neurotic conditions, such as phobias, obsessions, and compulsive behavior, are generally associated with extreme emotionality (see Neuroses). In addition, people who tend to become severely depressed often show the same high emotionality; however, in such cases this is combined with very low extroversion—that is, depressed personality types tend to be highly introverted. Hysterical people, on the other hand, show high emotionality combined with very high levels of extroversion (see Hysteria).

Psychotic individuals, such as psychopaths and schizophrenics, differ from neurotic, depressive, and hysterical individuals in that they are often unexceptional in their degree of

▲ *Those hardy individuals who sail single-handed around the world must have an unusual degree of self-reliance to endure the stark loneliness of months at sea on their own.*

▶ *Francis Chichester on his yacht Gypsy Moth IV, on his famous solo circumnavigation.*

emotionality and extroversion. However, they are rated as extreme for tough-mindedness—so much so that the scale for tough-mindedness is actually called the "psychoticism scale."

Many criminals have been found to rate extremely high on all three of Eysenck's variables.

Changing personality

To some extent, all forms of psychotherapy are concerned with modifying how a person acts, thinks, and feels. This, by definition, is changing that individual's personality. A marital problem or some other relationship problem may, at least in part, be caused by a so-called clash of personalities, and its solution may involve getting the partners to change the way they behave, think, and feel.

Phobias and similar problems are often treated by reducing the anxiety of the person in question—through behavior therapy, for instance. If this is achieved, the patient will, on a personality questionnaire, seem to be less emotional—that is, this aspect of his or her personality will have been changed.

▲ *It is sometimes suggested that personality is predetermined by the astrological sign of the zodiac (a cyclical chart of the 12 signs, or constellations, as shown above) under which a person is born. Astrologers believe that certain personality traits are common to people who share the same birth sign.*

One fact has arisen from therapists' attempts to facilitate such personality changes in their patients. The neurosis of a shy, reserved introvert is much easier to cure than a similar condition in a brash, outgoing extrovert. Similarly, it is generally easier for a therapist to change an introvert into something of an extrovert than to quiet an extrovert and give that patient the reflectiveness of an introvert.

Influences on personality

It has already been mentioned that personality is modified as a person matures; however, other influences can also have effects of varying magnitude. Long periods of stress will increase a person's emotionality and aggressiveness and may also make that individual more reserved (see Stress).

Patterns of upbringing will also have some effect on a child's personality, although it is not easy to predict what the effect might be. For example, a child may follow the pattern set by one or both parents, or may rebel against both. Certainly parental influence is a very important factor, particularly in the first five years of a child's life. Studies have shown that some patterns of behavior are repeated in succeeding generations.

There is also no doubt that personality in its widest sense can be affected by the long-term effects of alcohol or drug abuse, by traumatic shock, and by brain injury.

What is less obvious, however, is just how constant the broad outlines of the personality of an individual remain, even when he or she is faced with powerful outside influences. The personality does not change under duress; rather, people change the way they display their personalities.

See also: **Anxiety; Behavior therapy; Depression; Drug abuse; Genetics; Phobias; Psychoses; Psychotherapy; Schizophrenia**

Perspiration

Questions and Answers

I perspire heavily all year round, but I always feel more sticky and uncomfortable during the winter. What can I do?

In summer you probably wear light, loose-fitting clothes that allow air to circulate around your body, keeping you drier. In winter you wear heavier clothes to keep warm, but these trap perspiration, since little air can flow around your skin, making you feel sticky and uncomfortable. During the winter, try wearing looser clothes made of natural fibers, which allow freer evaporation of water vapor.

Whenever I take off my shoes and socks my feet are sticky and smelly. Is there anything I can do to stop my feet from sweating?

The short answer is no. The soles of your feet, like the palms of your hands, have many hundreds of sweat glands that are important for controlling your body temperature. As most people know, hands and feet also feel sticky when one is nervous or excited. You will feel less sticky if you wash your feet regularly with soap and water, dry them carefully, and then dust them with talcum powder. This is especially important if you wear nylon pantyhose or socks, and shoes made of plastic or another synthetic fiber. Cotton or wool socks and leather shoes are better for absorbing water vapor.

I find that I need to use the toilet more frequently during the winter, particularly when I am cold. Why does this happen?

Fluid loss from the body is a delicate balance between loss through perspiration, loss of water vapor from the lungs, and loss through feces and urine. When you are cold you lose very little fluid through perspiration and have to make up the balance through extra loss in urine.

Perspiration is one of the most underrated of all the vital functions of the body. Without the built-in thermostat of the sweat glands, people would overheat and eventually die.

Normal body temperature has been standardized at 98.6°F (37°C). Although there are variations and daily fluctuations from person to person, it is essential that the normal or core temperature is kept constant. If the outside temperature rises too much, the human body cleverly maintains its core temperature by losing heat through the process of perspiration.

How perspiration works

A small amount of body heat is lost each day directly through the lungs and the skin without involving the sweat glands at all. However, this is a fairly inefficient way of losing heat. It is not a very flexible method, because a person cannot increase his or her breathing, as a panting dog can, to lose excess heat if it gets too hot.

Most of the heat loss that occurs every day results from perspiration or sweat production from the sweat glands. However, the liquid sweat usually evaporates from the skin before it can be noticed, and for this reason it is called insensible perspiration. It is this evaporation that allows heat to be lost from the body.

Insensible perspiration works on the principle that liquid needs energy to help it evaporate, in the same way that boiling water transforms it into steam. In human beings, that energy comes

FUNCTIONING OF A SWEAT GLAND

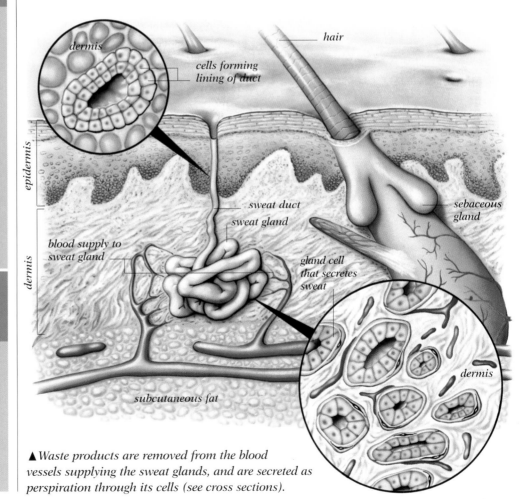

▲ *Waste products are removed from the blood vessels supplying the sweat glands, and are secreted as perspiration through its cells (see cross sections).*

My husband works in a steel mill, and a colleague was taken to the hospital with severe cramps. What caused them, and could my husband get them too?

If you work near a furnace, or even just live in a hot climate, when you are not used to it, you will perspire heavily. You lose more water than salt when you sweat, and too little of either can cause muscle cramps. It sounds as if your husband's colleague made the mistake of drinking lots of water without replacing the salt as well. If your husband gets very hot at work, make sure he takes extra salt as well as water.

I'm in my late forties and have just stopped having my menstrual periods. I also have hot flashes regularly, and I know this is normal during menopause. Sometimes I perspire a great deal as well. Is this normal?

Yes. During menopause, the hormonal and chemical balance in the body is disturbed. Hot flashes and sweats are caused when the body's thermostat overreacts to a garbled message. It's a bit like a furnace belting out heat because the thermostat registered that the room temperature had suddenly dropped to the freezing point. Cold sweats may also be a problem during menopause.

What's the best sort of deodorant or antiperspirant to use?

Body odor is caused by perspiration interacting with bacteria on the surface of the skin. Deodorants either mask the smell or inhibit the action of the bacteria, whereas the chemicals in antiperspirants stop the sweat glands from working by contracting the skin so that sweat cannot flow. Both types of protection can never be 100 percent effective and may cause irritation in people with sensitive skin. There is no substitute for regular washing with soap and water and for wearing clothes made from natural materials rather than from synthetic fibers.

► *During exercise, the human body can produce heat at a rate 10 to 20 times greater than when it is resting. To survive, the body must get rid of this excess heat, which is why people sweat so much when they are doing rigorous exercise.*

from the surface of the skin, and the effect of evaporating perspiration is to use up some of the heat and energy in the skin, leaving the person cooler. Once a person has become so hot that the perspiration is beginning to pour off his or her skin, the system has actually reached the stage where it can just barely cope. It takes only 1 calorie to raise 0.03 ounce (1 g) of water by 1.8°F (1°C), but it takes 539 calories to convert 0.03 ounce (1 g) of water from a liquid to a vapor state at the same temperature. This is the amount of heat that is taken from the body when each gram of sweat evaporates.

The sweat glands

The body is covered in sweat glands that produce liquid. Before puberty only one set of glands function, the eccrine glands. These are found all over the body except the lips and some parts of the sexual organs. There are many of these glands in thick-skinned areas such as the palms of the hands and the soles of the feet, and their activity is controlled both by the nervous system and by some hormones (see Feet; Hand). This means that as well as responding to changes in temperature they also react under other conditions—hence the sweaty hands when someone is excited and, later in life, the unexpected hot flash of menopause.

The other glands, the apocrine glands, are more complicated than the eccrine glands. Under a microscope they look like worm casts—highly complex coils. They develop and start to function during adolescence and are found in the armpits, the groin, and the areola (nipple) of the breast (see Adolescence). They are not associated with the nervous system, but the organic matter they produce does cause body odor if the body is not washed regularly. This is because organic matter reacts with bacteria in the skin, causing an offensive smell (see Bacteria).

Keeping clean

Normal sweating is an important function and should not be prevented completely. Washing daily with soap and water should be sufficient, though many people like to minimize the possibility of body odor by using a deodorant. However, never use a deodorant without washing first, since it could irritate your skin.

People who perspire heavily often want to reduce the wetness by using an antiperspirant, but some antiperspirants, particularly the roll-on variety, are not ideal because they work by blocking the glands and preventing the escape of sweat.

Continued use of antiperspirants could lead to irritation, particularly for those who have sensitive skin.

▲ The intense heat of the desert is made more bearable by the fact that the climate is very dry. Sweat can therefore evaporate more rapidly, cooling the skin.

Overheating

Perspiration from the eccrine glands does not consist simply of water; it also contains a wide range of chemicals found in the body, the most important being salt. People who perspire very heavily because of their work, or because they live in a hot environment, may lose up to 1.75 gallons (6.5 l) of fluid a day. They have to replace not only the lost fluid but the lost salt as well. They can either eat salty food or, if they can't keep food down, take salt tablets. Failure to do so can result in dizziness and headaches, a condition known as heat exhaustion. It is possible, however, to adapt to living in a hot environment; the body itself adjusts and excretes less salt.

If the body does not adapt fully to very hot weather, a person can run a slight risk of suffering from heatstroke. This is a very serious condition in which the body stops sweating completely, and the core temperature rises dramatically. If the person is not cooled down quickly, the result may be brain damage or even death. A far more common condition in hot weather is prickly heat. When exposed to the sun, the skin develops a red itchy rash. This happens because the sweat glands become blocked so that perspiration does not escape and an irritation occurs in the skin surrounding the gland. The best treatment is to stay out of the sun (see Prickly Heat).

Overheating can also occur when a person has a fever. Bacteria and viruses produce toxic substances that the body tries to kill by raising the thermostat. This raises the core temperature so that people with fevers sweat a lot.

Keeping cool

The body's cooling system works most efficiently in a drier atmosphere. If the atmosphere is humid as well as hot, perspiration cannot evaporate, and the film of perspiration that covers the skin stops the cooling process. This is why hot, humid climates are uncomfortable to live in, compared with hot, dry climates: it is impossible to remain cool. Likewise, tight-fitting clothes make people feel hot and sticky because their skin is bathed in a film of sweat, as if they were in a tropical rain forest. To stay cool in the heat, people should wear loose-fitting clothes so that air can circulate around their bodies. It is best to wear natural fibers, which will let the skin dry more easily.

See also: **Body odor; Feet; Fevers; Glands; Heat and heat disorders; Hot flashes; Menopause; Nervous system; Salt; Temperature**

Perthes' disease

Questions and Answers

My present doctor says that my five-year-old son has avascular necrosis of the head of the femur, which sounds rather worrying. My previous doctor said my son had Perthes' disease. Who is right?

Both. Perthes' disease is the same thing as avascular necrosis of the head of the femur.

What exactly is avascular necrosis?

Avascular means "without blood"; necrosis means "death." The term describes the effect on bone and cartilage of the loss of their full blood supply, which is necessary for healthy functioning. Normally only a part of the bone is involved and the rest remains healthy.

Is Perthes' disease painful?

Sometimes. The affected child may have an ache in the thigh or groin, or even in the knee, and movement of the hip can be painful. Surprisingly, however, pain is not a major feature of the disease.

My husband had Perthes' disease as a child and I'm worried that our son will have it too. Does the condition run in families?

Medical experts are not sure of this, but experience shows that it is rare for more than one member of a family to have the condition. Moreover, less than 10 percent of cases involve both hip joints. Thus it seems that the disease is unlikely to be hereditary, so you have no reason to worry.

Is it true that Perthes' disease affects boys more than girls?

Yes. The ratio of males to females with the disease is about four to one, although the reason for this is not known.

Perthes' disease is a disorder of the hip joint in which a segment of the rounded head of the thighbone (femur) loses its blood supply, becomes soft and crumbly, and no longer fits snugly into its socket. Usually, only one hip is affected.

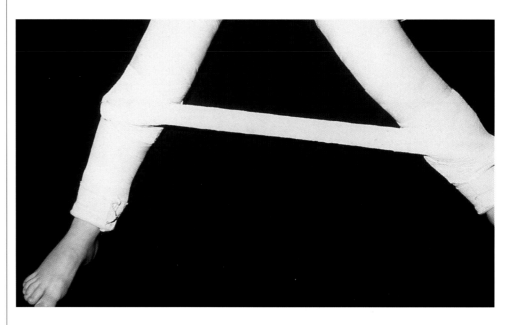

▲ *An orthopedic splint is used to reduce pressure on this child's diseased hip joint.*

Also called Legg-Calvé-Perthes' disease or avascular necrosis of the head of the femur (thighbone), Perthes' disease tends to appear between the ages of four and eight, although it can start as early as two or as late as 12. Although the shaft and neck of the femur have an excellent blood supply, the supply to the head of the femur is easily disrupted. How or why this happens is not known, but it has been suggested that injury, with bleeding into the joint, is the cause (see Joints). This theory seems to be supported by the higher incidence of accidents in boys; however, such bleeding always causes severe pain, which is not a major feature of Perthes' disease.

Perthes' disease usually starts with a painless limp that causes the child to lurch to the side of the affected joint. It has four stages. Stage one, which is visible on an X ray, is a widening of the space between the ball and cup of the hip joint (see Hip). Stage two is the appearance of a crescent of dense dead bone near the surface of the ball. In the third stage an extensive growth of new blood vessels occurs in the area, causing the dead bone to be reabsorbed. In the fourth stage, healthy new bone replaces the dead bone and reconstitutes the head of the femur.

Treatment and outlook

Treatment involves rest, followed by intermittent pulling (traction) on the joint over a 24-hour period. The patient may need to walk with a crutch until full movement is restored. If the soft top of the ball becomes flat, the cup will flatten also, so the joint must be retained in such a position that a round part of the ball joint presses against the cup. A splint may be used, or an operation may be needed to reposition the head of the femur.

Perthes' disease clears up by itself within two to three years, but early diagnosis is vital, since the joint distorts and may partially dislocate if the disease progresses unchecked. Both possibilities can cause degeneration, deformity, and later osteoarthritis. However, there may be few symptoms, even when the joint is deformed, so the disease can be overlooked. The outlook depends on how severely the head of the femur is damaged, but the younger the child, the better the outcome.

See also: **Bones; Limping; Osteoarthritis**

PET scanning

Questions and Answers

Positron emission tomography scanning is a sophisticated research tool that provides information about the dynamic functioning of the body. It may be used, for example, to detect a narrowed artery or the position of a tumor.

I am going to have a PET scan soon and I am a little apprehensive. Is it dangerous in any way?

No, not at all. Although PET scanning uses radioactive substances, the dose of radiation from material that is injected is negligible. In addition, the radiation lasts only for a very short period of time. Within minutes of completing the scan, all the radioactivity will have gone from your body. So having a PET scan is actually safer than having an X ray.

Does the patient feel anything during a PET scan?

As in other methods of body scanning, there is no physical sensation while a person is in the scanner. However, some people do suffer from claustrophobia. If the patient is worried about this, the doctor may prescribe a mild sedative. Also, before the scan, the patient will be given an intravenous shot, which may cause momentary pain.

I am due to have a PET scan of my brain. Will the doctors be able to read my thoughts?

Medical technology hasn't yet reached that stage and probably never will. PET scans simply give an indication of the metabolic activity of different areas of your brain by showing how much nutrient is being taken up in these areas.

I have been told I must go to a large hospital in another city to have my PET scan. Why can't I have it close to home?

Few hospitals are capable of providing PET scans because the equipment needed is so expensive and complex. However, recent advances in laser technology may make PET scanning cheaper and more widespread in the future.

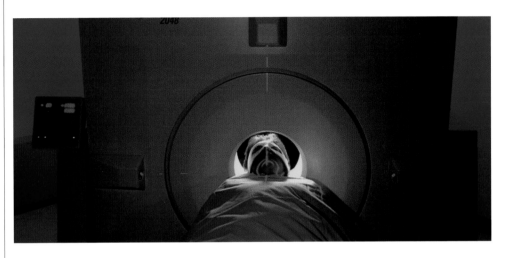

▲ *PET scanning is commonly used to monitor the biochemical activity of the brain.*

A positron is the antiparticle of an electron—that is, an electron with a positive charge instead of a negative charge. When a positron meets an electron, both are destroyed and gamma rays are emitted. In positron emission tomography (PET) scanning, a positron-emitting substance is introduced into the body and the amount of gamma radiation emitted is measured. This gives doctors an indication of the body's biochemical activity (see Metabolism).

Positron-emitting matter is made in a cyclotron—a powerful and expensive bombardment machine. This matter has a very short life, so the cyclotron must be in, or near, a hospital.

How is PET scanning carried out?
Positron-emitting isotopes can be incorporated into a range of biochemical substances, such as hormones or glucose. These substances are then injected into the bloodstream or inhaled.

Depending on the biochemical used, the positron-emitting material will quickly concentrate in selected parts of the body where, for a time, positrons will be given off. Each time a positron and an electron collide, a pair of gamma rays are given off. The patient is placed within a ring of gamma ray detectors, so that the point of origin of each pair of gamma rays can be determined. Tomographic (slice-oriented computer image construction) methods similar to those in CT scanning are used to build up, from the information, a picture of the biochemical activity of the area; the higher the concentration of gamma radiation, the greater the activity. Gamma radiation is converted into color-coded images to provide a graphic representation of activity.

Why is it done?
Biochemical activity is related to the amount of blood flow through the body tissue. If, for instance, a patient has a narrowed heart artery, the area of muscle supplied by it will have reduced biochemical activity. With use of a suitable isotope, this would show up on a PET scan.

An important application of PET scanning is in the investigation of brain activity. A PET scan can show the shifts of biochemical activity that correspond to different neurological functions. A PET scan can also show the difference in brain function between a person in normal mental health and someone with severe depression.

The outer edge of tumors often show higher metabolic activity than healthy tissue, so PET scans can indicate the exact site of a tumor.

See also: **Brain; Scans; Tumors**

Phantom pregnancy

Do any hormonal changes occur during a phantom pregnancy?

Relatively few studies of phantom pregnancy have been carried out, but a survey of the cases reported in medical literature of the 1960s revealed that many women did experience hormonal changes. Many of them had weakly positive pregnancy tests, suggesting that pituitary activity—which plays a major part in hormonal changes during pregnancy—was abnormal.

The pituitary gland influences menstruation by releasing a hormone that stimulates the development of a corpus luteum in the ovaries. If fertilization does not occur, the corpus luteum breaks down during menstruation, but in pregnancy it lasts for 14 to 16 weeks. Part of its role is to stimulate hormonal production until the placenta develops and takes over. Pregnancy tests are designed to detect the presence of these hormones.

Researchers believe that in a phantom pregnancy abnormal pituitary activity causes the corpus luteum to persist, as it would in pregnancy, so that it fails to stimulate menstruation.

How long does a phantom pregnancy last?

In the past, a diagnosis of pregnancy was largely dependent on observation and the woman's account of her symptoms. It was possible for the woman and her physician to persist in an incorrect diagnosis for the entire nine-month period, or longer. A famous case involved Mary Tudor, daughter of Henry VIII of England. She married Phillip II of Spain and first suspected she was pregnant in September 1554. It was not until July 1555 that her doctors admitted their diagnostic mistake. A second apparent pregnancy in 1557 was no more real, and some historians have speculated that it was ovarian or uterine cancer.

When a woman experiences false symptoms of pregnancy, she is said to have a phantom pregnancy. Although the physical symptoms are quite real, they are triggered by a powerful emotional disturbance.

A phantom pregnancy (pseudocyesis) is a rare psychosomatic illness, the symptoms of which may be so similar to those of a true pregnancy that they convince the sufferer and her relatives that the pregnancy is real (see Psychosomatic Problems).

Before the 20th century and the development of accurate methods of determining the presence and age of a fetus, experienced doctors and nurses could be taken in by a phantom pregnancy—only time would expose the illusion. Phantom pregnancies were rare even then, but they are even less common today.

Symptoms

A woman experiencing a phantom pregnancy may have every reason to believe that she is pregnant. She may fail to menstruate, or have scanty or wildly unpredictable periods. Her breasts may feel tender and appear enlarged and pigmented, and later they may begin to secrete milk. Morning sickness and a steadily enlarging abdomen are also characteristic of a false pregnancy. As time advances, the woman may even report quickening—the fluttering feeling caused by a fetus moving in the womb. Although this is usually caused by air and fluid moving in the intestine, or may merely be imaginary, it seems real enough to the woman, and without treatment, she may remain deluded.

Why does it happen?

Phantom pregnancy tends to occur in women who desperately want a child but seem unable to conceive, in women who are approaching menopause, and in women who have a deep-seated fear of becoming pregnant. It is also a sign of a deep emotional disturbance, tending to occur in women with hysterical personalities (see Hysteria).

▼ *A woman experiencing a phantom pregnancy will often have a distended abdomen.*

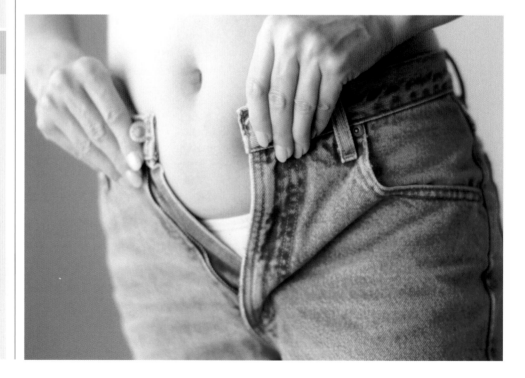

▲ *Mary Tudor, queen of England, was publicly humiliated when her celebrated pregnancies both turned out to be false.*

◄ *A woman's desire to have a child is a natural instinct, but in rare cases the craving may be so intense that it triggers a phantom pregnancy.*

The greatest problem a doctor faces is not diagnosing the condition, but convincing the woman of the diagnosis. Denying to her the reality of her deepest feelings can be difficult, since her sensations of pregnancy are not imaginary. Sixty percent of patients with symptoms of hysteria have distension of the abdomen, and 20–30 percent fail to menstruate. Even pregnancy tests may show weakly positive results. Indeed, the woman's strong conviction about her condition brings about the hormonal changes that cause her other bodily symptoms (see Hormones).

Diagnosis
Ultimately, it should be relatively easy for a doctor to determine whether or not the patient's symptoms indicate a true pregnancy. In normal pregnancies, tests may be only weakly positive at first, but the results become more strongly positive as the pregnancy advances. Also, although noticeable changes in the breasts and the cervix may be confusing, a careful manual examination in the first 14 weeks should quickly detect the presence, or absence, of a fetus. In a phantom pregnancy, the uterus never enlarges to a size of more than six weeks' pregnancy, however large the stomach appears. Moreover, should excessive fat, rigid muscles, or even a full bladder or intestine initially inhibit an internal examination, with time it soon becomes clear that the changes are not consistent with a true pregnancy.

What is the treatment?
If confronted by a patient with a phantom pregnancy, a doctor's first instinct should be to try to find the reason for it. By gaining the woman's confidence and patiently questioning her, a doctor might discover that she has a deep anxiety about either real or apparent infertility, or a strong fear of childbirth.

In time and with insight, the doctor may be able to suggest the truth about the woman's condition. Advice and reassurance can help to reduce any underlying anxieties in a patient who is not too deeply disturbed (see Anxiety).

Often, however, a woman with a phantom pregnancy may be unable to accept the diagnosis, or be unable to identify the emotional conflict over reproduction and the sexual role that the condition represents.

In extreme cases, psychotherapy or some other kind of therapy may be the only way in which such conflict may be resolved (see Psychotherapy; Therapy).

Does phantom pregnancy occur in men?
Male phantom pregnancies are so rare that they have become textbook curiosities, and few doctors have ever seen such a case. Curiously, however, most medical students are still taught to deal with the pregnancy symptoms, such as nausea, of expectant first-time fathers. Psychiatrists have traced the cause of male phantom pregnancy to role conflict: an anxiety state precipitated by either envy of, or distress over, the sufferer's partner's condition. This is significant testimony to the power of the unconscious mind.

See also: **Fetus; Menopause; Pregnancy; Psychiatry**

Pharmacy

I thought I was on a medication called propanolol, but my doctor wrote a different name on the prescription. When I had it filled I was given my usual pills. What was this all about?

This happens very frequently. When a new medication comes out, it is given an internationally accepted name (the generic name) that is used by pharmacologists, pharmacists, and doctors. However, the pharmaceutical company that manufactures the medication gives it a second name, the trade name. This leads to a confusing situation in which a medication has two names, and may have more if another company also decides to produce it. Your health plan may require the pharmacist to give you the generic drug unless otherwise instructed by your doctor. If you have any question as to whether you received the correct medication, ask your doctor or pharmacist.

Are there any tests that a doctor can do to see if someone is likely to suffer a reaction to a medication?

Yes, but there are only a few situations in which tests help to predict abnormal reactions. There are more situations in which a doctor can carry out tests during treatment to detect a reaction as early as possible.

Could something like the thalidomide disaster happen again?

When pregnant women took the drug thalidomide as a sedative, their babies were born with short, flipperlike limbs. As a result of this tragedy, far stricter regulations covering all new medications, especially those for pregnant women, were introduced. Despite the care that is taken with new medications, they can still turn out to have side effects that have not been found in any tests or trials.

Sometimes when people are ill, they are prescribed medication and expect it to make them well, never giving a thought to the process behind it. How are drugs developed, who makes drugs, and how are drugs dispensed?

▲ *Special bays are used for certain types of research work carried out by different pharmaceutical companies. The bays can be isolated by closing the shutter at the top.*

Until World War II, doctors had only a handful of truly effective drugs that they could rely on to treat diseases. In the 21st century, the situation is very different and doctors have hundreds of drugs to choose from, many of which come in a variety of forms. This enormous advance is a result of the work of pharmacologists—doctors and other scientists who study drugs—and the pharmaceutical industry, which does research and develops and manufactures drugs. Although this expansion has been of great value, it does create some problems. Both doctors and pharmacists, who are responsible for dispensing medications, need to keep abreast of all the new developments and be aware of the ways in which new medications can interfere with the action of other medications that the patients may be taking.

The process of making a medication from its basic ingredients and dispensing it from a drugstore on the doctor's instructions is long and complex, and it involves the expertise of many different people. In the past, the local pharmacy mixed up a prescription using a few basic ingredients. This procedure is rare now, and thus the job of the pharmacist has changed to one of dispensing ready-made ingredients from a manufacturer. However, dispensing has not become any easier, since there has been such a huge expansion in the number of medications.

Drug manufacture

The pharmaceutical industry has developed as part of a much larger general chemical industry. Many of the medications that are used around the world are made by large multinational companies that rival the huge oil companies in size and complexity.

When a pharmaceutical company produces a new medication, it can patent the process of manufacture for a period of 15 years. The patent allows the company to recover its investment in the research and development that led to the new medication. When a medication is no longer patented, any drug company can manufacture it, and there are many smaller companies whose trade consists entirely of making their own brands of tried and tested drugs, without ever developing anything new. These companies make drugs that are generally known by their internationally accepted generic name, rather than the trade name that the original company gave the drug when it was first introduced. The difference between generic and trade names explains why pills can be referred to by two different names—a situation that can often be of concern to a patient. Since different companies can make their own preparations, it is possible to be given a tablet that may be different in shape, size, and color from a previous prescription and yet still be exactly the same medication. There may, in some cases, be subtle but important differences between the generic and brand-name medications, such as the rate of absorption.

There are many stages that have to be gone through in the production of a medication. Although medicines can take various forms, ranging from aerosol inhalers to liquids, skin creams, and ointments to suppositories and drug-containing enemas, most of the medications used these days are taken in tablet or pill form (see Enema; Suppositories). Each tablet may contain only a few milligrams of the active compound. (Most tablets contain only one active compound, but there are many that contain a mixture of active ingredients.) The process of wrapping up these few milligrams of active compound into a pill that weighs hundreds of milligrams is called formulation. It is one of the traditional areas of interest to pharmacists, and many pharmacists work in the pharmaceutical industry developing formulations.

For a formulation to be effective, the final tablet has to be chemically stable enough to be left for a time on a pharmacy shelf. The tablet must also release the same amount of active compound

Who's who in the drug world

Pharmacist	The pharmacist has a degree in pharmacy and has studied all aspects of drugs, including their chemistry, pharmacology (see below), and formulation (the way drugs are made into pills and injections). Pharmacists are registered by a central authority in the same way that doctors, dentists, nurses, and physical therapists are registered.
Pharmacologist	Pharmacology is the study of the way drugs work on both people and animals. It is the basic science that enables us to build up our knowledge of drugs. Pharmacologists work both in industry and in universities. Most major hospitals have a department of pharmacology, which may also be part of a university to which the hospital is attached.
Pharmaceutical company	The pharmaceutical companies manufacture medications. There are many big multinational companies, but there are also a number of smaller companies that may produce only one or two medications. Much research that leads to the production of a new medication is undertaken by pharmaceutical companies that are often part of a larger general chemical concern.
Prescriber	The prescriber is the person who writes a prescription. This must be a doctor or dentist. Although the prescriber is responsible for the final effects of the medication prescribed, the dispenser (see below) is responsible for seeing that the instructions are followed accurately.
Dispenser	The dispenser fills the doctor's prescription. There are strict regulations about what must appear on the label of the container in which medications are dispensed. Very occasionally, a doctor or dentist may do his or her own dispensing, but otherwise this is done by a registered pharmacist in a drugstore, a dispensary within a health facility, or a hospital pharmacy department.
Toxicologist	Toxicology is a branch of pharmacology that studies poisoning. Drugs are a common cause, but by no means the only one.
Apothecary	This is an old-fashioned term to describe a person who not only practiced the sort of medicine that involved drugs (rather than surgery) but also made drugs up and dispensed them.

▲ *Many drugs are dispensed in pill form. The label on the drug's container will specify how many pills to take.*

▲ *During the process of creating an allergy vaccine, the allergenic material is dried in a greenhouse before it is converted into a concentrated extract.*

Questions and Answers

I have an old cure-all recipe from my grandmother. Will the pharmacist make it up for me?

The pharmacist would do this only if the medicine didn't contain substances that have to be obtained on prescription from a doctor. In that case you could buy all the ingredients and make it up yourself. However, many of these old-fashioned cure-alls are unlikely to be of much benefit, and could even be potentially dangerous.

My old prescriptions have all sorts of strange symbols written on them. What do these symbols mean?

In the past, a prescription was an instruction to the pharmacist to make up a complicated recipe of different ingredients. These days most medications come directly from a manufacturer, though the range of drugs is far wider. In a modern prescription, all the quantities are expressed in metric units: milligrams (mg) and grams (g) for weight, and milliliters (ml) for volumes of liquid. Sometimes the doctor uses the old apothecary's symbol for the number of tablets to be taken. These are like Roman numerals, with (ii) meaning 2, for example. The rest of the initials concern things such as whether the tablets should be taken before food, and how often they should be taken. These instructions are written on the label of the container.

On the container of the pills that my doctor prescribed for me it states that I must complete the course. How important is this?

Drug compliance, which means that the patient can be relied on to use a prescribed medication exactly as ordered by the doctor, is very important. Drugs are designed to work in specific ways for different conditions; some work on a sustained-release system, others are effective for a number of hours only. If you do not take all of the course prescribed, you may delay the cure.

▲ *Not all drugs come prepackaged, and a pharmacist may need to make them up by referring to a recipe.*

into the bloodstream after it is taken. Ideally, food should not affect the amount of drug that is released from tablets, but this ideal can be difficult to achieve. Therefore, the patient should always ask for and follow any instructions about whether the tablets are to be taken before, with, or after food.

An increasing number of drugs are being formulated in a special way so that the active ingredient is released slowly in the intestine and then absorbed into the bloodstream over the course of many hours. This is called sustained-release or delayed-action formulation. It allows the duration of action of drugs to be greatly extended so that people will not have to take tablets as often as they did before.

The mechanisms of commercial manufacture can make a great difference to the amount of active ingredient that is released into the body after a tablet is taken. It might be possible for two tablets to contain the same amount of active ingredient

The birth of a new drug	
The idea	Pharmacologists now know that the actions of body cells are controlled by hundreds of specific surface receptors for messenger substances and by thousands of enzymes. Greater knowledge of these receptors and enzymes has allowed pharmacists to develop chemical substances that activate, block, or modify the action of receptors or modify the function of enzymes so as to affect cell function usefully. Computers can be used to form models of these processes. "Virtual patients" or "virtual diseases" can be developed with software.
Toxicity tests	When a compound looks promising, the first step is to give it to animals (and, if it is successful, it is then given to humans at a later stage) to check that it does not cause any damage. In the final stages of development, more toxicity studies are done, including tests to see if fetuses are affected.
Volunteer studies	The first people to receive the compound will be volunteers. They will be monitored not only to see the drug's effect on the organ that it was designed to target (the heart or lungs, for example) but also to see whether there is any change in the standard tests of the function of the liver or kidneys, or in the number of the various cells in the blood.
Patient studies	By the time a drug has reached this stage, it has been intensively investigated to show that it has the desired effect and that there is no sign of serious toxicity. Carefully controlled trials are now carried out on patients who have the disease that the drug is designed to help. The situation is carefully explained to the patient, who gives what is known as his or her informed consent. Any study done on patients has to be approved by an independent hospital ethics committee.
Major trials	Following studies on small numbers of patients, larger trials are conducted. By this stage the drug has been shown to be of real value. The Food and Drug Administration (FDA) usually monitors each stage.
General release	After all these tests, the drug becomes available for general release and prescription by doctors. It is still kept under strict surveillance, however, and any side effects are reported to the FDA. General release is likely to occur several years after the drug was first developed.
Time and cost	Ten to 15 years, at a cost of about $250 million.

▲ *Prescriptions look mysterious to patients, but the signs and symbols are familiar to doctors and pharmacists.*

▲ *Druggists can recommend some medications that do not require a doctor's prescription for problems such as headaches, sore throat, stomach indigestion, or diarrhea.*

and yet one would release only half as much into the body. This is why manufacturing processes have to be standardized. There have been occasions in the past when companies have changed their manufacturing process and the strength of the tablets produced suddenly increased as a result. Because different manufacturing processes can produce tablets of different strengths, it is important that a patient should, if possible, continue to take the same brand of a particular pill if more than one brand is available.

Drug dispensing

Once a medication has been formulated into a satisfactory pill, it is sent out to hospital pharmacies and drugstores to be dispensed. Anyone dispensing a drug—that is, taking it from a shelf and putting it into a container that is then labeled and given to a patient according to the instructions on a doctor's prescription—has to be a registered pharmacist and also has to be working in registered premises. However, there are many active medications that can be bought over the counter from drugstores and do not require a doctor's prescription. These medications are typically used to treat minor conditions, and the drugstore pharmacist is often prepared to advise people about which is the most appropriate choice.

Drugstore pharmacists

The job of a dispensing drugstore pharmacist is more complicated than taking pills out of big bottles and putting them into smaller ones. The pharmacist has to be aware of all the correct doses of the many different drugs and, if unsure about a particular prescription, has to contact the doctor concerned to check a dosage. Pharmacists also keep up to date with the increasing number of ways that drugs can interact with each other, and for this reason also may contact the prescribing doctor if they know of a potential drug interaction.

In addition, the pharmacist has to make up various medications from ingredients that are supplied, and ensure that any special storage requirements for unstable drugs are met. There are also very stringent requirements about the way that certain medications, such as strong sedatives and morphinelike drugs, are kept secure. Additionally, pharmacists have to deal with the problems of supply that are common to any business. They have to know what medications are available and which are most likely to be used, so that they know which ones to carry.

Hospital pharmacies

For pharmacists who work in hospitals, the problems are very similar. Hospitals, however, use a much greater range of drugs, and considerable amounts of the drugs are needed. Certain specialized drugs are not very often required outside hospitals. The hospital pharmacy also has to supply all the various sorts of infusion fluid that doctors in the hospital may use (see Intravenous Infusion). Finally, the hospital pharmacist has to meet all the various drug requirements of special departments, such as the operating room and the neonatal intensive care unit.

Questions and Answers

My doctor's handwriting seems completely illegible. How can I be sure that my pharmacist is giving me the right medicine?

The pharmacist in your drugstore is probably practiced at reading doctors' writing and is able to decipher what you can't, particularly since he or she knows about medications and has some idea about what to expect. Moreover, a pharmacist will never dispense a drug unless he or she is sure about the doctor's intentions. This is why every prescription has to carry the doctor's address and, almost always, a telephone number as well. If a pharmacist is unsure, he or she will check with the doctor.

I was surprised when I heard my doctor call an ordinary aspirin a drug. You can't get addicted to aspirin, can you?

To a pharmacist or a doctor, a drug is any substance that is taken orally or applied to the skin to bring about some desired effect. If you think of it in this way, aspirin is one of our most powerful drugs, although you can buy it from a drugstore without a prescription. As far as addiction goes, only a minority of drugs are addictive. Although aspirin is not addictive, people can get into the habit of taking it in unhealthily large amounts. By and large, addictive drugs are those that give a lift to people who take them.

Is it usual for people to react differently to the same medication?

There is no medication that is entirely without side effects. There are two types of side effects. The risk of dose-related side effects is greater the higher the dose taken. If the dose was high enough, most people would be affected. To avoid side effects, whenever possible, doctors do not prescribe doses that are dangerous. With hypersensitivity or idiosyncratic side effects, a small proportion of people have a reaction, even when the drug is taken in small doses.

▲ *There are a number of manufacturing processes involved in the production of pills. Shown here are factory workers spraying on a special coating.*

Developing a new medication

There are many stages in the development of a new medication before it finds its way onto the shelf of a drugstore. The first stage is the development of the pure chemical substance that will eventually be formulated into the new tablets. Much of the work in the development of new medications is done by the pharmaceutical companies, but it all depends on the science of pharmacology, the study of the way drugs work. There are many departments of pharmacology in universities throughout the world, and in these the actions of drugs are explored without any commitment to the development of new products for sale. Most of the experimental testing of new medications is first carried out on animals, and exhaustive research is carried out not only to discover a drug's effectiveness, but also to see if it has any dangerous side effects (or toxicity).

A pharmacologist doesn't have to be a doctor: there are many scientists working in pharmacology who are concerned with very basic investigation of drugs, using either chemical testing methods or experimental techniques based on laboratory animals (see box on page 1552). However, medications given to humans must be prescribed by a qualified doctor.

After animal testing, there are three main phases of drug testing. The first phase, for safety and dosage, involves very few patients. The second test is for efficiency and involves a few patients. The third compares the new and the old drug. This is done on a large scale. Once a medication has reached the stage where it will be prescribed to humans, hospital specialists called clinical pharmacologists take over. Clinical pharmacologists specialize in the investigation of various medications, and departments of clinical pharmacology are usually found in teaching hospitals. The basic activities of pharmacologists and clinical pharmacologists overlap in many cases.

One of the most important techniques that pharmacologists use is sophisticated chemical testing to measure the levels of drugs in the blood. This enables them not only to look at the effects of new medications, but also to examine the different features of well-established medications, particularly the way they interact with other medications.

Pharmaceuticals have changed the face of medical treatment. Since the development of penicillin in 1941—a landmark in the history of drugs (see Penicillin)—a stream of effective remedies has been marketed for both old and new diseases: for example, selective serotonin reuptake inhibitors (SSRIs) such as Prozac (1987) and more recently Lexapro (2002) for the age-old disease of depression and Fuzeon (2003) for the relatively new disease of AIDS.

See also: Allergies; Hospitals; Medical ethics; Medical research; Medicines; Morphine; Poisoning; Sedatives; Side effects

Pharynx

Commonly referred to as the throat, the pharynx provides a vital link between the nose, mouth, and voice box. In so doing, it plays a major role in the essential tasks of breathing, eating, and speaking.

My son complains constantly of a sore throat. Does he need to have his tonsils out?

This is a question that only your doctor can answer, after having examined your son's tonsils. Constant sore throats in children are often caused by infections of the tonsils and disappear once the tonsils have been removed. However, this is not the only cause. If you are a smoker, it could be that inhaling your cigarette smoke is causing the problem.

Why is it that so many illnesses seem to start with a sore throat?

The reason seems to be twofold. First, some of the tissues found in the pharynx (throat) are part of the body's defense system against disease. These tissues become swollen and inflamed as they fight off bacteria and viruses. Second, if the body's defenses fail, disease-causing organisms attack the pharynx as well as other tissues.

When should I worry that a sore throat may be a strep throat?

Call your doctor if you cannot swallow liquids, if you have trouble breathing, if you have a fever over 101°F (38.3°C), if the nodes in your neck are swollen, if your tonsils are bright red or have spots of white pus on them, or if your sore throat lasts longer than a week. Children with sore throats should always get a throat culture.

My daughter's sore throat has developed into a middle-ear infection. Why?

This is a common complication of a sore throat because the infection travels easily from the pharynx to the middle ear via the eustachian tube. The condition is easily treated. You should consult your doctor as soon as possible.

The pharynx—usually called the throat—is the area at the back of the mouth that extends down inside the neck. Nearly everyone will have experienced a sore throat at some time—in most cases it is a symptom of the common cold or tonsillitis.

The pharynx is deep-lined with muscles and is shaped, very roughly, like an inverted cone. It extends for about 5 inches (12 cm) behind the arch at the back of the mouth to where it joins up with the gullet (see Esophagus).

The upper, wider part of the pharynx is given rigidity by the bones of the skull, and at the lower, narrow end its muscles are joined to the elastic cartilages of the voice box (see Larynx and Laryngitis). The outermost tissue layer of the pharynx, which is continuous with the lining of the mouth, contains many mucus-producing glands that help to keep the mouth and throat well lubricated during eating and speaking.

The parts of the pharynx

Anatomically, the pharynx is divided into three sections according to their positions and functions. The uppermost part, the nasopharynx, gets its name from the fact that it lies above the soft palate and forms the back of the nose.

▲ *Using a small flashlight and a disposable tongue depressor, a doctor can look at a patient's throat to check for inflammation. In children, the tonsils are often implicated.*

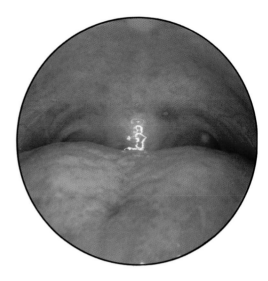

▲ *A form of pharyngitis called strep throat can be treated with antibiotics.*

◄ *Opera singers, such as the celebrated soprano Kiri Te Kanawa, must be careful to guard against infections of the pharynx.*

STRUCTURE OF THE PHARYNX

THE PHARYNX DURING SWALLOWING

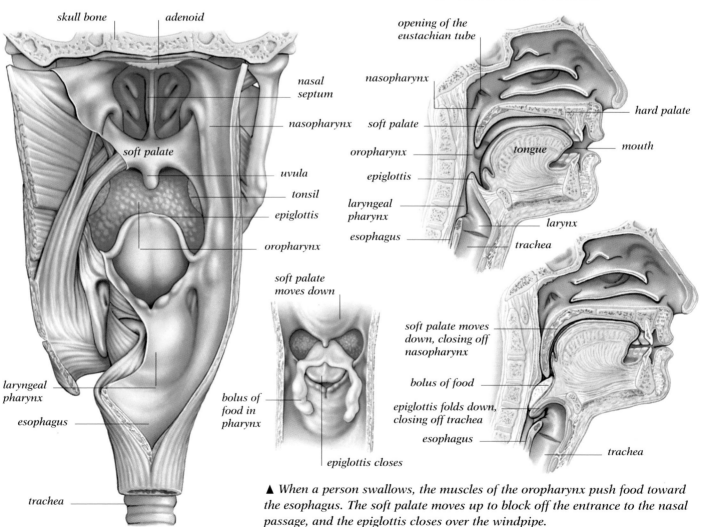

skull bone
adenoid
nasal septum
nasopharynx
soft palate
uvula
tonsil
epiglottis
oropharynx
laryngeal pharynx
esophagus
trachea

opening of the eustachian tube
nasopharynx
soft palate
oropharynx
epiglottis
laryngeal pharynx
esophagus
hard palate
tongue
mouth
larynx
trachea

soft palate moves down
bolus of food in pharynx
epiglottis closes

soft palate moves down, closing off nasopharynx
bolus of food
epiglottis folds down, closing off trachea
esophagus
trachea

▲ *When a person swallows, the muscles of the oropharynx push food toward the esophagus. The soft palate moves up to block off the entrance to the nasal passage, and the epiglottis closes over the windpipe.*

Small fish bones and other similar objects can get stuck in the throat very easily. If this happens, the best course of action is to eat one or two mouthfuls of bread and then take a drink of water. If the bread and water do not move the offending object, always seek medical help rather than try to get it out yourself. One reason for this is that the bone may not actually be stuck at all—instead it may have grazed the pharynx itself, leading to a sensation that mimics a stuck bone.

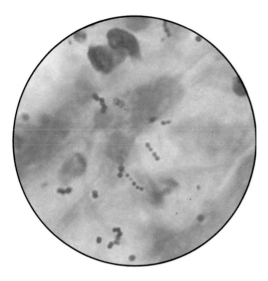

▲ *A magnified view of streptococci, the bacteria responsible for causing strep throat.*

Below this, the nasopharynx is bordered by the soft palate itself. Upward movement of the soft palate closes off the nasopharynx when a person swallows, and this prevents food from being forced up and out of the nose. A failure in this coordination leads to the discomfort that is sometimes experienced when a person sneezes.

In the roof of the nasopharynx are the adenoids, two clumps of tissue that are most prominent in childhood. The nasopharynx also contains, on either side of the head, an entrance to the eustachian tube, the passage between the middle ear and the throat. Disease-causing microorganisms of the mouth, nose, and throat have easy access to the ears and can cause middle-ear infections (see Otitis).

The oropharynx, the area of the pharynx at the back of the mouth, is part of the airway between mouth and lungs. It is much more mobile than the nasopharynx. The squeezing actions of the muscles of the oropharynx help shape the sounds of speech as they come from the larynx. With the aid of the tongue, these muscles also help to push food down toward the entrance to the esophagus.

The most important organs of the oropharynx are the tonsils, two masses of tissue that are often implicated in the sore throats common in childhood. Like the adenoids, the tonsils are composed of lymphoid tissue characteristic of the body's defense system. This tissue produces specialized white blood cells that engulf invading bacteria and viruses.

The lowermost or laryngeal section of the pharynx is involved entirely with swallowing. This section lies directly behind the larynx, and its lining is joined to the thyroid and cricoid cartilages. The movements of these cartilages help in the production of sounds. Contraction of the muscles helps to propel mouthfuls of food through this part of the pharynx. Just above the laryngeal part of the pharynx is the epiglottis, a flap of tissue that closes down over the entrance to the airway as a person swallows and thereby prevents food from getting into the lungs and causing choking.

What can go wrong?

By far the most common problem of the pharynx is inflammation, known medically as pharyngitis and experienced as a sore throat. Pharyngitis can appear suddenly (acute), or it can persist over several months or even years (chronic).

The most usual cause of acute pharyngitis is the common cold. A sore throat is a telltale sign of an impending infection, even before the first cough or sneeze. The common cold is caused by a virus. However, there are also bacteria—called streptococci—that can cause a form of pharyngitis known as strep throat.

As well as a direct infection, pharyngitis can be a subsidiary symptom of other diseases. Inflammation and infection of the parts of the body next to or within the pharynx, including the larynx, mouth, sinuses, and tonsils, can result in pharyngitis.

Other diseases that usually include pharyngitis as one of their many symptoms are glandular fever, measles, and rubella (German measles). Scarlet fever, once a lethal childhood disease but now easily controlled with antibiotics, is confined to the nose and throat; it is also associated with severe pharyngitis.

The chief culprits in the case of chronic pharyngitis are smoking and excessive drinking. Cutting down or—particularly in the case of smoking—stopping altogether is necessary for a cure. Another common cause of chronic pharyngitis is postnasal drip—a constant drip of fluid from the back of the nose. This results from persistent mouth-breathing due to a blocked nose. There are many causes of this, and a doctor will make a diagnosis.

Smokers may develop cancer of the pharynx. In the very obese, the neck flops in on itself, obstructing the pharynx, causing snoring, sleep apnea, and other sleeping disorders.

Treatment

Treatment depends on the cause. First, there is the treatment of conditions caused by viruses, such as the common cold, none of which respond to antibiotics. Second, there is the treatment of bacterial cases, such as strep throat, which can be cured with antibiotics.

People should use common sense in deciding whether or not they or their families need medical attention. When an acute sore throat first occurs, it can be soothed by sucking lozenges. If the discomfort persists, or if the patient has a very high fever, then medical advice should be sought.

See also: **Adenoids; Common cold; Palate; Sore throat; Streptococcus; Throat; Tonsils**

Phenylketonuria

I am pregnant and worried about my baby. Is phenylketonuria a common problem?

Phenylketonuria is a rare disease, affecting about one in every 15,000 babies born in the United States. It is detected a few days after birth by a simple screening test. In the unlikely event that your baby has PKU, the appropriate dietary treatment can be started.

Is the impairment that is caused by phenylketonuria permanent?

The way to prevent the effects of this disease is by screening and a special diet. Tests are carried out on newborn babies in many countries. If the condition develops untreated, intellectual impairment is 97 percent likely, and most sufferers are affected severely. A diet low in the amino acid phenylalanine can improve matters but will not restore a child who is badly affected.

My baby has phenylketonuria. Will I be able to breast-feed her?

No. Human milk contains phenylalanine, an amino acid that your baby's body cannot handle. The high levels of this amino acid that occur in the first few months or years of life lead to intellectual and developmental impairment. The brain is at its most sensitive at this time in a child's life. Your baby will have to be given a special formula diet.

Does someone suffering from phenylketonuria have to stay on a special diet for an entire lifetime?

Dietary restrictions are usually relaxed between the ages of six and 12, after which time a child can eat normally. Women should go back on the special diet before becoming pregnant; otherwise, the fetus will be affected.

About one in every 15,000 babies born in the United States has phenylketonuria, a disease that causes intellectual impairment. Testing newborns and putting those with the disease on a special diet now ensures normal development.

Phenylketonuria, or PKU, is a rare inherited disease caused by the absence of an enzyme for dealing with the amino acid phenylalanine. If it is not detected, the condition leads to brain damage in the affected child. However, screening at birth and then putting a child with the condition on a special diet will ensure that his or her brain develops normally.

Causes

Phenylketonuria is part of a group of diseases that are known as the inborn errors of metabolism. Such a disease is present from birth and is one in which the body is unable to handle a particular chemical constituent.

In phenylketonuria, the chemical is the amino acid phenylalanine. In most people, the enzyme phenylalanine hydroxylase acts on this amino acid to convert it to another amino acid called tyrosine. However, because a patient with PKU lacks phenylalanine hydroxylase, none of the phenylalanine is converted to tyrosine. As a result, high levels of phenylalanine accumulate in the affected person's blood.

The accumulation of phenylalanine causes damage in a young child's developing brain, which is particularly susceptible to the effects of a raised level. Also, because the phenylalanine is not being converted to tyrosine, there is a lack of this amino acid in the tissues. Tyrosine is

▲ *Before a woman who was born with PKU becomes pregnant, she must go back on a protein-restricted diet that is low in phenylalanine. Special foods are now available for people affected by PKU, such as a type of bread that is low in this amino acid.*

▶ *A baby may look healthy, but a tiny percentage of newborns have PKU. A heel-prick test is used to assess the level of phenylalanine: the blood sample is sent to a laboratory for analysis.*

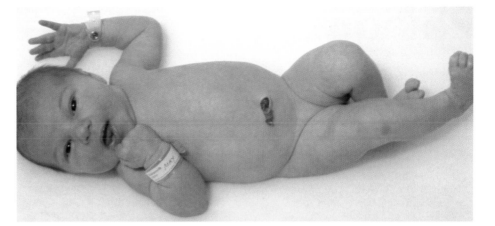

responsible for making melanin—the body's dark brown pigment—so children who are affected by PKU all tend to have blue eyes, blond hair, and fair skin (see Melanin).

PKU is one of 50 known inborn errors in the handling of amino acids and is inherited in a recessive way: for a child to actually inherit the disease, the abnormal gene has to be inherited from both parents.

If a couple has one child with PKU, there is a 25 percent risk that further children will be affected. The mother should be tested as soon as possible if she gets pregnant again.

Symptoms

Babies affected by PKU are normal at birth. Brain damage begins when they start to take in phenylalanine—that is, when they are fed. If they are left untreated, babies with PKU grow into severely impaired individuals with an IQ of less than 30.

PKU babies often have bad eczema. They might also suffer from seizures, and they tend to show no interest in other people.

Dangers

Phenylketonuria is dangerous in that it can be passed on to children unnecessarily. Any woman who was born with the disease and treated with a special diet as a baby should go back on that diet before she becomes pregnant. The level of phenylalanine in her blood must be kept within strict bounds throughout her pregnancy so that the developing fetus does not become affected.

People with PKU are unlikely to pass the disease on unless they have a child with a carrier of the abnormal gene. The same applies to the brothers and sisters of affected people. Nevertheless, people should have genetic counseling if there is PKU in the family and they themselves wish to start a family.

Treatment and outlook

All newborn babies are screened at or around the fifth day of life with a simple heel-prick test. If positive results are obtained from this test, treatment will be started immediately.

A child who is affected by PKU must be given a special formula that is usually made from beef serum and is low in phenylalanine. Other than this, his or her diet should not contain any protein, since phenylalanine is a common constituent of protein in both animal and vegetable foods. Therefore, both breast milk and cow's milk must be avoided.

When the baby is three months old, the situation is reassessed. At this stage, some babies—who have a minor form of the disease—can tolerate normal levels of phenylalanine in their formulas and begin to eat normally. Other babies, who have a high level of phenylalanine in their blood, must remain on the special diet.

When they are weaned, children who are still affected will be allowed more normal foods, but they can have no high-protein foods other than the special formula. Breakfast cereals, milk, and potatoes are rationed because they all contain a lot of phenylalanine. Butter, jelly, candy, and sugar drinks, on the other hand, can be taken in unlimited amounts, as they are low in phenylalanine. Children are also permitted some special brands of bread, flour, cookies, and pasta. The sweetener Nutrasweet must be avoided.

Between the ages of six and 12, the diet of a PKU-affected child is allowed to return to normal. However, if there is any deterioration in schoolwork or the child's general behavior, there should be an urgent reassessment. The special diet should start again if tests show that the blood levels of phenylalanine are very high.

Very recent research suggests that tetrahydrobiopterin, a substance that is a cofactor in the conversion of phenylalanine to tyrosine, can significantly lower levels of phenylalanine in the blood of patients who are suffering from a mild form of the disease. Gene therapy may be possible in the future.

See also: Eczema; Enzymes; Genetic diseases and disorders; Genetics

Phlegm

Phlegm is a sticky substance containing mucus and other particles and fluids. Various conditions can cause a person to produce phlegm, although a phlegm-producing cough is commonly associated with heavy smokers.

Phlegm—or sputum, as it is called medically—is any material that is produced as a result of coughing. Phlegm may contain mucus, saliva, pus, particles of inhaled dust or fiber, blood, or shreds of tissue from diseased parts of the respiratory tract.

The main constituent of phlegm tends to be mucus, which is secreted by glands in the membrane lining the respiratory tract. The mucus acts both as a general lubricant, which forms a protective coating over the delicate lining, and as a sticky fluid that traps any unwanted and potentially dangerous debris so that it can be eliminated from the body by coughing (see Mucus).

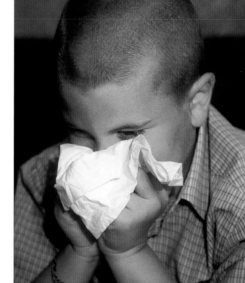

▲ *Coughing is the body's way of eliminating phlegm from the respiratory tract.*

Types of phlegm

The most common type of phlegm, known as white or mucous sputum, is translucent, white, and often frothy. Its presence indicates that there is inflammation somewhere in the respiratory passages. White sputum may come from the pharynx at the back of the throat. When a person has a cold or hay fever, white sputum may come from the back of the nose and run down to the throat. White sputum that originates in the lungs is commonly the result of asthma, smoking, chronic bronchitis, or the early stages of ordinary bronchitis.

If the phlegm contains yellow or green puslike matter it is called mucopurulent, and it indicates that an infection has developed in some part of the respiratory tract (see Pus). Common causes are bronchitis, bronchopneumonia, and sinus infection.

Other discoloration of the phlegm usually stems from the air that is breathed. Coal miners often have black phlegm due to particles of coal dust, and the sputum of city dwellers may be similarly discolored because of air pollution (see Air Pollution).

People who cough up bloody phlegm should see a doctor. The most common cause of blood-streaked phlegm is energetic coughing, which can damage some of the tiny blood vessels lining the respiratory tract. This normally lasts only a day or two. More heavily bloodstained phlegm or coughing up pure blood may have more serious causes and should be investigated immediately.

Diagnosis and treatment

Examining a patient's phlegm can provide a doctor with considerable information about what is wrong with the patient. Microscopic examination and laboratory tests enable the doctor to look for certain types of cells that indicate which diseases or germs are causing an infection. Abnormal cells in the phlegm can also be used to diagnose lung cancer.

A person who has been coughing up phlegm for two weeks should always see a doctor, who can deal with the cause of the phlegm and prescribe an appropriate cough medicine if necessary.

See also: Asthma; Bronchitis; Chronic obstructive pulmonary disease; Common cold; Coughing; Lung and lung diseases; Pharynx; Pneumonia; Smoking

Phobias

Thousands of people suffer from phobias—irrational fears. The wide spectrum of phobias includes fear of open spaces, cats, and public speaking. Fortunately, treatment is always possible.

A phobia is an intense and irrational fear of an object or situation. The word "phobia" comes from the Greek *phobos*, which means extreme fear or terror. The fear can be of things that are harmless, or it may concern things or situations that are potentially harmful.

Fears, however, are not classed as phobias when there is good reason to be afraid: a soldier who is terrified in combat does not have combat phobia. Similarly, an obsession is not a phobia. Obsessive people do not fear an object or situation; they fear only its consequences.

Who gets phobias?

Phobias are fairly common—nearly 8 percent of all adults have irrational fears. Some phobias, such as a fear of certain animals or of school, tend to start in childhood. Others, such as agoraphobia (fear of open spaces) or social phobia, may not develop until after puberty. Often, these phobias are linked to an emotional or introverted personality.

▲ *Ailurophobia—an irrational fear of cats—is a common phobia. It has been suggested that the way a cat stares may be at the root of this fear.*

Questions and Answers

I can understand why people have phobias about cats and dogs, because they bite and scratch, but I suffer with agoraphobia, a fear of open spaces that seems to be irrational. Why is this?

Agoraphobia is not just a fear of open spaces; it is also a fear of meeting people and coping with the world. The reason you have acquired this phobia is unique to yourself, but it may well be based on some distressing event outside your home which made you fear that you would be unable to cope if it happened again. Treatment is possible and the outlook for a permanent cure is good.

How can I help my three-year-old son overcome his fear of the dark?

You should leave an electric nightlight in his room, or leave the door ajar and keep the light outside on. Never ridicule your son for fearing the dark, but behave calmly and reassuringly when you put him to bed. Don't rush upstairs every time he calls, or he'll have you looking into his room all night. Instead, reassure him by calling to him so that he knows you're nearby.

Do phobias run in families?

Phobias are not hereditary. However, children do tend to copy their parents' behavior, and if either parent shows unusual fear over some situation, the child may develop the same fear, even if only temporarily.

Is it true that some phobias are harder to cure than others?

Yes. Probably the easiest to cure are phobias involving animals—spiders, snakes, rats, bats, and so on. One of the toughest phobias to treat is agoraphobia—the fear of having to engage in social interactions.

Signs and symptoms

In the presence of the object or situation that causes the phobia, the phobic person may experience emotions ranging from frank distaste to panic and even pain. Symptoms include increased and uneven heartbeat, pallor, sweating, muscle tension, a tightness in the chest, and difficulty in breathing to the point of fainting (see Anxiety). As a result, the seasoned phobic will usually have developed ways of avoiding the object or situation.

Agoraphobia

Agoraphobia literally means "fear of the marketplace," but it is really several fears rolled into one. Primarily it is a fear of open spaces, but underlying this is a fear of large spaces, being in crowds, meeting people, shopping, traveling, and traffic. It is the most common of all phobias, affecting 60 percent of phobic people.

Agoraphobia usually starts as an unexpected panic attack, with sensations ranging from a pounding heart to fainting. Sufferers usually associate their fear with the place where the first attack happened, and many find their lives become increasingly restricted. Some even end up housebound.

Claustrophobia

Claustrophobia is a fear of confined spaces. Most people will acknowledge a slight feeling of claustrophobia in a crowded subway

◄ *Claustrophobia—a fear of confined spaces—can restrict a person's life dramatically. Even something as mundane as using an elevator becomes terrifying.*

▼ *Many people are afraid of lightning, with good cause: it can be very dangerous. However, if the fear is such that the person is terrified to go out in the rain, it constitutes a phobia.*

▶ *Imagine being so terrified of crowds that you end up housebound. This is one of the symptoms of agoraphobia, and the fear is compounded by the fact that getting treatment in a clinic would entail traveling through crowds.*

or elevator, but some react with panic, preferring to use flights of stairs rather than take the elevator.

A characteristic of claustrophobia is its tendency to be triggered by situations unconnected with the event that started the phobia. For example, claustrophobia that started in an elevator might develop until the affected person is unable to use public transportation, enter small rooms, or even wear tight-fitting clothes.

School phobia

Most children go through a period of not wanting to go to school, perhaps because they have not studied for a test or because they are being bullied. However, this is not a phobia.

School phobia is intense and long-lasting, and it embraces all situations connected with school. It often produces physical symptoms such as a headache, upset stomach, nausea, and vomiting. These problems are real: they are not troubles invented in an attempt to avoid going to school.

School phobia occurs in nearly 2 percent of children. It is thought to develop from the child's anxiety at being separated from his or her mother, and the mother's anxiety about the child's ability to cope at school. Mother and child gradually become dependent on each other for reassurance, and increased anxiety occurs with each separation.

Social phobia

Social phobia is a fear of being in the presence of other people or of having to interact with them. It affects men more than women, and it is often a combination of a severe lack of confidence, anxiety, and a feeling of being socially inadequate. Symptoms may include a fear of social gatherings and an inability to look people in the eye or to talk with them on a personal or public level.

These fears may then become linked to other activities that are carried out in front of other people, such as eating out or using public transportation. The fear then transfers to these other activities, so that eating and traveling begin to produce anxiety.

As might be expected, such anxieties often develop during adolescence, when the individual may become painfully aware of a need to do or say the right thing among his or her peer group. A fear of sex can develop in the same way.

Although social phobics can go out of the house on their own, they often become housebound because they have difficulty being with other people.

Animal phobias

Spiders, snakes, rats, bats, insects, horses, dogs, cats, and birds can all cause phobias. Many people are frightened of certain animals, but when this fear turns into an obsession and a need to avoid a particular animal, it has developed into a phobia. For example,

people with a bird phobia may scream and cover their heads when a bird flies near them. Most people who fear animals manage to live with their phobia by trying to avoid the object of their fear.

Childhood fears

Fears of ghosts, witches, the dark, or being lost are common in young children. However, these are not phobias, because they disappear as a child matures. Any childhood fears that remain beyond age six may indicate that a child needs a little help, but simply talking about the problem with the child is usually enough.

Treatment

There are two schools of thought about treating phobias: one maintains that phobias can be treated by psychoanalysis; the other suggests that behavioral therapy is more effective.

Psychoanalysts take the view that phobias are symbols of deep-rooted conflicts. The fears associated with the objects or situations are based on childhood experiences and may relate to conflicts about the person's sexual feelings or aggression. Critics argue that psychoanalytic approaches have not proved particularly helpful in treating phobias (see Psychotherapy).

Behavioral therapists have an opposing theory; they believe that a phobia is an acquired habit of responding with fear (see Behavior Therapy). Cognitive behavior therapy is the most effective behavioral approach to treating phobias.

See also: **Psychology; Therapy**

Photosensitivity

Why does my daughter get a lumpy, itchy rash in early summer?

This sounds like polymorphic light eruption, which is more common in girls. It starts with the first summer sun and can last up to a week. However, with gradual exposure it can be avoided, and by late summer your daughter should be able to tolerate the sun. You may find that tablets containing beta-carotene, a pigment present in carrot juice, will help.

Why can I develop photosensitivity through my clothes?

Photosensitivity is mainly caused by the sun's invisible rays—called ultraviolet (UV) light—not by visible light rays. Penetration of light rays varies with their wavelength. The shorter UV wavelength can pass not only through thin clothing, but also through glass. Make sure that any protective clothing you wear is thick enough to cast a shadow.

Can the contraceptive pill cause photosensitivity?

Only rarely. It occasionally affects the liver, and this situation results in changes in chemicals that cause photosensitivity. More commonly, the Pill may cause chloasma—a blotchy pigmentation that appears particularly on the face.

What is melanin?

It is a dark brown skin pigment present in varying amounts in all races. Melanin absorbs energy from the sun's rays and lessens their harmful effects. Fair-skinned people, who are less able to produce melanin, may burn easily in the sun. Photosensitivity is simply an exaggerated reaction in people who are displaying an abnormal sensitivity to light.

Photosensitivity—a heightened sensitivity of the skin to light—can be an inherited abnormality, but is more often acquired later in life. It may cause an itchy rash to develop after only brief exposure to sunlight.

Photosensitivity is an abnormal reaction to light that causes an itchy rash to appear on areas of skin that are exposed to the sun. However, with adequate precautions and treatment, the effects of photosensitivity can be kept under control.

Sunlight and photosensitivity

Ultraviolet (UV) rays—that is, the invisible part of the sun's rays—cause sunburn and photosensitivity reactions. Although the sun may feel pleasant and relaxing, too much sunlight can be damaging. The skin gives people some protection against the sun by producing a dark brown pigment called melanin. The energy from the sun's rays is absorbed by the melanin so that it does not cause any harmful effects. Dark-skinned races and some individuals have plenty

▲ *Although air feels cool to skiers, the ultraviolet rays in sunlight are made more intense by reflection from the snow. Sunburn and photosensitivity reactions are more likely in these conditions, and an efficient sunscreen should always be worn.*

▲ *Differences in skin color are due to different levels of melanin. Melanin granules are made in the epidermis by cells called melanocytes. Exposure to sunlight speeds up the action of the melanocytes, which produce more melanin.*

▶ *This patient's rash was caused by a photosensitizing drug.*

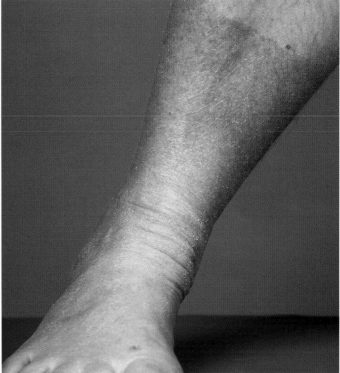

of melanin, but fair-skinned people are less able to produce enough of the pigment to protect their skin. In light-skinned individuals, the excess energy is taken up by other molecules that, when activated and altered, may trigger a very itchy skin rash.

Acquired photosensitivity

The type of photosensitivity seen most often by doctors is called polymorphic light eruption. The condition usually starts around puberty and is seen most commonly in girls who are fair-skinned. It occurs characteristically in spring and early summer. Instead of the normal redness of sunburn, itchy spots appear on the sun-exposed areas, such as the face and outer arms. The rash may leave a distinct line around the ends of sleeves and necklines. This condition is quite common but is not always recognized by the sufferer, since it can occur any time from two hours to two days after exposure to the sun. It persists for two to seven days and tends to recur every year.

The other photosensitivities that most commonly occur are those resulting from contact with photosensitizers—chemicals that alter and increase sensitivity to sunlight—or from the use of medications such as the tranquilizer chlorpromazine, or an antibiotic called tetracycline. The reason why some people are affected by these medicines, while other people are not, is still not known. However, such reactions are thought to be related to the duration and dosage of the photosensitizing drug that is involved.

Contact photosensitivity

There are many substances that cause photosensitivity when they come into contact with the skin. In such cases, the rash appears in sun-exposed areas of the body where the substance has been applied. For example, the dye eosin, which is used in lipstick, can cause a photosensitive rash on the lips.

There are 25 different substances in tar that can cause contact photosensitive reactions. The effects are seen commonly in people who use wood preservatives as part of their job. Certain plants can cause a severe reaction—typically a streaky rash in exposed areas,

usually on the neck. Common culprits are parsnip, giant hogweed, cow parsley, celery, limes, and some oranges. Antibiotic and antihistamine lotions and creams can also cause photosensitivity, as can antiseptics, but such reactions are rare. Bergamot oil, which is used in some perfumes, can cause a streaky redness, followed by pigmentation around the neck.

Sometimes acquired photosensitivity can be a sign of a general disorder such as lupus erythematosus. With this condition, a rash appears on the nose and cheeks after exposure to the sun. Doctors call it a butterfly rash (see Rashes).

Inherited photosensitivities

Photosensitivities that are inherited are rare. The major group is called porphyria. This is an abnormality in the chemical pigment porphyrin, one of the components of the red blood cells.

The origin of the mythical werewolf is sometimes attributed to a very rare type of porphyria. Sufferers were so sensitive to sun that their skin blistered and became scarred and deformed if they went out in daylight. Because of this, they went out only at night. This type of porphyria also caused excessive growth of hair.

Treatment

Treatment depends on the type of photosensitivity. In cases of polymorphic light eruption, gradually desensitizing a person to light by slowly increasing exposure over a period of weeks can be effective. Tablets containing beta-carotene, the same pigment that can be found in carrot juice, may also help the condition (see Vitamin A).

When contact photosensitivity is the problem, avoidance of photosensitizing substances is important. Sensitive people should also take other general precautions to better protect themselves against sunlight.

See also: Melanin; Skin and skin diseases; Sunburn

Physical examination

Questions and Answers

Most of the time I just don't feel very good. Do you think I should ask my doctor to give me a thorough physical examination?

Any first-time visit to a doctor usually includes a physical examination. If you feel bad for any length of time it is also important that you go to your doctor to find out what is wrong. Normally he or she will be able to assure you that there is nothing wrong. However, if there is any doubt, the doctor will probably recommend a full physical examination.

Many medical experts recommend regular checkups as a form of screening to detect medical problems. A checkup is important because it can detect problems such as cancer before they become well established and thus more difficult to treat.

My father had a full physical at work and was told that his health was excellent. Then a week later he died from a heart attack. How could this happen?

No system of screening or physical examination, no matter how detailed or thorough, can reveal exactly what is happening in every part of all the body's complex and diverse mechanisms. Therefore, it is possible to have a full checkup that reveals nothing, and then to die after leaving the doctor's office. It may seem that regular checkups are a waste of time, but this is a shortsighted view. The information about preventable diseases that is provided by having a thorough checkup still makes it worthwhile.

In addition, a full physical examination confirms that all the systems and parts of the body are functioning normally. In the final analysis, with regular checkups it is possible that a number of wholly treatable diseases will never be allowed to develop to the point where people become so sick that their lives are endangered.

A doctor may give a patient a physical examination to find the cause of an illness, but even when a person is in good health, regular checkups can help prevent many conditions from developing—or ensure successful treatment.

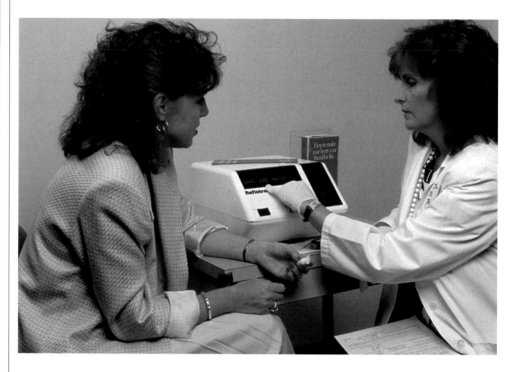

▲ *Blood cholesterol level is measured in a sample of blood taken from a finger prick. The machine analyzes the sample and automatically displays the result.*

A physical examination is usually the second part of a patient's consultation with the doctor. It is normally preceded by the doctor's listening to a description of the symptoms and, if this is the patient's first visit, taking a medical history. The doctor may also ask the patient about aspects of his or her life (such as work) that have a bearing on health. This information enables the doctor to pay special attention to any likely areas of trouble during the examination.

After the examination the doctor will be able to assess the state of a patient's health, diagnose any illness, and advise the patient about its management or treatment. The doctor may also be able to give a prognosis, a forecast of how the illness is likely to affect the patient's life, if at all, and how long it is likely to last.

When it is necessary

The most common circumstance in which people need a physical examination is that they are feeling unwell; the examination is carried out as part of the process of finding out what is likely to be the cause of the trouble and where in the body it is situated.

With some diseases, called local conditions, only one particular part of the body is involved, and so it is necessary to examine only the affected area. However, there are other conditions that affect the whole body and make the patient feel generally sick. Such conditions usually require an examination of the entire body. A full physical is also necessary if there is any doubt about what is wrong with the patient or if the illness does not fit clearly into the normal pattern of a particular disease. In such situations, the examination is likely to be lengthy and detailed, since the doctor will have to search for clues to the underlying problem.

However, many physical examinations are carried out when people feel quite well. The object of such examinations is to make certain that the person really is as healthy as he or she appears

Conducting a physical examination

PROCEDURE	WHAT IS INVOLVED	WHAT IT CAN SHOW
Examination of mouth and throat	Tongue held down with wooden spatula and interior of the mouth examined with the aid of a flashlight	State of teeth, gums, tongue, tonsils, and back of throat
Examination of nose	Interior of the nostrils is examined under a light	Inflammation of nose and sinuses, nasal polyps, source of nosebleeds
Examination of eyes	Eyes examined with ophthalmoscope Patient asked to look from a near to a distant object and back and follow movements of examiner's finger Light shone into eyes	Abnormalities of lens and retina Abnormalities of focusing or eye movement Pupil reactions, nerve connections for the light reflex, abnormalities of adjustment to light and dark
Examination of ears	Ears examined under a light shone into a small conical tube placed in the ear	Inflammation of the ears; wax; condition of eardrum; possible perforation
Hearing test	Listening for whispered words and tuning fork notes; tests with earphones	Various types of hearing defect
Examination of chest	Visual inspection Palpation—feeling the chest Percussion—tapping the chest Auscultation—listening to chest with a stethoscope	Abnormalities of shape, breathing movements, rashes, lumps, and pulsations Position of maximum heartbeat and thus size of heart; lumps, especially in women's breasts Presence and site of some lung diseases; position, size, and shape of heart Presence, site, and type of some lung and heart diseases
Examination of pulse	Feeling a pulse point	Abnormalities of heart rate and rhythm; state of arteries
Measurement of blood pressure	Cuff bound around upper arm and inflated—tight feeling but not painful	Normal, raised (hypertension), or low (hypotension) blood pressure
Abdominal examination	Visual inspection Palpation Percussion Auscultation	Abnormalities of shape; rashes, sores, lumps, movements Lumps, presence and stage of pregnancy, site and type of any tenderness Presence of fluid; state of bladder Presence or absence and type of noises from intestines and therefore abnormality of gut action
Rectal examination	Gloved finger inserted into the rectum—unpleasant but not painful	Size, shape, and any tenderness of prostate gland; any lumps. High percentage of rectal and (in men) prostate cancers are detected this way. Screening stools for blood is a test for some intestinal cancers, ulcers, and other diseases.
Vaginal examination	Gloved fingers, possibly with the aid of a speculum, inserted into vagina—uncomfortable but not painful	Abnormalities of vagina, womb, fallopian tubes, and ovaries
Examination of nervous system	Muscles are put through normal range of movements Testing sensitivity to light touch, very mild pain (pinprick), temperature (hot water), and position Testing reflexes by tapping elbows, wrists, knees, and ankles with hammer; tickling soles of feet	Action (motor) message systems are working normally Sensory message systems are working normally Reflex or rapid-response systems are working normally
Blood tests	Collecting a specimen, by either pricking fingertip or inserting needle into the vein at front of elbow	Anemia and other blood disorders; liver, kidney, and metabolic diseases
Chest X ray	Patient holds a deep breath while X rays pass for a fraction of a second through the upper trunk	Lung disease; size and shape of heart; breast disease
Electrocardiogram (ECG)	Being wired up to recording apparatus—painless	Abnormalities of action of the heart

Someone told me that all children should have an annual physical examination. Is this right?

Certainly it is wise for children to have regular medical and dental checkups to make sure that they are developing normally and that there are no signs of disease. It is not usually necessary, however, for these to be done as often as once a year. It is desirable that adolescents have a check twice a year during their time of most rapid growth.

My company wants me to have a medical examination, although as far as I know, there is nothing wrong with me and I haven't had a day off work for over 10 years. I'm afraid something negative about my health, or something that will affect my chances of promotion may show up in the examination. Do I have the right to refuse to be examined?

You can certainly refuse to be examined. Legally, it is an assault for a doctor to examine anyone against his or her will. The exception is a situation in which the person is likely to have committed a criminal offense in circumstances that make the medical evidence vital to the process of justice. This is why you are usually expected to sign a consent form beforehand that allows the doctor to go ahead with an examination.

If you do refuse a medical examination, however, your company may regard your refusal as sufficiently important to dismiss you. Whether or not the company would succeed in this would depend on the terms of your employment. If you feel strongly about not being checked over, you might be able to give the company a report from your own doctor.

In general, company medical examinations are more concerned with keeping you in good health than with finding reasons for getting rid of you, and your suspicion, although it is understandable, is probably quite misplaced.

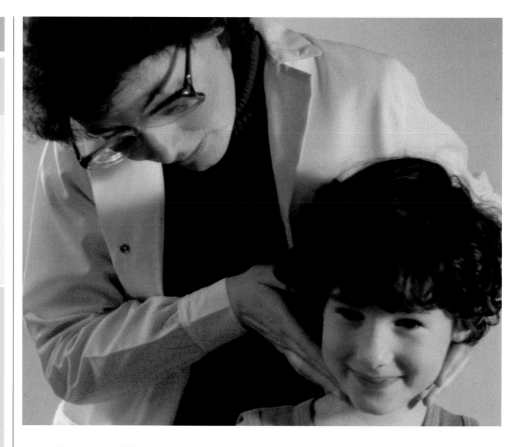

▲ *Children should have regular physical examinations to make sure that they are developing normally and that there are no signs of disease.*

to be. The examination confirms that all the systems and parts of the body are functioning normally and that there are no indications of an unsuspected condition or disease.

Most children have examinations of this type at intervals during their school years. They are carried out by a pediatrician to make sure that the child is developing normally and that there are no signs of problems that may arise in the future (see Child Development). This is essentially a screening process during which the doctor pays particular attention to looking for and eliminating any indications of the most common dangerous diseases. It is now recognized that such examinations play a valuable part in monitoring the child's physical and mental progress.

Such examinations may seem unnecessary and a waste of time. However, many serious diseases can be prevented from developing any further or can be completely and permanently cured if they are detected at an early stage, often before a person is aware that there is a problem. This may not be possible if the disease has been allowed to develop to a stage where a person is so sick that he or she has no alternative but to consult a doctor.

Provisions for examinations

Physical examinations are provided for the employees of many organizations, including private companies, the military, and police departments. They are carried out in the interests of both the individual and the organization, since the maintenance of good health and the early detection and treatment of disease are important to the prosperity of both. For similar reasons, many employers insist on establishing that prospective employees are in good health before they are hired. Satisfactory physical examinations are sometimes also required before a student is accepted into university or college courses, as part of enrollment.

At present, there is no national provision for regular physical examinations to check people's health once they have left school. In some areas there are women's clinics where women can have regular gynecological and breast examinations (see Breasts; Gynecology), but there are few comparable facilities for men. Therefore, many people wishing to take sensible precautions for their health by having regular checkups must make their own arrangements. In the absence of symptoms, a check should generally be made annually.

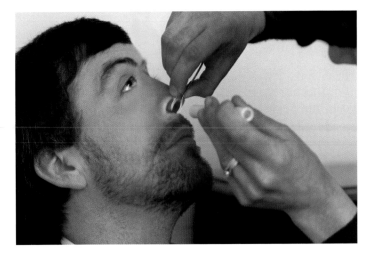

▲ *A thorough physical examination involves using a light to examine the nose for any inflammation or nasal polyps.*

▲ *The doctor measures the blood pressure of a patient using an instrument called a sphygmomanometer.*

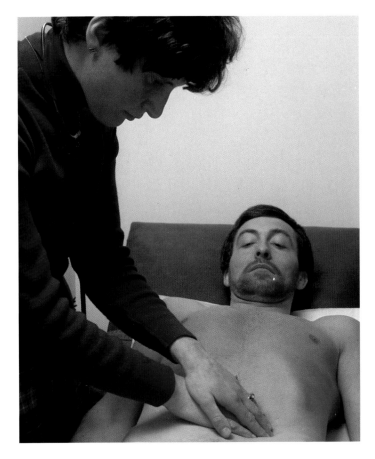

▲ *The abdomen is palpated to detect tenderness or swelling.*

Having an examination

Before the doctor actually performs a physical examination, he or she will take a general look at the patient. What appears to the patient to be a quick glance may be the most informative part of the examination. For example, the doctor may pick up signs of abnormalities such as anemia, jaundice, or a raised cholesterol level in the blood (see Anemia; Cholesterol; Jaundice); and by noticing the patient's gait—the way he or she walks—the doctor may see indications of diseases of the nervous system.

A physical examination may be carried out in one of two ways. Some doctors work on a head-to-toe basis; others take a physiological approach and explore each of the body's systems, such as the nervous system, circulatory system, and gastrointestinal system, in turn, moving up and down the body and back again as necessary.

Whichever method is followed, the doctor's basic approach is the same. First, he or she looks at each part of the body for any abnormality in its appearance, such as spots, rashes, lumps, or swellings. Second, he or she feels, or palpates, the part to discover any area of tenderness, internal swelling, or other suspicious conditions. Third—though this usually applies to the chest and abdomen only—he or she taps, or percusses, the area. This tapping produces sound vibrations that enable the doctor to evaluate the size, borders, and consistency of some of the internal organs, and to detect whether there is any fluid present (and how much) in the thoracic or abdominal cavity. Fourth, the doctor uses the stethoscope to examine the sound-producing organs, such as the lungs, heart, and intestines. Variations in the normal sounds or the presence of additional noises can provide valuable indications of what is going on in areas that cannot be seen.

The examination is usually completed by measuring blood pressure; testing hearing, eyesight, and urine; and measuring height and weight. More extensive tests may include measuring lung function, assessing heart function (see Electrocardiogram), and taking X rays of parts of the body. Tests in women may include examination of the breasts, and material from the vagina and the cervix (see Cervix and Cervical Smears; Pap Smear; Vaginal Discharge).

A physical examination is not usually painful or unpleasant. The apprehension and nervousness that some people feel beforehand often tends to be the worst part of the experience. People often feel good afterward if they are told that they are in fine health; and if any abnormality is discovered, they will be reassured to know that its early detection means there is the best possible chance of curing the problem.

See also: Blood pressure;
Diagnosis; Eyes and eyesight;
Health care system; Hearing;
Pediatric medicine; Reflexes;
Stethoscope; Symptoms; X rays

Physical fitness

Questions and Answers

How quickly will my body adapt itself to my new fitness regimen? At the moment I ache all over.

You may be doing too much too soon; slow down a bit. As you get fitter, you will be able to do more without feeling such ill effects. Your body has probably been under-used for a long time; don't expect it to be in prime condition after only a few days or weeks. There shouldn't be too much suffering involved in getting fit; more discomfort should be felt during exercise than afterward.

Does the ability to remain fit lessen as you get older?

Yes, it is more difficult to get fit and stay fit as you age, so you should exercise regularly as the years go by. You don't need to do this to excess, but anyone over 70, for example, should make a habit of walking a few miles every day.

Are children naturally physically fit or do they have to work at fitness?

The younger children are, the less they have to work at their physical fitness. As they grow older, though, the situation changes; there will be a noticeable difference between the performance of teenage athletes and their untrained friends. People from their twenties onward definitely need regular exercise for real fitness.

I used to jog a lot before I became pregnant. Is it OK to continue?

If you have not had any problems during pregnancy or any bad pregnancies previously, there is no reason why you should stop. If you have had trouble, you should cut down or stop for the first trimester. During the second trimester you will probably feel fine; by the final trimester you may feel a bit large for too much exercise.

All age groups are much more concerned with physical fitness now than ever before. However, people should ensure that if they embark on a fitness program, they choose one to suit their age and capability.

There is no doubt that to see someone like Michael Johnson sprinting his way to a world record in his prime was to witness one of the fittest people who ever lived. However, it is equally obvious that people do not all need to be so fit to lead a happy and contented life. How much exercise does a person need to keep the body fit enough to deal with the demands of everyday life, and what is the best way of getting that exercise?

▲ *Few people are at the peak of their physical fitness throughout life. However, only top athletes need to be supremely fit. For other people, gentle, regular exercise is all they need to feel and look healthy.*

Getting fit

DO

Do warm up properly. Injuries occur when you start a heavy workout without an adequate warm-up period. Runners should do a few stretching exercises to keep supple and repeat these during the cooling-off period.

Do use proper equipment. This is particularly important in relation to training or running shoes. Always buy the best shoes for your feet.

Do eat sensibly. If you are overweight you must not combine a crash diet with a sudden fitness program; in fact, your appetite may increase if you exercise more than usual.

DON'T

Don't rush into your fitness program; you could injure yourself. The older you are, the more slowly you must start; if you are over 35 and are concentrating on jogging, for example, you should start with a week of brisk walking.

Don't exercise if you have a cold or flu, or if you feel an infection coming on.

Don't get cold. Injuries can be prevented by wearing warm clothes in cold weather.

▲ *Regular exercise doesn't have to be boring. Thousands of people take up physical activities for recreation, either through clubs or with friends.*

Generally, it is true to say that most of the people would feel a lot fitter, and maybe live longer, if they exercised regularly and took more care of their bodies.

Keeping fit is very much concerned with the way that a person chooses to lead his or her life. An office employee whose only exercise is walking between the subway station and home will not be as physically fit as a bicycle courier who rides many miles in a day.

Fitness has two roles to play in each person's attitude toward positive health. First, a person must keep up a minimum level of fitness to keep the body looking good and feeling well so that he or she can enjoy life to the fullest. Second, a person must be physically fit enough to be able to manage the physical loads that his or her daily activities and leisure pursuits demand.

Why bother to keep fit?

There are two important reasons why people should always try to remain physically fit. By far the more important is that they will simply feel better; the ordinary tasks of everyday living seem so much easier to cope with when the body is in good shape. The main reason why so many joggers have taken to the parks and sidewalks is that they have discovered this simple fact.

The second important part of keeping fit is the effect it is thought to have on life expectancy. If physical fitness does prolong life, that result is almost certainly due to the benefit fitness gives to the heart, lungs, and blood vessels, which are all involved with delivering oxygen to the tissues (see Oxygen).

Ideal pulse rates during exercise		
AGE	**MINIMUM**	**IDEAL**
Women		
20–30	130	155
30–40	125	150
40–50	115	140
50–60	110	130
60–70	100	129
70+	95	115
Men		
20–30	135	165
30–40	130	160
40–50	125	150
50–60	115	140
60–70	105	130
70+	100	125

This panel shows the pulse rate you should be aiming for if you are trying to do your heart any good.

Any exercise that increases the heart rate is useful, even brisk walking. The easiest way to take your own pulse is to stop exercising and time your pulse over the next six seconds, multiplying by 10 to get the heart rate in beats per minute. The minimum column shows the lowest effort that will improve your heart; the figures in the ideal column are about three-quarters of the maximum possible rate, and this level does the most good.

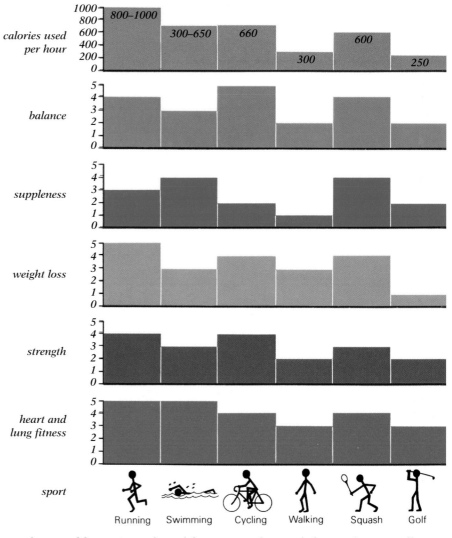

GETTING THE MOST FROM EXERCISE

▲ *Each area of fitness is graduated from one to five, with five as the most effective.*

It is a simple fact that people who live in the West are most likely to die of a disease affecting the heart or the blood vessels caused by the twin evils of high blood pressure and atherosclerosis. If exercise does have a helpful effect on life expectancy, it acts by preventing or delaying the effects of these disease processes. However, physical fitness certainly has no known effect on the chances of suffering from other fatal diseases, such as cancer.

Scientific studies

Scientists (epidemiologists) who study the effects of disease on the population as a whole have for some years been looking at the possible beneficial effect of physical fitness on the heart and blood vessels. There are many different studies that indicate a reduction in the number of heart attacks in people who are physically active compared with those who are less active, or sedentary. One study showed that people who were on the move and ran up and down stairs several times a day were less likely to develop heart trouble than people who were simply sitting down all day. And while it is too early to say that exercising definitely reduces the chances of having a heart attack, there is a definite correlation between fitness and avoiding heart trouble (see Heart Attack).

How can people tell if they are fit?

When people talk about physical fitness, they usually have some specific objective in mind. Sports people will get fit in time for the baseball or football season, for example, and the level of fitness that they accept as adequate will depend on what they want to do and on how well (and at what level) they want to perform. Perhaps a better question is: how can a person tell if he or she is unfit?

The main signs of unfitness are breathlessness and sweating on relatively minor exertion (see Perspiration). If a person cannot climb up three flights of stairs without breaking into a sweat, then he or she is unfit; also, if a person gets so breathless when walking up the same three flights that he or she cannot carry on a normal conversation, he or she is also unfit.

Apart from the ability to exert a lot of energy in a short time, when a person climbs stairs, for example, he or she should also have a reasonable amount of endurance. Nobody under the age of 70 (who is not disabled) should feel unable to manage a level four-mile walk at a reasonable pace. For more active sports, a person would have to be much fitter.

Finally, there is the question of actual physical strength. In these days of relatively mechanized living, there are few tasks that need an enormous amount of physical strength. Many people have felt the worse for wear as a result of moving some heavy piece of furniture at some time, and this is fairly normal.

When people's bodies are not up to the physical tasks that they attempt, it is of course reasonable to say that they are unfit. However, there is no reason to suppose that people are improving their life expectancy by building up muscular strength; it is the fitness of the heart and lungs that probably matters more from this point of view (see Heart; Lung and Lung Diseases), although there are actually few forms of exercise that do not increase muscle strength to some degree.

How do you get fit?

The capacity of the heart and lungs to carry oxygen to the tissues of the body seems to be the key to the sort of fitness that leads to physical well-being and possibly a longer life. Scientists can measure this by looking at the amount of oxygen the body can consume during the course of one minute while someone is exercising hard. In a healthy 20-year-old man this may be around 1½ fluid ounces (45 ml) of oxygen consumed per 2.2 pounds (1 kg) of body weight during the course of 1 minute; the figure for women is about 0.3 fluid ounce (10 ml) per minute less. Oxygen consumption falls in everyone after the age of 20. In a highly trained endurance athlete, such as a top-class marathon runner, the figure may be as high as 2½ fluid ounces (80 ml) per 2.2 pounds (1 kg) per minute. Very unfit people can sink to a figure of around 0.85 fluid ounce (25 ml).

The type of exercise that improves the degree of oxygen uptake and the overall efficiency of the heart and lungs is called aerobic exercise. In simple terms, this means the sort of exercise that makes a person breathless while he or she is doing it. Endurance exercises—such as running, swimming, and walking, as well as the many ball games and team games that involve a lot of running—are all good forms of exercise that improve oxygen uptake and therefore the level of fitness of the heart and lungs. The most efficient, convenient, and inexpensive form of exercise for most people is probably running. However, the most important thing about choosing a basic form of exercise in a fitness program is that it should be an exercise that the person enjoys and is prepared to go on doing for years.

Nevertheless, improvement of the function of the heart and blood vessels is not the only thing that matters when overall fitness is considered. It is also important to develop the body so that it is well balanced and supple, as well as being reasonably strong. Running or jogging does all of these things, except developing suppleness; therefore, some stretching exercises must be done for overall fitness. Swimming, on the other hand, is a particularly good all-around approach to achieving fitness; and for those who are motivated best by some direct form of competition, all the common racket games like squash, tennis, and badminton have excellent effects on fitness. Finally, for those who find fitness easiest to achieve when some form of travel is involved, hiking and cycling are the obvious activities.

Whatever form of exercise a person chooses, it has been shown that any reasonably intensive training program will improve oxygen consumption of the body by as much as 30 percent in the course of a few weeks. In middle-aged men who were given a very gradual increase in the amount of exercise that they were doing, it was found that increases of up to 20 percent could easily be obtained.

▲ *There are hundreds of activities that promote physical fitness. The keynote is activity, whether in the workplace or at play. Getting any sensible regular exercise is going to be good for people, so they should choose the type that best suits their age, lifestyle, and preference. Physical fitness will improve a person's health and outlook and may even prolong life— whether a person is 25 or 75.*

The main thing to remember about starting to get fit is not to expect too much too soon. However, with perseverance it should be possible for a person to produce a noticeable change in his or her feeling of well-being in the course of only a few weeks by a simple program that involves walking and running.

One noticeable change that has taken place in Western society in recent years has been in the number of people who are prepared to take hard exercise to keep themselves physically fit. Although they may have no thought of going out and winning world-class athletic events, these people are motivated by the thought that, through being fit, they can function better in business and socially; and, of course, in the process they realize that they might well be prolonging their lives.

> *See also:* Aerobics; Arteries and artery disease; Blood pressure; Exercise; Jogging; Life expectancy; Muscles; Physical fitness testing; Pulse; Wellness

Physical fitness testing

Questions and Answers

My husband is into bodybuilding. He insists that he is very fit, but I disagree. Apart from working on his muscles, he gets no exercise at all. Am I right?

Yes, very likely you are. Physical fitness has little to do with mere muscle bulk. Fitness mainly involves the heart, the lungs, and the blood vessels.

I have always thought myself reasonably fit and I get plenty of exercise, but now I find I get breathless more easily than I used to. Am I losing my fitness?

Not necessarily. Increased breathlessness from standard exertion is certainly a basic and useful measure of fitness, but there are many other possible reasons. Increased breathlessness could be caused by lung, heart, or other problems, so it would be safer to go to see your doctor for a checkup.

Is it true that athletes have naturally slow heart rates?

Yes, up to a point. Long-distance runners have slow pulse rates, often below 50 beats per minute, but this is not due just to nature. Heart efficiency improves with training so that the heart can perform the same work at a lower speed. Successful athletes owe about half their advantage to training and half to heredity.

My wife calls me a couch potato. However, I always maintain that I am fit enough to do all the things I want to do. Why should I bother to get any fitter?

There are many reasons. They include the effect on quality and duration of life, physical appearance, avoidance of disease, a positive state of mind, and a general feeling of well-being.

Physical fitness is not a state that a person can take for granted. Without regular exercise, a person will become unfit and more prone to disease. Fitness testing is an important, and possibly lifesaving, way of measuring health.

Lack of exercise increases a person's susceptibility to a variety of diseases, including heart disease, osteoporosis, obesity, and diabetes. It is a highly unnatural state, and a drawback of civilization. Thousands of years ago, humans had to hunt for food and had no aids for transportation. They had to be fit to survive.

For hundreds of years humans have enjoyed the physical benefits of civilization but have ignored the need for the natural maintenance of physical fitness. Inevitably, such neglect leads to physical deterioration. It is important, therefore, to understand exactly what is meant by physical fitness, how it is maintained, and how it can be measured.

There is much more to physical fitness than bulky muscles and the ability to run marathons. The term "fitness" should be taken literally; it applies to all aspects of life, work, leisure, and recreation. However, physical fitness has implications well beyond the purely physical. Nearly everyone who makes a determined effort to get fit enjoys an upswing in mood and a significant decline in depression. In some cases, persistent depression can be effectively treated simply by getting regular vigorous exercise. The reason for this is that an increase in physical fitness implies improved functioning of far more than just the muscles; it is essentially a matter of increasing the oxygen supply to all the various tissues and organs of the body.

The importance of oxygen

Of all the elements required for the maintenance of life and health, oxygen is by far the most important. This is because the chemical energy required for every cellular and bodily function is

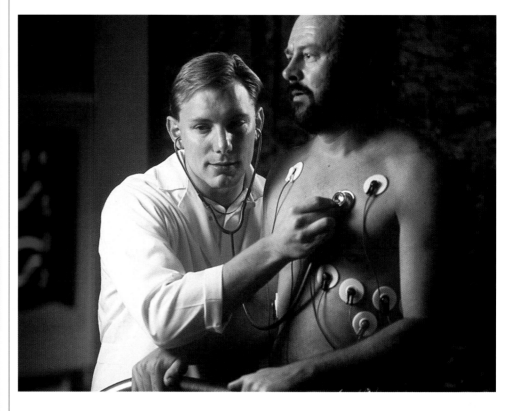

▲ *A doctor uses a cardiac stress test to measure the heart's electrical activity. This fitness test is often carried out on patients who have chest pains or breathlessness.*

derived from a combination of oxygen and body fuels, such as glucose, in a process called oxidation (see Glucose).

Oxidation releases energy and can occur only if there is an adequate supply of oxygen. Deprivation of oxygen for more than a few minutes may be fatal. At the least, it is likely to cause severe damage to the brain, which has the highest energy requirement of any organ in the body.

However healthy a person may be, the chances are that if the oxygen supply to the tissues of the body can be improved, he or she will be healthier still. The measure of the efficiency with which oxygen is distributed to all parts of a person's body is what is ultimately meant by "physical fitness."

Aerobic fitness

During aerobic exercise, the increased oxygen needs of the body are fully met. Unlike nonaerobic exercise, it is a form of exertion that can be continued for long periods. This is because nonaerobic exercise is limited to a few minutes at a time, since available oxygen is used up quickly and energy runs out.

During aerobic exercise, however, the volume of air that moves in and out of the lungs is increased, the volume of blood pumped by the heart in a given time increases, and the amount of blood flowing through the muscles also increases (see Circulatory System; Heart). In this way, sufficient oxygen is transported from the atmosphere to the working muscles to meet their requirements. As a person systematically continues to engage in aerobic exercise, the oxygen transport system becomes increasingly efficient by a process of gradual adaptation. In this way, enough oxygen can be supplied with progressively less change from the resting state. Less exertion is needed, and the business of exercising generally becomes progressively easier.

Regular vigorous aerobic activity improves both the performance of the exercise and the amount that can be performed before it becomes limited by breathlessness. This limit imposed by breathlessness is called "exercise tolerance."

Increasing breathlessness is an indication that the body, whether healthy or not, needs more oxygen. Although people with respiratory, heart, or circulatory problems should not exercise without medical supervision, the health of people with, for example, angina pectoris (heart pain), caused by an inadequate blood supply to the heart muscles, can be improved by aerobic exercise. The same applies to people with leg pain (intermittent claudication) caused by partial obstruction of the leg arteries, and to people with persistent lung airflow obstruction from bronchitis, emphysema, or other lung disorders. Through exercise, ordinary daily activities may become significantly easier for such people.

The improved oxygen supply also contributes notably to weight control, promotes a sense of well-being, and may even reduce a tendency to diabetes by improving glucose tolerance. None of these benefits, either for healthy people or for those with medical problems, will be achieved unless the exercise is regular and involves significantly more exertion than that encountered in everyday life. Nothing is gained without breathlessness.

Warning

People who suffer from heart, lung, or any other major disease, who are 45 or older, or who are significantly unfit should consult their doctors before embarking on any exercise program. While almost

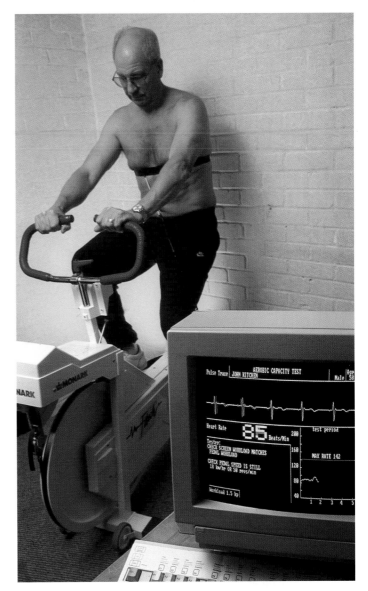

▲ *An aerobic capacity test measures the activity of this subject's cardiorespiratory system. The test assesses stamina and is often used in assessments at fitness centers.*

everyone, healthy or less than healthy, and of any age, can benefit from exercise, in some conditions it may be dangerous.

Measurement of fitness

So far as the physiologist is concerned, aerobic fitness is measured by determining the greatest rate at which oxygen can be used up during continuous exercise. This rate of consumption increases with regular sustained exercise and decreases in people who are sedentary. The decrease is greatest in people who remain at rest in bed.

Such changes can occur quite quickly. A 30 percent increase or decrease in a person's oxygen utilization rate can occur in a few weeks; and if the change in exertion is considerable, the difference may be as high as 100 percent within two to three months.

Direct measurement of oxygen consumption rates can be made while the subject is walking or running on a treadmill, using a stationary cycling device known as an ergometer, or stepping on and off a raised platform.

▲ *Being physically fit has implications beyond the purely physical. Exercise increases the oxygen supply around the body and often results in a more positive outlook on life.*

The subject carries a large bag from which oxygen is breathed through a tube. In this way, actual consumption can be measured. Such tests show that an average healthy young man might have an average oxygen consumption rate of 3⅓ quarts (3.15 l) per minute. A long-distance runner might have a rate of 5¾ quarts (5.5 l) per minute. About half of the difference between these two rates is the result of physical training.

To measure such a person's progress in training rather than to assess maximal fitness, it is necessary to determine how long he or she can sustain a high level (perhaps 80 percent of maximum) of oxygen consumption. The result indicates to what extent that person has reached his or her full potential for aerobic fitness.

Short-term high rates are important for short-distance runners but may give little indication of the improvement appropriate to marathon runners. Most people who take up jogging find that, in

time, they are able to improve their longer-distance performance. Such improvement is due to an increase in the length of time for which the higher rate of oxygen usage can be sustained.

When muscles are forced to work with not enough oxygen, glucose fuel is broken down abnormally and lactic acid is formed. This may cause pain, but if not, low levels of lactate can be assessed from a blood sample. Therefore, sustained activity fitness is measured by the percentage of the maximum oxygen consumption rate that can be sustained before the lactic acid levels in the blood begin to rise.

This measurement may be important for professional marathon runners. An athlete in training might, for instance, show no change in his or her top rate of oxygen usage, but might show a rise of from 75 percent to 80 percent of this rate before the blood lactic acid begins to rise. Such an increase would be associated with a small but, over long distances, highly significant increase in average running speed.

Clinical measurement of fitness

Physiological measurements of the kind described above are used in research laboratories, but they are seldom used by doctors because indirect methods are more convenient. A doctor might check the pulse rate, put the patient through an exercise routine, and then check exactly how long it takes for the pulse rate to return to normal. This gives quite a useful clinical guide to physical fitness (see Pulse).

Doctors also rely heavily on the clinical history of exercise tolerance to assess fitness and to monitor progress in disease. In people with angina or claudication, for instance, the doctor is interested in how far the patient can walk, under standard conditions, before the pain starts.

Breathlessness with various amounts of exertion is of great concern. Doctors will question a patient about the exact amount of exertion required to bring on breathlessness (see Breathing). The scale used starts with vigorous exercise, such as running, then goes on to brisk walking, normal walking uphill, walking on the level, strolling, sitting in a chair, and lying in bed. It is normal to become breathless while running, but many fit people can walk briskly without breathlessness. A person who is breathless while walking normally on the level is grossly unfit but may not be suffering from any disease; a person who is breathless while sitting or lying is certainly ill.

Fitness and the heart

Oxygen can be supplied to the muscles only when it is carried in the circulating blood. Blood coming from the lungs is normally saturated with oxygen, therefore if more oxygen is to be supplied in a given time, more blood must flow (see Blood). Paradoxically, athletic training does not increase the maximum heart rate; it reduces the maximum rate.

There is a definite limit to the rate at which the heart chambers can contract efficiently. Above a certain pulse rate, the chambers cannot fill properly, so the output falls. To achieve an improved rate of blood flow, the output per beat, called the stroke volume, must be increased. This is where training comes in. Training achieves an overall increase in the size of the heart and a more efficient and complete emptying of the heart chambers with each beat. Trained athletes have a better stroke volume at every heart rate. This is part of the reason why the heart rates of long-distance runners and others engaged in sustained exertion are lower. The increased heart output implies a greater oxygen uptake at any given heart rate, so the rate can be lower for the same amount of oxygen supplied.

Fitness and the muscles

Everyone knows that training can increase muscle bulk. The increase, called hypertrophy, is due to an actual increase in the size of individual muscle cells (fibers). However, there is more to it than that. Well- exercised muscles are more efficient in extracting oxygen from the blood flowing through them. The actual profusion of tiny blood vessels (capillaries) increases with exercise so that the oxygen is brought nearer to the muscle fibers and the distance it must diffuse to get to them is less (see Capillaries).

Diffusion is a relatively slow process, so the reduced distance is important. Muscle cells contain numerous tiny bodies called mitochondria. These are the powerhouses of the cells, the actual sites of energy production by the oxidation of glucose (see Cells and Chromosomes). With training, the number of mitochondria in each muscle cell increases. The quantity of the enzymes that activate the chemical reactions of oxidation also increase. Athletes' muscles therefore require a smaller total blood flow to achieve the same rate of oxygen consumption and the same power.

There is another factor. The principal fuel of the body is glucose, but fatty acids can also be oxidized to provide energy. This process, however, requires a greater oxygen consumption than the use of glucose. Training is believed to increase the ease with which fat can be used as a source of energy during prolonged exercise, thereby sparing the relatively limited glucose stores and postponing fatigue. Training increases the quantity of the enzymes that move fatty acids into the mitochondria and those required for fatty-acid oxidation (see Fats).

Training for the nonathlete

These various advantages of training are available to everyone and may offer distinct benefits even to people whose quality of life is damaged by disease. A good oxygen supply to all parts of the body is vital, and if the supply can be improved, the advantages are considerable. Physical fitness implies far more than simply the ability to excel in competitive games; it affects every aspect of life.

An adequate standard of physical fitness for the nonathlete can be maintained by a relatively limited training program. Regular aerobic exercise, such as brisk walking, jogging, swimming, dancing, skipping rope, cycling, rowing, skating, and even climbing stairs, will lead to improved performance in daily living and a generally improved state of mind. For many people, just half an hour three times a week may achieve these effects and reduce the risk of serious disease. Weight control programs are unlikely to succeed unless supplemented by deliberate regular exercise. Contrary to popular belief, regular training does not increase appetite but makes it easier to maintain a reduced food intake.

It has been medically proved that people whose walking range is limited by the gripping chest pain of angina pectoris or the leg pain of intermittent claudication can improve their endurance by exercising. In these cases, exercise cannot improve the flow of blood through narrowed arteries, but it can increase the ability of the muscles to extract oxygen from the blood available. In the case of nonathletes, formal testing of physical fitness is unnecessary; the person concerned will quickly become aware of the improvement both in physical capacity and in the sense of well-being.

▲ *A doctor uses a piece of equipment called an adipometer to measure the percentage of fat stored in an athlete's arm. This information is used to tailor exercise regimes to the specific needs of the individual.*

Other aspects of fitness

The concept of fitness involves, in addition to heart and muscle strength, such factors as the regulation of body composition, flexibility, agility, coordination, balance, reaction time, and psychological endurance (see Balance; Coordination). Most of these concern only professional athletes, but some, notably body composition and flexibility, should concern everyone.

Body composition is the ratio of lean weight to fat. This is measured by determining the body mass index (BMI): the weight in pounds (kilograms) divided by the square of the height in feet (meters). The higher the BMI, the greater the proportion of fat. Because the height is squared, the index has little correlation with stature. A person with a BMI above 28 for men and 27 for women is considered obese (see Obesity). These figures represent a weight 20 percent above ideal. High body fat renders a person unfit in a variety of ways and is a significant risk factor for various diseases.

Flexibility is an aspect of fitness that is often disregarded, especially by older people. However, it is important because, unless deliberately maintained by regular exercising, the range of joint movement decreases progressively throughout life (see Joints).

Loss of flexibility is easily measured; a person simply needs to explore the range of joint movement, especially spinal movement, of which he or she is capable (see Movement; Spinal Cord). Comparison with what a small child can do can be painfully revealing. Flexibility exercises or hatha yoga, however, can increase the range of joint movement (see Yoga). Some therapists have noted that a correlation exists between the flexibility of the body and the flexibility of the mind (see Mind-Body Therapy).

See also: **Aerobics; Arteries and artery disease; Exercise; Jogging; Lung and lung diseases; Metabolism; Muscles; Osteoporosis; Oxygen; Physical fitness**

Physical therapy

Physical therapy has to do with mobility. It uses physical methods, including manipulation and massage, plus a range of other techniques, to give relief from pain and restore movement after an injury or disease.

Questions and Answers

Is it true that electrotherapy treatments can be dangerous?

In unskilled hands, electrotherapy could be dangerous. However, physical therapists are trained in the use of this equipment and will ensure that the patient is protected.

After nine holes of golf my hip begins to ache and sometimes gets quite painful. I try to keep playing and work the pain away. Is this sensible?

Pain is usually a danger signal that something is wrong. It would be advisable to see your doctor and not to try to work through the pain, since this may make the problem worse. Your doctor may think that physical therapy will help with this problem.

I recently had a gallbladder operation and have been told to do breathing exercises. Why?

Pain in the abdomen will make you breathe more shallowly. This can cause some of the small air spaces in your lungs to collapse and can lead to pneumonia. Deep breathing helps prevent this.

My child suffers from cerebral palsy and has regular physical therapy. Will she ever be able to manage without it?

A child with cerebral palsy has to learn to sit up, walk, and control bodily movements until he or she gains independence. This requires an intensive course of treatment in the early years. As the child is more able to fend for him- or herself, the physical therapist will teach the parents how to encourage the child further, and gradually there will be no need for continuous treatment. However, you can always ask a physical therapist for advice.

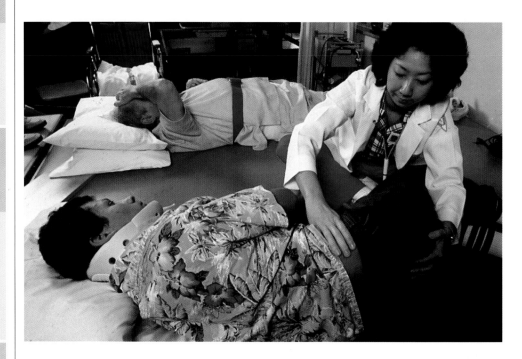

▲ *A physical therapist works to mobilize a patient's lower spine. Back pain can be highly disabling, but manipulation may resolve the problem and bring welcome relief.*

For many people, the words "physical therapy" conjure up an image of an arthritic limb being massaged, but in fact such therapy covers a broad range of treatments. The term "physical therapy" is derived from two Greek words: *phusis*, meaning nature; and *therapeutike*, meaning healing.

Physical therapy is a necessary adjunct to many treatments of disease, disability, and injury. In addition to its traditional role of treating rheumatic aches and stiff joints, physical therapy can help restore limbs to their normal function after an injury, help pregnant women to prepare for childbirth, and teach children with physical disabilities to control their limbs. Physical therapy also helps many postoperative and bedridden patients to breathe, trains those who have suffered brain or spinal damage to relearn mobility, and teaches paralyzed patients to use other muscles so that they can have more independence and control over their lives.

Physical therapists are highly trained health care personnel. They study anatomy (the structure of bones, muscles, blood vessels, and nerves), physiology (how the body works, including breathing, digestion, and circulation), pathology (how disease affects the body), and psychology, as well as therapeutic exercises and techniques of healing. In addition to their wide variety of manipulative skills, they have machines and aids at their disposal. They use treatments that range from simple to highly complex and include various techniques to strengthen muscles; mobilize joints; relieve aches, pains, and stiffness; and teach coordination and walking.

Methods

Physical therapists' work involves manipulation, mobilization, and massage, to get the patient and his or her temporarily immobile limbs moving. Manipulation is a method used to make joints and tissues more flexible (see Joints). Finger and hand movements are used to apply pressure, for example, in cases where joints, although not dislocated, have moved slightly out of alignment and have become stiff or fixed (see Stiffness). Many back complaints benefit from this treatment. Forceful, finely isolated pressure can relieve pain when a nerve has become inflamed or pinched. Skill is needed to know precisely where and how to apply pressure to obtain a satisfactory result. Unskilled manipulation can be dangerous. Similar skills are used to mobilize joints and relieve pain. Often, less force and more gentle pressure are needed than in manipulation, and the benefit comes not from one or two treatments by the physical therapist, but from repeated movements in which the patient has to work with the therapist. Exercises are used to restore strength to weakened muscles. Hands are used to massage and manipulate soft tissues around the joints to improve blood flow and assist limb movement. Some modern massage techniques are based on Swedish methods (see Massage).

Techniques

In addition to their manipulative skills, physical therapists use a range of techniques that require specialized equipment. The most recently introduced technique is electrotherapy or electroshock therapy, in which low- or high-frequency electricity is used for its healing effect on the skin, muscles, and other tissues.

Electrotherapy comes in a variety of forms. Shortwave diathermy is a high-frequency current that penetrates deep into the tissues and is used to relieve deep-seated pain in joints such as the hip. Pulse magnetic field therapy, in which pulses of magnetic energy are passed through the limb, is used to heal fractures. A combination of high- and low-frequency currents that penetrate deep into the tissues is used in inferential therapy to increase circulation and reduce pain (see Pain). Low-frequency currents initiate muscle contractions in limbs that have been affected by disease or injury.

Pain can also be reduced by transcutaneous nerve stimulation, in which a low electric current is passed through the tissues, thereby stimulating nerves near the surface of the skin.

Ultrasound is used on soft tissue, muscles, and ligaments; high-frequency sound waves cause vibration and a warming effect to relieve pain, decrease inflammation, improve circulation, and restore movement in the fluid components of the tissues (see Ultrasound). For pain relief and improved circulation, infrared irradiation from a lamp, or a hot pack, can be used. There is also a wide range of traditional treatments. Cold therapy is applied in the form of ice wrapped in towels or crushed ice in water, and it is used to suppress pain and relieve swelling (see Swellings). By reducing blood flow, cold therapy can reduce inflammation, and it is a convenient method of treating hand, foot, and knee injuries.

Hydrotherapy involves exercising in warm water in special pools. The heat helps muscles to relax and relieves pain. Exercises aim to restore muscle power and make movement easier. Hydrotherapy is widely used for paralysis and rheumatic disorders.

Paraffin wax can be used to treat painful joints in the hands. Hot wax is molded around the fingers, and since it prevents heat loss, the heat is retained for a long time. Finally, there are techniques that can be used to facilitate movement. Facilitatory techniques are used when there is abnormal movement or no movement of a limb; the aim is to make the limb more efficient by working through nerve reflexes and nerve stimulation (see Movement).

A combination of all these techniques may be used. The choice will depend upon the physical therapist's assessment of the patient's condition and his or her knowledge of which techniques produce beneficial results. Weakened and damaged muscles and

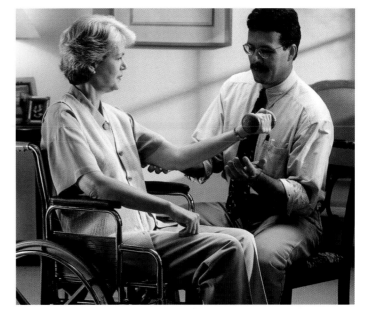

▲ *A wheelchair-bound woman keeps in shape with physical therapy. A range of equipment and techniques are used to strengthen joints and muscles and restore normal movement.*

tissues cannot be strengthened by the physical therapist alone; effort has to come from the patient too. The physical therapist will teach, assist, encourage, and demonstrate, but the patient must follow the treatment consistently and make an attempt to fight his or her way back to health.

Uses of physical therapy

Physical therapy is used in a wide range of problems that may arise because of disease, disability, or injury.

Neurology: Neurological conditions occur in the central nervous system, when the nerves in the brain or spinal cord are damaged by disease or injury, or when there are disorders of the peripheral nerves. Central nervous system disorders can have such diverse causes as traffic accidents, strokes, and congenital or birth disorders such as cerebral palsy. Muscles cannot move unless messages are transmitted to them along the spinal cord (see Cerebral Palsy). Muscles will also not be able to move if nerves are damaged. If a nerve in a finger is cut, it will cause a loss of sensation and a loss of movement in the finger. Much more serious paralysis results if the spinal cord is cut or if certain areas of the brain that control movement are affected. If the spinal cord is cut below armpit level, paraplegia is the result. Injuries higher up produce tetraplegia or quadriplegia. Damage to the brain from a stroke or severe head injury can produce hemiplegia (see Paraplegia).

Paralysis can result from congenital conditions such as spina bifida, or diseases such as multiple sclerosis, in which the myelin sheath that allows the nerve to conduct its electrical message becomes damaged and prevents proper functioning of the nerve.

A patient with hemiplegia may suffer from visual disorientation, in which he or she sees only half of each visual field. This is distressing, and the patient will have to be trained to adjust to the environment. In all cases, the therapist will try to stimulate the nerves, inhibit abnormal movements, correct imbalance, or improve the strength of normal muscles to take over extra work from those that are permanently damaged. For instance, the arm muscles of a

Questions and Answers

I always thought that an osteopath was the same as a physical therapist, but a friend said this was wrong. Who is right?

Your friend is correct. Osteopaths are physicians who have been through medical school; physical therapists have not.

Physical therapists cover a wide sphere of practice, specializing in manipulation and often working as part of a health care team. Osteopaths treat skeletal disorders.

My father recently had a stroke and has lost movement and feeling in his right arm. How can physical therapy help him when he cannot feel anything?

Physical therapists are trained to treat not only loss of movement but also loss of sensation. They will be able to help your father by retraining the nerve pathways that have been affected by the stroke to adapt to new patterns of movement.

I am paralyzed from the waist down and am confined to a wheelchair. Is there any point to physical therapy when I'll never walk again?

Many patients who are confined to wheelchairs live full, active lives. Some travel, play sports, go to work, and raise children. To help such people achieve independence, a physical therapist teaches them the basic activities that will produce the strength and stamina to maneuver their wheelchairs, so they will be able to engage in activities as fully as possible.

I woke up the other morning with a stiff and painful shoulder. Could a physical therapist treat this?

Yes. It would be best to see your doctor first, and if he or she thought it warranted further treatment, he would refer you to a physical therapist who would find the source of the pain and treat it.

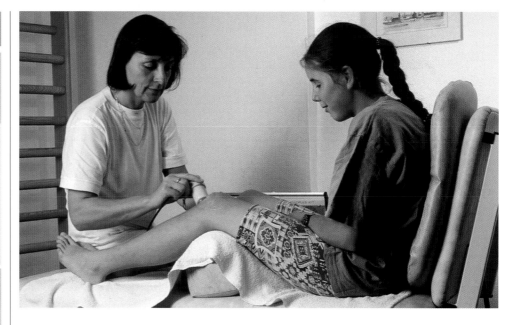

▲ *Ultrasound is an addition to the physical therapist's armory for treating damaged tissues—particularly in arthritis. Very-high-frequency sound waves are passed into the body, decreasing inflammation, improving circulation, and relieving pain.*

patient whose legs are paralyzed can be strengthened to enable him or her to propel a wheelchair, and to transfer to a toilet, bath, or bed (see Paralysis).

Obstetrics and gynecology: Some physical therapists work chiefly with pregnant women. At prenatal classes they give information about relaxation, breathing, how to push and use muscles correctly during labor, and what actually happens during birth. Therapists can give advice about correct posture, so that the extra weight of the baby in the womb will not lead to backache. Postnatal sessions not only improve general physique but also teach the importance of exercise to restore the normal strength of the pelvic floor muscles, which support the abdominal organs, including the bladder. Weakness following childbirth can lead to urine leaking from the bladder, a condition called stress incontinence. Guidance can also be given on the correct way to lift and carry, so that lifting the baby will not lead to aches and pains.

Orthopedics: This branch of medicine deals with deformity of the bones because of accident, disease, or congenital complications. These deformities, which include fractures, sprains, and amputations, can be treated surgically or by mechanical means (see Sprains). Broken bones generally require support from a plaster cast, and the limb may be immobilized from three weeks to two months or more. When the cast is removed the limb is stiff, and treatment is needed to strengthen and restore it to normal mobility. Different techniques of manipulation, mobilization, and massage will be needed depending on whether or not the affected limb is weight-bearing(as a leg is, for instance; see Fractures). Less severe than broken bones, but more common, are injuries to ligaments and muscles. It is important that these are treated quickly, especially for injured athletes, so that the full function of the limb can be restored.

When a patient has lost a limb, the physical therapist will be involved in choosing an appropriate artificial limb (see Prostheses). The patient is taught to move the limb correctly so that bad habits do not develop in the early stages of rehabilitation. With the right prosthesis and physical therapy many patients are able to resume normal activity and live full and active lives.

Pediatrics: Pediatrics covers diseases and injuries to children. Many of the techniques used for adults also apply to children, but there may be complications because the child is still growing. Physical therapists work very closely with other members of the health team, such as play therapists, occupational therapists, and speech therapists, so that a full relationship with the child is developed and he or she suffers as little as possible during treatment.

Respiratory care: Physical therapy is necessary when respiration is impeded, because in such cases, chest diseases, such as asthma, bronchitis, and pneumonia, can occur.

Following surgery, the effects of an anesthetic can produce secretions that need to be removed from the lungs. In all of these cases, the physical therapist will teach the patient postural drainage

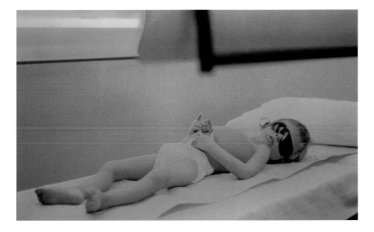

▲ *In liver disease, bilirubin causes yellow staining in the skin (jaundice) and itching. Blue light therapy converts the bilirubin to a form that can be excreted in the urine.*

techniques to remove the secretions. In conditions such as cystic fibrosis, it may be necessary to percuss the chest (a form of beating) to dislodge the mucus from the bronchi (see Cystic Fibrosis).

Intensive care: Patients who are seriously ill are cared for in an intensive care unit, where a physical therapist is an important member of the extended team. He or she works with patients who have been involved in serious accidents, when there may be severe head injury, and on patients who have had chest, heart, or abdominal surgery. Physical therapists keep the limbs of unconscious patients mobile and monitor any chest condition. Patients in intensive care units are often on respirators, and a physical therapist must work to keep the airways clear and the chest free of secretions, both by agitating the chest with hand massage and by using suction methods.

Rheumatology: This encompasses a group of diseases including rheumatoid arthritis and osteoarthritis. Rheumatoid arthritis (inflammation of the tissues around the joints) attacks several joints at once, such as the fingers and toes, whereas osteoarthritis usually attacks a single joint that has previously been damaged through injury or wear and tear. The term "rheumatism" is often used to cover symptoms that arise from these conditions, such as lumbago (see Lower-Back Pain, Osteoarthritis, and Rheumatoid Arthritis). If a patient has a painful joint in the hand, wrist, elbow, or foot, a physical therapist can support the joint with a splint.

Burns: Physical therapy is important in the treatment of burns. When the burn covers a joint, the scar tissues contract as they form across the joint, and this will restrict movement. During the healing process, the soft area underlying the skin has to be mobile. Massage is needed to keep the tissue stretched, and exercises are used to keep the joint moving. When a patient has extensive burns, the exercises may be done under water in warm saline baths, after the dressings have been removed. The warmth of the water relieves pain and aids movement. Ultrasound is also often used to soften scar tissues by agitating the cells of the tissues to decrease inflammation and improve local circulation (see Scars).

Intellectual impairment: There are various degrees of intellectual impairment, which are usually classified into two main groups: the severely impaired, who require constant care and attention because serious brain damage prevents them from responding to treatment; and those who are intellectually impaired but can still learn to wash, dress, and feed themselves with a minimum of help.

If a child is intellectually impaired, treatment starts very early. The child will be encouraged to learn the simple, everyday movements of sitting, standing, walking, and climbing. Treatment is aimed at giving the child maximum independence as early as possible so that he or she will be able to carry out simple activities such as going for walks, taking a bus, or going to the store.

Frequently, mental impairment is combined with motor disability. In this condition the skilled techniques of the physical therapist can help correct imbalance and achieve normal movement patterns.

Cancer: Many forms of cancer can now be cured, but the disease can result in paralysis, pain, muscular weakness, and fractures. Even when a patient has a terminal illness, the physical therapist will use massage, mobilization, and exercise to retain full movement of the limbs for as long as possible.

Geriatrics: Geriatric medicine is the care of elderly people. During the aging process elasticity in tissues lessens, and the result can be stiffness and pain. The physical therapist will treat these symptoms with massage, mobilization, or other techniques, such as one of the forms of electrotherapy (see Aging).

Lack of mobility in older people, however, can lead to other symptoms. For example, a broken leg considerably limits movement, and this limitation in turn can lead to circulation problems and result in congestion of the lungs. In this instance, patients will also need to have respiratory care. Age can cause problems with balance, and patients may need to be retrained to control their balance by following a specific exercise program, usually done in front of a mirror (see Balance).

One neurological disease that sometimes affects older people is Parkinson's disease, which produces a tremor in the limbs. A number of facilitatory techniques, which have been developed through many years of research, are used to teach patients how to easily change their walking pattern.

Cardiac surgery: In the cardiac unit the work of the physical therapist begins two or three days before surgery. Physical therapists will get to know the patient and teach him or her certain movements and exercises. These will help the patient as soon as he or she regains consciousness following surgery. The patient will need to know how to handle a machine that will assist his or her breathing, how to carry out exercises that will help him or her to breathe properly, and how to cough. It is very painful to cough following major heart surgery, but coughing is necessary to remove secretions from the lungs. When the patient is able to get out of bed, he or she will be given a program of graduated exercises to help improve stamina and regain normal patterns of movement.

Physical therapists work closely with their colleagues in the health care team, including occupational therapists and, when the patient has had a stroke, speech therapists. All of these therapists could be involved in assessing the patient's needs in preparation for his or her discharge from the hospital.

Aside from specialized functions of physical therapy, simply getting a patient out of bed regularly is very important. Pneumonia, deep vein thrombosis in the legs, and bedsores are just a few of the problems that can be avoided in this way (see Bedsores; Pneumonia; Thrombosis).

See also: **Heat treatment; Hydrotherapy; Manipulation**

INDEX